Magic Moments

Magic Moments

The Perry Como Story

Matthew Long

BLOOMSBURY ACADEMIC
NEW YORK • LONDON • OXFORD • NEW DELHI • SYDNEY

BLOOMSBURY ACADEMIC

Bloomsbury Publishing Inc, 1359 Broadway, New York, NY 10018, USA
Bloomsbury Publishing Plc, 50 Bedford Square, London, WC1B 3DP, UK
Bloomsbury Publishing Ireland, 29 Earlsfort Terrace, Dublin 2, D02 AY28, Ireland

BLOOMSBURY, BLOOMSBURY ACADEMIC and the Diana logo are trademarks of Bloomsbury Publishing Plc

First published in the United States of America 2025

Copyright © Bloomsbury Academic, 2025

No rights are claimed or implied by the supplying of the photos, but all are from physical copies, either from the author's own collection or from the collection as credited.

Photo restoration: Matthew Long

For legal purposes the Acknowledgements on p. xiv constitute an extension of this copyright page.

Cover design: Sally Rinehart
Cover image © ZUMA Press, Inc. / Alamy Stock Photo

All rights reserved. No part of this publication may be: i) reproduced or transmitted in any form, electronic or mechanical, including photocopying, recording or by means of any information storage or retrieval system without prior permission in writing from the publishers; or ii) used or reproduced in any way for the training, development or operation of artificial intelligence (AI) technologies, including generative AI technologies. The rights holders expressly reserve this publication from the text and data mining exception as per Article 4(3) of the Digital Single Market Directive (EU) 2019/790.

Bloomsbury Publishing Inc does not have any control over, or responsibility for, any third-party websites referred to or in this book. All internet addresses given in this book were correct at the time of going to press. The author and publisher regret any inconvenience caused if addresses have changed or sites have ceased to exist, but can accept no responsibility for any such changes.

Library of Congress Cataloging-in-Publication Data to come

ISBN: HB: 978-1-5381-9563-5
ePub: 978-1-5381-9564-2
ePDF: 979-8-8818-5654-0

Typeset by Deanta Global Publishing Services, Chennai, India
Printed and bound in the United States of America

For product safety related questions contact productsafety@bloomsbury.com.

To find out more about our authors and books visit www.bloomsbury.com and sign up for our newsletters.

*This book is dedicated to my wonderful grandparents
Emily and Barry Clark
who were instrumental in my introduction to Mr. Como.*

They are forever in my heart.

For Thomas—
Do what you love and follow your heart.
Love, Daddy
xx

Contents

Foreword xi
Acknowledgements xiv

Introduction 1
Record and Broadcast Industry Abbreviations 7
Recommended Listening and Song Index – Abbreviations and Key 9

1   That Old Gang of Mine 11
    Recommended listening 1938–41 24

2   Till the End of Time 25
    Recommended listening 1943–9 39

3   Some Enchanted Evening 43
    Recommended listening 1950–4 66

4   Magic Moments 69
    Recommended listening 1955–9 84

5   The Sweetest Sounds 89
    Recommended listening 1960–8 109

6   How Beautiful the World Can Be 113
    Recommended listening 1970–7 136

7   The Best of Times 139
    Recommended listening 1980–7 154

8   When You Come to the End of the Day 157
    Recommended Christmas listening 1946–82 173

Appendix: The songs he loved and more 177
Notes 243
Bibliography 252
Index 254

Foreword

I have very fond memories of, as a child, watching the Perry Como Show every week with my dad. He was a doctor who came from a musical family, and he had a very good ear. He taught me how to distinguish between flat or sharp singing by listening to Perry and his guests on the show. Perry didn't do either of those things. He almost always sang dead centre of the note. Dad thought that was pretty important, so I wanted to do that too. And I did! Perry taught me that. He also sang with such ease and seemed like such a nice man. I just loved him!

Fast forward to 1975, when I was invited to do a guest appearance on a television special that Perry was taping in Lake Tahoe, Nevada. The first time I saw him, he was rehearsing on stage at Harrah's Hotel, and I was in the audience listening and waiting for my turn to rehearse. He couldn't see me because the room was dark but I was mesmerized by the power of his voice. As I remember it, for some reason, he wasn't even using a microphone. I knew about the ease of his singing, but the power took me aback.

Perry finished rehearsing, and I was just sitting, waiting for my turn, when I felt someone come up behind me and put their hands on both of my shoulders. An unmistakable voice said, 'You must be Anne'. What a way to introduce himself! So warm and welcoming. I already felt that he was like that from watching him on television, but how wonderful to know that he really was like that. That's the way it went for the rest of the special.

I worked with Perry again in 1979 on a Christmas special that he did in Santa Fe. Life had changed a lot for me by then. I had just had my second baby, and travelling was difficult for me, but as for Perry, it was the same thing... the same warmth. It was like going home to be and sing with him. What a treat.

Perry and Anne Murray during the taping of Perry Como's Christmas in New Mexico, *1979. Photo courtesy of Anne Murray.*

Later, I owned a home in Jupiter, Florida, where Perry lived, and my mother spent winters there. She was a devout Catholic, and almost every Sunday she saw Perry in church. One time, she stopped him and said, 'I'd like to introduce myself. I am Anne Murray's mother'. He paused briefly in observation and responded, 'so you are . . . so you are!'

Perry was a huge influence on me. As a kid, I knew and sang along with all of his songs. He was a crooner and I loved the crooners. In 1993 I recorded an album called *Croonin'* that was full of 1950s songs, including Perry's songs 'Wanted' and 'Round and Round' . . . all songs of my childhood. Of all my albums, that was my true labour of love.

Meeting and working with Perry Como was a dream come true for me and I feel privileged to have had the opportunity to spend time with such a talented and wonderful man.

Anne Murray
February 2025

Anne Murray is a four-time Grammy-winning Canadian singer whose albums have sold more than fifty-five million copies worldwide and had more than twenty number one hits during her forty-year career. Among her greatest hits are 'Snowbird', 'Danny's Song' and 'You Needed Me'.

Acknowledgements

Through my passion for and research of the Perry Como legacy, I've had the great fortune to meet many lovely people around the world. To one extent or another, they have all played their part in this wonderful journey, and I would like to take the following paragraphs to express my thanks to all of them.

I would like to start by extending a special thank you to Malcolm Macfarlane and Ken Crossland, the authors of *Perry Como: A Biography and Complete Career Record* (McFarland, 2009). Malcolm and Ken generously gave permission for my use of the research from their book, which has served as an excellent supplement to my own research.

A special thank you is also due to the American Music Research Center at the University of Colorado, Boulder, and in particular, staff members Kelly Brichta, John Dziadecki, JoAnna Ramsey and Jennifer C. Sanchez, who have all been generous with their time and prompt to respond to my enquiries.

From other universities in the United States, I would like to thank Rebecca Williams from Duke University, Durham, North Carolina, who has been very conscientious in her efforts to assist my enquiries. And from the University of Missouri-Kansas City, the assistance of Stuart Hinds and Nikki L'Amour was most prompt and courteous.

Turning to the music world, Anne Murray and her secretary Diane Stewart were most generous with their time. Anne was kind enough to agree to an interview and graciously provided a heartfelt foreword for the book. I am most grateful to them both for making this possible.

Also from the entertainment industry and archival community, I'd like to thank Michael Biel, Mark Cantor, Ray Charles, Bill DiCicco, Ethel Gabriel, Mickey Glass, Adrian Goldberg, Alexandra Henwood, Tom Hercock, Anne Hopper, Anita Kerr, Ian Marshall, Des O'Connor, Sammy Jones, Tommy Loftus, Nick Perito, Matthew Price and Guy Worsick. At different stages in my development and across various related endeavours (including this project) they've all been most helpful and supportive.

On a more personal basis, I must extend my sincere gratitude to my friend and mentor George Townsend, webmaster of the Perry Como Discography and Digital Companion (www.kokomo.ca) who has been a constant source of advice and guidance to me for over twenty years. Recording dates for Perry's RCA Victor recordings are provided courtesy of his excellent website and the Como Circle headed by Martha Gerhard, who conducted the original log sheet research.

It is and has been a pleasure to know and correspond with friends, family and admirers of Perry's over the years (some of whom also work within the industry and whom I am proud to count among my friends). I would like to express my thanks to all of the following people for their friendship and valuable contributions over the years.

Sylvia and Tony Arnone, Jonathan Arthur, Ron Baker, Doug Bell, Charlene Blassingham, Hans Jeff Borger, Gene Como, Melanie Como, John Corrado, Adrian Daff, Adrian DeBee, Michael Dunnington, Florence Gill, Steve Goddard, Giuliana Gorlei-Pittsey, Bill Hodges-Smith, Charlie Honold, Lucinda Cummings Kilmer, Liam Logan, Christopher Logan, Linda Maxom, Leslie Rowland McCarthy, Gil Nelson, Lamar and Sabrina Pecorino, Larry Posner, Yasuo Sangu, Michael Schnurr, Tommy Sheldon, Carlo Stevan, Cassie Miller Thornberg, Joan and Howard Turvey, Lucinda Terrill Wahl, John Walton, Willy Wettergren and Colleen Zwack.

And last but in no way least, there are two people I don't know what I'd do without: my Mom and Dad – Ann and Peter Long. They have supported me all the way in every respect of my interests and passions, and I am forever grateful for their love and guidance.

Introduction

It's a distinct challenge to write a fitting book on someone such as Perry Como. The most important balance I feel is taste and respect. On the one hand, Perry had no desire for any books to be published about him. On the other, his career is highly deserving of serious commentary. I've agonized for a long time over this conundrum. The balance that I speak of I sincerely believe is achieved by drawing upon Perry's own public commentary on his life and career. 'I think my private life should be my own', said Perry. 'I get myself in trouble once in a while feeling that way, because people who write and people on television wanna know all about ya and I tell 'em just as much as I think they should know'.[1] It is on precisely this basis that I have approached the writing of this book.

One might then ask how you make a story interesting without being intrusive. That's not difficult where Perry Como is concerned. For Perry's story not only encapsulates the true spirit of the American dream but is also a career that flourished and sustained across many decades. He remained relevant and a constant presence through eras of great social and technological change, and he did so without compromising his personal or professional integrity.

This poses one further question: How then does one avoid making a glossy account of such a person's life? My aim has been to achieve this by drawing upon personal accounts and viewpoints from people within the industry who understand the ingredients of what makes a successful career, the difference between a good recording, a bad one and a mediocre one, and what the true markers of success are.

There is much that has been said about the career of Perry Como over the years. People with even the most introductory knowledge of the Como legacy will probably know that he was a barber – a pretty good one too by his own assessment and never hesitant to demonstrate his ability. If you know that he was a barber, you probably also know that Perry was born and raised in Canonsburg, Pennsylvania – a band singer in the 1930s who entered the world of mega-stardom in the 1940s and went on to countless major successes on records, radio and television. The story has adorned the rear of many an album cover through the decades. For the purposes of continuity and context, there are certain aspects of this story which are integral to the narrative which shall be discussed in detail; but it is hoped that this text will give a broader insight into the ingredients which made Perry Como's career such a special one.

The desire is to also dispel a few myths relating to the Como methodology. One such misconception is that Perry would record any song that was brought to him. This is simply not true; Perry was very selective about the material he recorded for commercial release, as will be explored. Another is that Perry recorded some of his biggest hits in one take. Although this is a myth that was often indulged by Perry himself, it is also not true.

Something seldom acknowledged is just how influential and extensive Perry Como's contributions to popular music were. He perfected the style of ballad singing with clarity and sincerity – without any excessive affectations or false modesty. He rode the waves of change in popular music and was very much a part of the current musical scenes. It's a testament to Perry's musicianship that he was able to apply his craft to numerous musical styles with superb results. Some of the novelty songs might well have been throwaways in less capable hands, but Perry brought quality and integrity to each one, plus an audible wink of good humour.

In the recording studio, Perry didn't simply go through the motions. A couple of dozen takes in some instances was by no means unusual for him, but there was more to it than that. Greatness is almost always the result of a team effort, and the Como legacy is no exception to that rule. Perry surrounded himself with people whom he trusted and valued, technically and artistically – each played a key role in his recordings. Orchestral leaders such as Mitchell Ayres and Nick Perito, choral leader Ray Charles, arrangers including Joe Lipman and Jack Andrews; producers Charlie Grean, Chet Atkins, Andy Wiswell and many others, all played an integral part in the vast Perry Como legacy.

On television, Como found a home to which he became instinctively attuned. The voice, the looks, and the personality all came naturally to Perry. The medium also proved the perfect model for promoting his recordings. At his peaks on both radio and television, a preview of a newly released song on his shows would almost guarantee a chart entry. Perry, however, was not concerned with record charting positions nor with listening to his own records. His choral director Ray Charles once observed that the charts as a whole represented 'the best of the bad!'[2]

Como's greatest achievements on disc are surely to be found within his studio albums. When writing about Perry in 1968, music critic Gene Lees suggested that 'Perhaps the reason people rarely talk about his formidable attributes as a singer is that he makes so little fuss about them'.[3] This was one of Perry's most endearing qualities. There was no ego with Perry – he did what he did to the best of his ability and then he went home, to his family. In a world where many would sell their souls for a taste of fame – Perry succeeded on his own terms without ever compromising his integrity.

My own awareness of the Como legacy began in the late 1990s. Many of my fondest childhood memories are of summer holidays spent with my grandparents. They were like a second Mom and Dad – I make no exaggeration. They were also my best pals. We had so much fun together! Popular music of the early to mid-twentieth century was very much a part of the back and foreground of these visits. My grandad Barry had a particular fondness for the deep baritones of Vaughn Monroe and Al Jolson, as well as the bass tones of Paul Robeson. My nan Emily was more an admirer of the great pop vocalists: Perry Como, Nat King Cole and Andy Williams among them.

One afternoon at my grandparents' house, while my Nan tended to some ironing, I vividly remember her listening to an audio cassette that my Grandad had compiled from their own record collection. As the cassette side was changed and with the reels in spin, in a matter of seconds I was greeted with the lush sound of strings and brass, then the warm, rich voice of Perry Como singing 'It's Impossible'. I was hooked! Before too long, my Grandad was up in their loft and he got the records down for me . . . and there it was among them: 'Perry Como – 40 Greatest' a double LP compilation on the K-Tel label, released in 1975. This was my introduction to Perry Como. I knew nothing particular about him personally at this point, but I adored his voice and I started to collect. That I was to learn what a fine gentleman he was in due course, was the metaphorical icing on the cake. Since that tender age of

Gene Como (Perry's brother) and Matthew Long at the Perry Como statue in Canonsburg, Pennsylvania, 2006. Author's photo.

ten, my passion has gone from strength to strength, never waning – testament surely to the timeless quality of Mr. Como's music.

In the many years since, and particularly so with the ever-expanding internet, I have had the honour and privilege to correspond with fans and colleagues around the world, and all through this time I have continued to collect, research, and preserve. This book is the result of more than twenty-five years of admiration for a man whose music is very dear to my heart. It is intended as a one-stop guide to the core of what made Perry Como so special – but also as an objective testament to his talent. If you are just learning about Perry Como, then I hope this book will serve as a basis for discovering his catalogue of music. For the already initiated, I hope the book will provide fresh insights and context to the music you already know and love. Perry Como's music has received very little scholarly attention over the years. My intention is to change that and hopefully, in doing so, introduce the Como legacy to new generations of fans.

It's amazing how one can feel a close connection with a person, without ever having known them. That's part of Perry's genius. He didn't sing at you or through you – he sang *to you*. I will be forever grateful to this very special gentleman of song – for the fine example he set as a person and as a professional, and for the multitude of magic moments his music has brought me. Thank you, Perry. You are never far away from me!

Matthew Long
February 2025

For more information about Perry Como and his legacy, you can write to Matthew at: perrycomomagic@outlook.com

Record and Broadcast Industry Abbreviations

ABC	American Broadcasting Company
AFM	American Federation of Musicians
AFRS	Armed Forces Radio Service
ASCAP	American Society of Composers, Authors, and Publishers
BBC	British Broadcasting Corporation
BMI	Broadcast Music, Inc.
CBS	Columbia Broadcasting System
EP	Extended Play vinyl record
HMV	His Master's Voice
LP	Long Play vinyl record
NARB	National Association of Radio Broadcasters
NBC	National Broadcasting Company
PBS	Public Broadcasting Service
RCA	Radio Corporation of America
RIAA	Recording Industry Association of America

Recommended Listening and Song Index

Each chapter of this book contains a list of recommended recordings by Perry Como from the years indicated. The intention is to provide an overview of the length and breadth of recorded material from the era, combining artistic achievements and commercial successes with Perry's personal favourites and songs that are autobiographical in nature. The song index follows the same template but with an added emphasis on the most recurrent songs in Perry's repertoire.

Abbreviations

BB	Beat the Band
CPPC	Columbia Presents Perry Como
CSC	The Chesterfield Supper Club (radio)
CSC TV	The Chesterfield Supper Club (television)
PC CBS	The Perry Como Show (CBS)
PC NBC	The Perry Como Show (NBC)
PC KMH	Perry Como's Kraft Music Hall

Key

★   A perennial Perry Como performance
■   Recorded for a film soundtrack
■*   Recorded for a film soundtrack but omitted from the final cut
●   Recorded for RCA Victor
●*   Recorded for RCA Victor but not originally released

Song title
   Composer (m), Lyricist (w) ('mw' if combined), copyright year
   The larger work from which the song originates (if applicable).
   Recording date - commercial release title and catalogue number
   Show - date of broadcast [collaborating artists where applicable]

e.g.   **I Love You** ● ★
   mw Cole Porter, 1944
   From the musical Mexican Hayride.
   8 Feb 1944 - PC Sings Just for You CAL-440
   CPPC - c. 1944 / PC KMH - 28 Mar 1966

All recording dates credited (in the example above '8 Feb 1944') refer to RCA Victor recordings, with the exception of songs recorded up to the end of 1941, which were made for Decca. For these recordings, the nominated release catalogue number is preceded by the label name: e.g. '5 Oct 1939 - Decca 2919'.

1

That Old Gang of Mine

Saturday 4 March 1933, was a prestigious day in Washington, DC. Several bands were assembled to play at the inaugural ball of the newly elected president Franklin D. Roosevelt. Appearing at the ball was a band known as the Freddie Carlone orchestra, and their featured vocalist was a young man named Perry Como. It was quite the opening gig for the just-turned professional singer!

Perry Como had come to the attention of Freddie Carlone earlier that year when Carlone opened the floor to any budding singers at a local gig. Perry's friends encouraged him to get up and sing with the band. Reluctant at first, Como headed for the stage prompted by the insistence of his pals. He sang 'More Than You Know' to the cheers of his friends and made a considerable impression on Freddie, so much so that Carlone contacted Perry soon after to ask if he would like to join his band for $28 a week – and in that moment Perry Como entered show business.

Born Pierino Ronald Como on 18 May 1912, Perry, as he became known, was born to Italian immigrants Pietro and Lucia Como in the coal-mining town of Canonsburg, 18 miles southwest of Pittsburgh, Pennsylvania. Perry was one of thirteen children and the first of his siblings to be born in the United States. According to Como legend, he was the seventh son of a seventh son. Local records, however, dispute this. As a child, Perry spoke only Italian until he started school. The Como parents originated from Palena in the Abruzzo region of Italy and were married there in 1901.

Many Abruzzese, like the Como's, left their lives in Italy with the hopes of a more prosperous future in the United States. As was a common practice for immigrants, Pietro came over on his own first with very few possessions: the clothes he was wearing, a small amount of cash and the desire to build a new life. Pietro arrived at Ellis Island in New York on the *San Giovanni* in May 1910. Once settled in the United States, Lucia joined Pietro along with their three surviving children. The Como's had tragically lost their firstborn child and two twins, all when they were less than two weeks old. Infant deaths were an all-too-common occurrence at the time.

Pietro worked as a millhand at the Standard Tin Plate Corporation in Canonsburg. The company had been formed in 1903 by a group of local businessmen for the purpose of producing tin-plated, thin-gauge steel for supply to companies that produced tin cans.[1] Perry had very fond memories of his father.

> He was a very gentle, very kind man; and he was very busy with thirteen children! I think that's where I get most of my supposedly relaxed attitude – 'cause he was very calm, nothing bothered him. But we always knew he was the big chief! . . . . I don't think he ever raised a finger on any of the youngsters but there was a respect there . . . you knew he was the boss![2]

The Como family home was very much an Italian household. An abundance of hearty, home-cooked food and a warm welcome awaited family and guests alike. They might start a meal with eight or nine people for dinner and end up with twenty-five, applying to the traditional Italian adage, 'Twenty? Forty? What's the difference?' Anyone who visited could go into the family kitchen, fill up a plate, sit down and eat.[3]

Music was an important feature of the household. Pietro Como was a great admirer of the famous tenors Enrico Caruso and Beniamino Gigli – he also sang himself, although not professionally. The music of Caruso and Gigli would have emanated from the family gramophone, forming Perry's introduction to the world of music. Pietro encouraged his children to learn to play instruments, so Perry began to establish both a musical ear and theoretical understanding from a young age. The Como's had an organ which Perry used to play, he also played in the Canonsburg Italian Band and performed at local fraternal events.

The Freddie Carlone orchestra, based in Cleveland, Ohio, was primarily a territory band, performing in their native state of Ohio, but also further afield. The band's musicians included saxophonist Nick Lovano, trumpeter Lennie 'Buzz' Lenassi and pianist Fred Kaiser. During this time, Perry began to develop his musicianship. He learnt to read music, built confidence as a vocalist, and adapted to the life of a touring musician. It proved an excellent platform for the young singer and Perry spoke with much fondness and respect for Freddie.

The year 1933 was equally important to the Como story for another reason, for it was also the year he married his childhood sweetheart, Roselle Belline. Roselle, who hailed from the neighbouring town of Meadow Lands, had met Perry at a wiener roast on the banks of Chartiers Creek in the late 1920s. Roselle was Perry's rock and one of his biggest supporters. She believed in him, even when he was doubtful of his own ability. 'She's been wonderful for me and . . . she's a great lady . . .' said Perry in 1984. 'We'd have our fusses', he said, but added, 'You show me two married people who don't fuss with each other occasionally, and I'll show you two people who aren't married'.[4]

Reflecting on the eve of his twenty-fifth wedding anniversary, Perry said:

I'm probably the only husband who can boast that he's been married three times – to the same girl! The first time we were married, Roselle and I eloped and were married by a justice of the peace. Our parents kind of suspected that we would run off because we had been going together since we were fifteen and saw so much of each other that both sets of parents realized we were serious. So when we announced that we had married, nobody was really surprised. The only thing that bothered them was the fact that we hadn't married in church. So we had to get married a second time in church. It wasn't a big wedding, just the family, and then we went home to dinner and had a little wine.

In the early 1950s, Perry and Roselle married for a third time when they renewed their wedding vows. 'We've had such a wonderful marriage that we thought we'd like to take those vows all over again, so we flew down to Palm Springs – didn't even tell the children until we got back – and got married again'.[5]

Perry's first career, though, was as a barber. His father felt that a trade of some form was essential for his young son, and through the connection of a dear family friend, Steve Fragapane, Perry opted for a career in barbering, beginning work at the age of eleven and working before and after school in Mr Fragapane's shop for 50 cents a week. He started off by cleaning the mirrors in the morning, polishing the doors and sweeping up, later graduating to shaving, which was a primary source of custom for the shop at the time. Within three years, Perry had his own two-chair barber shop, gradually turning his extracurricular venture into a solid business, earning a sizeable income of $125 a week.

But the call of music was clearly a strong one, and Perry's musical activities developed throughout. In fact, a vivid memory of Perry's from this period concerned his time as a double-bell euphonium player. A fellow from the Canonsburg Italian Band (led by Stan Vinton, father of singer Bobby Vinton) was establishing his own band and asked if Perry would like to perform with him. It was during Ferragosto (15 August), a big feast in Italian tradition with fireworks, parades, food and music. It was a busy and tiring experience for the young Mr. Como. 'I'll never forget it', said Perry.

> We used to buy instruments in those days – $5 down and $2 a month . . . I left for three days, I came back just fractured . . . . He [the leader] came around a couple of weeks later to pay me off and he put $26 on the table . . . and my dad was so upset, he said '$26 for three days work? You lost close to $100 in the barber shop!' It didn't add up to him . . . So without saying a word to me, he goes down and gets a big saw and he cuts off the two bells. 'Course it destroyed me because I hadn't paid for the damn thing yet! . . . But he was so sweet, I remember him with very fond memories, he was a good man. I couldn't really get mad at him, but I said 'Pop! Look what you're doing! . . .' And I think I paid $200 for the instrument – but he didn't care, he didn't want me to play anymore because he thought I was just too young to be running around. So he made wine funnels out of the bells, which is kinda silly, but he had the bells and he'd kinda hold 'em in, so he'd transfer his wines from one barrel to another and it got so wild I couldn't get mad with him – and I think I'm still paying for it!

Perry began to combine his tonsorial talents with those of his vocal cords during this same period. He would often sing for customers in his barber shop,

The Sons of Italy, Canonsburg, Pennsylvania – one of the fraternal organizations at which Perry sang during his formative years. Author's photo.

sometimes even simultaneously – crooning hits of the day. Differing from his father, Perry's musical ears were particularly attuned to the vocal stylings of Bing Crosby, Russ Columbo and the newly emerging art of crooning, pioneered by the likes of Gene Austin, Rudy Vallée, Nick Lucas and many others. This new approach to singing found its beginnings in the late 1920s, owing to the advances in recording technology and the introduction of the microphone. While in the first quarter of the twentieth century it had been essential for a singer to be able to project loudly to ensure a good reproduction on disc, it was now possible, thanks to electrical recording, for a much more intimate sound to be achieved, reminiscent of the 'bel canto' style which means in English 'beautiful singing'. This style of singing originated in Italy during the seventeenth century and is a technique that combines an emphasis on purity in tonal quality with perfection in vocal control. It proved an excellent fit with the improvements in recorded sound – and so, the crooner was born.

Perry also dipped his toes into the world of vaudeville during his formative years. Como, along with a friend named Lou McHugh (possibly an Americanized variation of the last name Marchione), established a routine in their spare time. They named their act 'Perry & Lou – The Comedy Boys'. Perry was the straight man who sang and played guitar, while his friend Lou was the comedian, who wore a funny hat and spoke in broken English. Perry described Lou as a very short man with a cherub-looking face. Their theme song went as follows:

> *How do you do everybody, how do you do?*
> *We are the medley boys, Perry and Lou!*
> *From Maine up to Alaska, this is all we wanna ask ya:*
> *Howdily do, a-do-a-do-a-do-a-do . . .*

This would then lead into some patter. For instance:

> **Lou**: Perry, you know – I was arrested goin' on a streetcar this morning?
> **Perry**: Well, why were you arrested?
> **Lou**: Well, err . . . You know that sign that says-a 'Don't-a spit on-a the floor?'
> **Perry**: Yes, but what's that got to do with it?
> **Lou**: So, I spit on the seat!

From 1933 to 1935, Perry toured with the Freddie Carlone band throughout Ohio and the neighbouring states of Pennsylvania and West Virginia until one night in December 1935, the Como singing career would take its first steps towards national exposure. Bandleader Ted Weems heard Perry singing with the Carlone orchestra at a casino in Warren, Ohio and was immediately impressed. He was seeking a new singer following the departure of Art Jarrett from his own ensemble and offered Perry a job there and then. Concerned over his loyalty to Freddie, Perry was initially hesitant of the idea, but Carlone was insistent that this was not an opportunity that Perry should pass up, so, Perry joined Ted's orchestra.

The Ted Weems Orchestra already had a national following and more than a decade of recording and personal appearances to their credit. The band's first major hit, 'Somebody Stole My Gal', recorded in November 1923, reached No. 1 in 1924, and many more hits were to follow. By the mid-1930s, the Weems band had evolved from its jazz roots into a unique entertaining group and featured talents including whistler Elmo Tanner, saxophonist, comedic singer and songwriter Red Ingle and bassist Country Washburn, among many others.

On 15 May 1936, Perry made his recording debut in Chicago as vocal refrain with the Weems ensemble. This first session for Decca Records resulted in six recordings, two of which contained Como vocals – 'Lazy Weather' and 'You Can't Pull the Wool over My Eyes'. These first Como outings are a fascinating listen. Even at this early stage, there were hints of the Perry Como magic to follow. Perry's vocal flows easily along with the gentle foxtrot rhythm of 'Lazy Weather' and he is accompanied on disc for the first of many times with Elmo Tanner in the whistling role. By contrast but equally effective is Perry's vocal on 'You Can't Pull the Wool over My Eyes'. The faster, driving rhythm proved a good vehicle for the dexterity of the Como voice and something that would become a regular feature of Perry's single records in the 1950s. The stylistic influences on this first recording session were clear, though – echoes of Bing Crosby, Russ Columbo and Al Jolson can be heard. Throughout the remainder of the year, Perry recorded six additional vocal titles with Ted Weems plus one cameo on the novelty number 'Knock, Knock, Who's There?', which enjoyed some chart success.

The first couple of years with the Weems band were challenging – Perry was finding his own style vocally, and on both records and radio, his sound and enunciation were under scrutiny. Ted Weems had just signed with Decca

Records, the label Bing Crosby was already recording for. Because of the perceived similarities between Como and Crosby at the time, Decca were opposed to recording Perry. During one of his early sessions, Dave Kapp (brother of Decca president Jack Kapp) exclaimed to Weems, 'Why are you letting him sing? Hell, we got one Crosby'. Perry had not heard this in the moment but had observed the confusion, and an engineer relayed what had been said later. Perry said, 'It was like someone was stabbing me ... here I was trying to get on record'.[6]

While fulfilling a regular engagement at the Palmer House in Chicago in 1936, the Weems band were threatened with dismissal if their new male singer did not improve his diction. Ted recalled that:

> Without his [Perry's] knowing it, I had some records made of our broadcasts, and one night I asked Perry to stay after the show to hear them. He was crushed—by his own voice, 'Funny,' he said 'I can't understand a word I'm singing'. Then I told young Mr. Como to cut out the vocal tricks and give his fine voice the freedom it deserved. 'Just open up' I suggested 'and sing the words from the heart.' He did just that. His enunciation and performance improved overnight. He was on his way.[7]

These early experiences in broadcasting proved a vital learning curve for Perry that would serve him well as he developed his singing style.

That same year, Ted Weems and his orchestra took over musical support duties on the *Fibber McGee and Molly* show on the NBC Red Network. Commencing on 15 June 1936, the Weems outfit became the resident band, leading to Perry's first regular, national radio exposure, singing a vocal with the band as a weekly interlude to the classic comedy series. *Fibber McGee and Molly* were the real-life couple Jim and Marian Jordan, who had their beginnings in vaudeville. The series centred around the misadventures of a suburban couple from the fictional town of Wistful Vista and their neighbours and was built around the tall tales (i.e. 'fibbing') of McGee and the abrupt but loving temperament of his wife, Molly. The series ran for over twenty years on NBC, beginning in 1935 and continuing until the late 1950s.

Perry's first vocal outing on the show took place on 22 June 1936, during which he sang 'Twilight on the Trail' – a song which he would return to several

Ted Weems and his Orchestra, c. 1936. Perry is seated on the front row, third from right.

times over the years in broadcasts and on record for his first stereophonic album, *Saturday Night with Mr. C.* in 1958. The show gave Perry an opportunity to be heard performing such classic standards as 'These Foolish Things (Remind Me of You)', 'You Turned the Tables on Me' and 'I've Got You under My Skin', the last of which became a staple of Perry's concert performances in the 1970s and beyond.

Perhaps most significant, though, is a performance of 'The Way You Look Tonight' on the 12 October 1936 edition of *Fibber McGee and Molly*. As with 'I've Got You under My Skin' it was a staple of Perry's concert performances and clearly a favourite, but it also holds the distinction of being one of the longest recurring entries in the Como repertoire. The song was new at the time of the broadcast, having been featured by Fred Astaire in the film *Swing Time* that same year. Fifty-seven years later, Perry was still performing the song during his final tour of Japan in 1993 – a testament surely to the timeless combination of music by Jerome Kern and lyrics by Dorothy Fields.

Perry continued with *Fibber McGee and Molly* until November 1937, when he broke off with a handful of solo broadcasts for WMAQ in Chicago. Irish tenor Clark Dennis took up the mantle for the remainder of Weems' residency with the McGees, which concluded in January 1938.

During the same month, the Weems band played a week at the Chicago Theatre. It was Perry's first live performance in a theatre setting, and the young singer was petrified of the new surroundings. In the past, he'd been singing in ballrooms, where patrons danced, and the band was closer together. Now, Perry was on the stage of a seated theatre with a large orchestra pit. He approached the microphone and proceeded to sing a romantic ballad, still suffering badly from stage fright. As the song progressed, he could soon hear laughter coming from the audience. Bemused by the whole experience, Perry couldn't understand why the audience were laughing. There was nothing mildly humorous about the song.

After a while, Perry's youthful feistiness took over, and in upset, he walked over to the stands where fellow performers Red Ingle and Elmo Tanner were positioned. Now with his back to the audience, Perry looked at Elmo and said, 'What in hell are they laughing about?' and very quietly, Elmo answered, 'Your fly's open!' The audience didn't hear this exchange, but as soon as Perry began to adjust his dress, they laughed again, to which Ted remarked, 'Keep it in!'[8]

In the spring of that year, Perry was given his own radio show, with broadcasts on a more regular basis for station WCFL. The show, which was a commercial one, was sponsored by a hair oil preparation manufacturer, beginning on a twice-weekly basis, airing on Tuesdays and Thursdays with some variation later. The sponsorship proved a very apt pairing of Perry's new and former trades, and although the programme was short-lived, it was another step up for the Como career. Ted's advice had paid off. The Como voice was maturing, and people were beginning to take notice.

Throughout the late 1930s, Perry continued to develop and polish his vocal style. He steadily began to ease away from the vocal fluctuations of his early efforts to a far more consistent and rounded tone. By 1939, his vocal style was coming into its own, and a pair of sessions in early October of that year proved particularly fruitful. One recording, 'I Wonder Who's Kissing Her Now', on which Perry is joined by a glee club vocal ensemble of the Weems band, would go on to be a big hit for him when reissued (along with a new solo recording of the song) in 1947. The song was also featured by Perry and the band in the Universal film short *Swing Frolic*, released in 1942, in which Perry made his film debut.

Radio came calling again in 1940 when a new musical game show titled *Beat the Band* began. Sponsored by General Mills, makers of the then-new breakfast cereal Kix, and hosted by Garry Moore, the show featured Ted Weems and his orchestra. For the game, listeners would send the band questions, and each answer was a song title. For example, in a sample question Garry Moore asks, 'When a mother punishes her small boy by keeping him in the house, what does his gang ask when they see him in the window?' and Elmo Tanner answers, 'Ain't ya comin' out?' – which was the correct answer. Any listener whose question was used on air would receive $10. If a member of the band couldn't answer the question correctly, the listener (who had 'beat the band') received $20 plus a case of Kix, and the band member had to throw a half-dollar coin into the bass drum as a forfeit.

Following a successful audition show, *Beat the Band* made its formal debut on NBC radio on Sunday 28 January 1940, less than two weeks after the birth of Perry and Roselle's son, Ronald (known as Ronnie), born on 15 January. The show proved to be an excellent platform for promoting the Como voice, and he performed solid versions of such hits as 'Mister Meadowlark', 'Faithful Forever' and 'Blueberry Hill' during the series. The show enjoyed a successful run throughout the year, airing each Sunday from 5.30 pm to 6.00 pm. At the beginning of 1941, however, a dispute between the National Association of Radio Broadcasters (NARB) and the American Society of Composers, Authors and Publishers (ASCAP) resulted in the formation of Broadcast Music, Inc. (BMI). Consequently, the Weems band could only play tunes registered with BMI over the airwaves, which quickly presented difficulties, and the final edition of *Beat the Band* aired on 23 February 1941.

It was an unfortunate end for what had been a highly entertaining and engaging radio series. Ted Weems and his orchestra would continue with many live engagements throughout 1941, playing a series of one-nighters in states across the breadth of the United States, taking in locales from California to Pennsylvania and many states in between. Sessions for Decca Records topped and tailed the year and represent what are undoubtedly the most distinctive and recognizable of Perry's records from the era. Perry was now well and truly his own man as a vocalist. Gone were the vocal tricks and overly affected delivery. In its place was a warm, rich baritone that was confident, sincere, and heartfelt. This was our first taste of pure Perry.

Perry's tenure with the Weems band continued throughout 1942, but with the entry of America into the Second World War following the Japanese attack on Pearl Harbor, Ted Weems disbanded his orchestra in December 1942, with most of the band joining the Merchant Marine. Perry spent Christmas Eve alone that year and would later recall it as the loneliest Christmas he'd ever spent. Reflecting on the occasion in 1976, Perry recalled:

> I had just left the band, I was in Chicago and it was Christmas Eve, and I was in one of those Horn and Hardart [a food services company who introduced the first coin-operated, automatic food dispensers] by myself, having a bowl of soup, Christmas Eve, sitting there like a big dummy, and I think that's what got me away from travelling. My wife wasn't there, no

friends 'cause everybody was having dinner at their own homes, and I'm sitting there and I thought to myself, 'Boy, I tell you one thing, if I live through this, this is the last Christmas that I'll be away from home.'[9]

Perry was disheartened by the whole experience. 'Roselle kept telling me that I had something – that we were young and that it was worth the gamble to see if I could go on singing as a career', said Perry. 'I was all set to go back to barbering in Canonsburg. I was happy barbering'.[10] It was Roselle's faith in her husband's talent that stopped him from returning to the barber business. While he might not have realized it at the time, he was on the cusp of a solo career. The touring schedule and the weekly broadcasts on NBC had served as an excellent catalyst to his vocal apprenticeship. He was now ready to take centre stage. Within four months he had his own radio series on CBS and within six, a record contract with RCA Victor. Perry Como, the solo artist had arrived.

Quintessential Como
Recommended listening 1938–41

Darling, Not Without You
m Abner Silver, w Edward Heyman
and Al Sherman, 1936
27 Sep 1936 - Decca 959

A Gypsy Told Me
m Sam Pokrass, w Jack Yellen, 1938
From the film Happy Landing.
22 Feb 1938 - Decca 1695

In My Little Red Book
mw Al Stillman, Ray Bloch
and Nat Simon, 1938
23 Feb 1938 - Decca 1695

Simple and Sweet
m Abel Baer, w Bud Green, 1938
23 Aug 1938 - Decca 2019

Class Will Tell
m Joe Burke, w Edgar Leslie, 1939
11 Mar 1939 - Decca 2365

Goody Goodbye
m Nat Simon, w James
Cavanaugh, 1940
4 Oct 1939 - Decca 2794

That Old Gang of Mine ● ★
m Ray Henderson, w Billy Rose
and Mort Dixon, 1923
4 Oct 1939 - Decca 2829
11 Jan 1951 - 47-4035

I Wonder Who's Kissing Her Now ● ★
m Joseph E. Howard and Harold Orlob,
w Will M. Hough and Frank R. Adams, 1909
From the musical The Prince of Tonight.
5 Oct 1939 - Decca 2919
29 May 1947 - 20-2315

May I Never Love Again
mw Sano Marco and Jack Erickson, 1940
27 Jan 1941 - Decca 3627

Rose of the Rockies
mw Nick Kenny, Charles Kenny
and Allie Wrubel, 1940
28 Jan 1941 - Decca 3628

It All Comes Back to Me Now
mw Hy Zaret, Joan Whitney
and Alex Kramer, 1940
28 Jan 1941 - Decca 3627

Angeline
m Edward Ross, w Si Rothman, 1941
9 Dec 1941 - Decca 4131

Having a Lonely Time
mw Paul Gibbons and Roy Ringwald, 1941
9 Dec 1941 - Decca 4131

Deep in the Heart of Texas
m Don Swander, w June Hershey, 1941
9 Dec 1941 - Decca 4138

2

Till the End of Time

After a lonely end to the year in December 1942, Perry Como was intent on returning to Canonsburg, Pennsylvania, to set up a new barber shop and resume his first career. War had always been a nasty business, and the Second World War had ripped its way through Europe. The United States entrance into the war would prove to be a big turning point, but not without great cost. As a married man, maintaining a bona fide family relationship, with a child and in a non-essential industry, Perry was considerably down the list of priorities for drafting into the war, as outlined by the Clarification Directive issued in the United States. He decided to wait to be drafted but never was.

Back home in Canonsburg at the beginning of 1943, Perry had made enquiries about the purchase of a new barbershop. Fate, however, had a very different plan in store for him. Before Perry had time to return to the barbering business, he was contacted by Tommy Rockwell of the Rockwell-O'Keefe Agency with the offer of representation. The Rockwell-O'Keefe Agency (who had managed the Ted Weems Orchestra) already represented Bing Crosby, Ruth Etting, and the Mills Brothers, among many others. Perry was tired of the constant travelling though, and the one-nighters of a touring band. He wanted more stability and a base to live for an extended length of time with his young family. Tommy was able to give him the assurance of this, and in the Como family's case, this base would be New York – the state they called home for over twenty years. 'I liked Tommy right away,' Perry reflected. 'He became my agent, but he became more like my father. He steered me. All my major career moves, he made. He had everybody. I'd have been a fool not to go with him.'[1]

There were three core elements to establish in Perry's opening solo year – a recording contract, radio broadcasts and concert performances. Radio came first. Following a couple of stand-alone broadcasts in March, Perry began a regular series of shows on CBS starting on Monday, 12 April 1943, under the title *Columbia Presents Perry Como*. The shows which were 15 minutes in duration consisted of three songs sung by Perry, with an instrumental tune in between. The programmes were always opened and closed by an announcer (the first of whom was Warren Sweeney), but between these points, Perry handled the music and introductions himself. Very quickly he was referring to his listeners as friends – something that would become an integral part of the Como style. This relaxed and sincere approach served Perry well as he made his way in radio, and it would transfer with exceptional effect to television.

The accompaniment on *Columbia Presents Perry Como* was provided by the Raymond Scott Orchestra. Scott, an accomplished musician and pioneer of sound effects, had not long joined CBS as a musical director at the time of Perry's arrival. Together over the course of several months, Perry and the band collaborated on a combination of gentle swing and romantic ballads, plus a good helping of revivals. Perry quickly settled into the format – performing smooth and melodious versions of such current hits as 'It's Always You', 'You'll Never Know' and 'It Can't Be Wrong'. Songs making a revival were clearly dear to Perry's heart, and this sense of nostalgia would have surely struck a chord with audiences listening during wartime America. Songs like 'For Me and My Gal', 'Girl of My Dreams' and 'My Melancholy Baby' were featured alongside new material, including 'I Have Faith' and 'In My Dream of Tomorrow' – both of which captured the sentiments of hope during a troubled time. Perry's love for the early popular song is perhaps best exemplified in one of his first album collections, *A Sentimental Date with Perry Como*, originally released in 1949 and expanded in 1956.

The guitarist in the Raymond Scott Orchestra was Tony Mottola. Tony was a talented musician in his own right who would go on to record many solo albums. He became a long-standing member of the Como team and is particularly remembered as principal guitarist on the 'Sing to Me, Mr. C.' segment of Perry's television shows sponsored by Kraft Foods. Tony's association with Perry would continue on radio, records and television well into the 1960s. Mottola also worked extensively with vocalist Frank Sinatra. Like Perry, they both also shared their cultural heritage with Italy.

Another of Como's core collaborators first worked with Perry at this time too, pianist Billy Rowland. Como and Rowland can be seen together in the 1943 newsreel film 'Upbeat in Music' (part of the *March of Time* series) in which Perry is featured in a segment highlighting the development of a song from plug to performance. The featured song, which appears to have been written specifically for the film, was 'Now', composed by Jack Shaindlin with lyrics by Marcel Vavin. Billy would continue to work with Perry on radio and join him in the transition to television. As with Tony Mottola, he worked with Perry into the 1960s. Loyalty for Perry was a very important thing. If Perry liked someone and they worked well together, it was likely that their association would last a very long time.

By the summer of 1943, the second of Perry's new priorities came to fruition. Following the submission of a demo provided by Tommy Rockwell, Perry was offered a recording contract with RCA Victor and signed with the label on 17 June 1943. Three days later, on 20 June, the first Como recording session took place in RCA Victor's Studio 2 in New York City. Arriving at 11.30 am for rehearsals, Perry began recording at 1.30 pm. It was to prove a challenging day, but ultimately successful.

Due to a recording ban by the American Federation of Musicians (AFM) that had commenced in August 1942 and which was in force at the time of Perry's signing with RCA Victor, it was necessary for singers to record with vocal backing only, or occasionally, a single guitar played by the singer or group. Vocalists, who were not considered musicians at this time, were exempt and as such could record. The ban was instigated by James C. Petrillo (the union's president) when a dispute over composer royalties with the record labels could not be settled. Consequently, AFM members were not permitted to make commercial recordings. The ban did not, however, extend to other forms of musical activity, such as radio broadcasts and live concert performances.

The necessity of strong vocal backing during the ban encouraged inventiveness. Sounds of an onomatopoeic nature (such as 'do's and 'bom's) were a familiar feature among such recordings. Vocal groups such as the Mills Brothers took the opportunity to innovate – mimicking muted trumpets and rhythm sounds to great effect. 'That was murder', recalled Perry of his first solo recording session. 'I had two boys with me who had perfect pitch, so I put them next to me, but it was hard because if the singing got too loud, you'd get a little sharp. We messed up take after take'.[2]

At this point in time, recordings were made with the same core principles which stemmed from the introduction of the flat disc gramophone record, invented by Emile Berliner in 1887. The fidelity and frequency range of recordings had changed vastly over the years, especially with the introduction of electrical recording, but one aspect remained very familiar – that of the cutting lathe and the wax blank disc. A cutting stylus attached to a lathe would make impressions in the smooth, flat surface of a rotating wax disc seated on a platter while the artist in the studio performed. This left an analogue waveform embossed in the wax, which, following a series of mouldings and electroplating, would result in a master recording from which duplicates called stampers could be made and used to press the recording onto a surface of shellac. By its very nature, each take was a potential final or unusable take, depending on how the performance went. If someone went slightly off-key or slipped up on a lyric, the disc was likely to be rejected.

Despite the difficulties and challenges, both artistic and technical, by 11.45 pm that night (more than ten hours after recording commenced), the session had yielded three completed recordings, two of which would be paired as the first Perry Como record in the RCA Victor catalogue – 'Goodbye Sue' backed with 'There'll Soon Be a Rainbow'. The single was well received upon release and reached No. 18 on the Billboard music chart.

The recording ban continued for the first year and a half of Perry's solo recording career. A further six titles were recorded a cappella before the dispute was resolved (in RCA Victor's case) on 8 December 1944. Before then, Perry enjoyed further chart success, most notably with his recording of 'Long Ago (and Far Away)' from the film *Cover Girl*. Perry's recording became his first top ten hit in the United States. The song on the other side of the disc 'I Love You' was from the musical *Mexican Hayride* and written by Cole Porter. The song which was clearly a favourite of Perry's was performed by him on radio and television no less than nineteen times. In fact, Cole Porter is one of the most frequently recurring songwriters in Perry's career, with more than three dozen titles to his credit.

Just a week before signing with RCA Victor, Perry embarked on his first solo concert engagement at the Copacabana nightclub in New York on 10 June 1943. The engagement had initially been for two weeks but was substantially extended due to the success of Perry's performances, running until mid-August. The Copacabana engagement was a major success. Harriet Van Horne of the *New York World-Telegram* found Perry to be

> darkly handsome, pleasantly wholesome, and mercifully unaffected. His voice is clear, full-throated baritone, and when he sings he appears to be suffering no pain at all. Not even that private exquisite pain that is peculiar to nightclub crooners.[3]

Variety magazine's Abel Green was equally favourable, stating that Perry 'has poise, showmanship and unction. . . . He croons with intelligence'.[4]

A return engagement at the Copacabana and engagements at other prestigious New York venues, such as the Versailles Club and the Paramount Theatre, were to follow. Perry's first season at the Paramount took place from 14 July to 8 August 1944 as a cine-variety show alongside the film *And the Angels Sing* starring Fred MacMurray, Dorothy Lamour and Betty Hutton. Perry was supported in the performances by the backing of clarinettist Jerry Wald and his orchestra.

While working at the Paramount Theatre, Perry encountered an usher by the name of Vito Farinola. One day after Perry had finished his show, Vito was taking Perry up to his dressing room and stopped the elevator between floors. He sang a few lines of 'There Must Be a Way' and stopped. 'Go ahead, go ahead, sing!' said Perry. Vito sang some more and stopped again. 'Sing it! Finish it! Finish it!' said Perry. Vito finished the song, and Perry said, 'No kid, you gotta keep singing! You've got a nice voice'.[5] Such was the benevolence of Perry's support for new talent. Farinola later changed his name to Vic Damone, and the rest, as the saying goes – is history.

During this early period in his solo career, Perry invited his Dad along to a performance he was giving in the local vicinity and made sure Pietro had a seat in the front row. As soon as Perry came on stage, the audience went wild. This was the era of the bobby-soxer – a term which originated in a *Time* magazine article in 1943. The name was derived from the ankle socks often worn by teenage girls, usually along with loafers or saddle shoes. The bobby-soxer referred usually to female high school students who swooned to the romantic vocal stylings of the crooner. Audiences would jump, scream and cry for their performing idols.

Perry had barely got through his opening number when Pietro left the theatre, shocked by what he had experienced – something totally alien to what he was accustomed to. When the crowds had settled down, Perry looked over to where his father had been seated and was alarmed to see that he wasn't there. After the show, concerned for his father's whereabouts and keen for his appraisal, Perry headed back to the Como family home in Canonsburg. When he got there, he found his father sitting in the house. 'Where did ya go?' asked Perry. 'I got frightened', said Pietro, 'I thought those kids were crazy!' But what Perry really wanted to know was, what did his father think of his singing? Pietro paused calmly for a moment, looked at his son and said 'e brava' (which roughly translates as 'good' or 'nice'). For Perry that qualified as excitement from his father, who would not usually offer comment on such things. He was glad to have his father's quiet approval.[6]

The package was now assembled – records, radio and in-person appearances, but another medium was to present itself too: motion pictures. Before the conclusion of his engagement at the Copacabana, Perry signed with Twentieth Century-Fox in July 1943. It would prove to be Perry's least favourite venture of his entire career. He found the process of making movies boring: 'Half a page and you work a week!'[7]. He also felt that to truly get on in Hollywood, living there on a permanent basis with directors getting to know you was important.

Over the course of the next two years, Perry appeared in three films for Twentieth Century-Fox, all directed by Lewis Seiler. The first was *Something for the Boys* (1944), featuring Perry in a cameo role as a soldier. While his dialogue was brief, the film did produce two standout vocals from Perry, 'I Wish We Didn't Have to Say Goodnight' and 'In the Middle of Nowhere'. While based on the short-lived musical of the same name, the only original Cole Porter song in the film is the title song, with the soundtrack composed primarily by Jimmy McHugh with lyrics by Harold Adamson.

Next was *Doll Face* (1945) based on a play by Gypsy Rose Lee. Perry's dissatisfaction with the life of an actor was beginning to grow, and he appeared uncomfortable in the role. Nevertheless, he again delivers solid vocal performances for another McHugh and Adamson soundtrack, including 'Here Comes Heaven Again' and 'Dig You Later (A Hubba-Hubba-Hubba)' – the latter becoming a major hit on disc for him, achieving gold record status.

Portraying a character other than himself on screen was not Perry's style. He had, however, made considerable improvements in his acting skills by the time of his final film for Twentieth Century-Fox, *If I'm Lucky* (1946) in which he plays a young crooner who ends up running for governor. An added star attraction is trumpeter and bandleader Harry James. Perry's co-stars throughout the three films were Vivian Blaine and Carmen Miranda, with Phil Silvers appearing in the first and last of the outings. *Doll Face* and *If I'm Lucky* also feature the earliest known stereo recordings by Perry, from a time when there was much innovation in sound design at film studios.

Perry returned to movie-making once more for his final feature film appearance. Working this time for Metro-Goldwyn-Mayer, he appeared in the 1948 fictionalized biopic of the songwriting team Richard Rodgers and Lorenz Hart titled *Words and Music*. The storyline was criticized at the time for being excessively fictionalized, but despite criticisms of the narrative, musically, the film is a feast in glorious Technicolor. It features an array of MGM talent from the era. Rodgers is portrayed by Tom Drake and Hart by Mickey Rooney. The film is packed with memorable performances – not a bad one among them. These include interpretations by Judy Garland ('Johnny One Note' and 'I Wish I Were in Love Again' – the latter with Rooney), June Allyson and the Blackburn Twins ('Thou Swell'), Lena Horne ('The Lady Is a Tramp' and 'Where or When') and Mel Tormé ('Blue Moon'). Perry's contributions were 'Mountain Greenery' (with Allyn Ann McLerie), 'Blue Room' (with dancing by Cyd Charisse) and 'With a Song in My Heart', which tops and tails the closing montage. With *Words and Music* complete, Perry closed the door on his acting career for good.

Mr. Como had far more suited avenues to demonstrate his talents. He had already proved his personable skills on his CBS radio show. Combined with a strong following and several prestigious engagements to his credit, he was a clear choice to host a new music variety program, sponsored by the Liggett & Myers Tobacco Company and specifically their Chesterfield brand of cigarettes. It was an association that was to last for over a decade.

The *Chesterfield Supper Club* had its first broadcast on Monday, 11 December 1944, on NBC. At this early stage, the show was hosted by disc jockey Martin Block, whose career in broadcasting had begun in 1934. The guest on opening night was Jimmy Savo, the first of many guests to visit the show over the next six years and a frequent return visitor. Savo, who guested on the show no less than twenty times, was a vaudevillian whose on-air persona was that of a meek and bashful character of a youthful disposition. He is perhaps best remembered for his performance of the novelty song 'One Meat Ball'. Also guesting in the *Supper Club*'s opening week were singers Connee Boswell, Miguelito Valdés and Marion Hutton, plus comedian-pianist Victor Borge.

The shows were broadcast live and transcribed by NBC. The Friday 15 December broadcast was the first to be repackaged by the Armed Forces Radio Service (AFRS). The AFRS was established by the US War Department in May 1942 for the purpose of informing and entertaining the American forces. Over the next five years, hundreds of editions of the *Chesterfield Supper Club* would be edited and compiled by the service for rebroadcast over the AFRS network. It was a highly productive and successful year for Perry, capped off by being voted 'Most Romantic Singer of 1944' in a national poll.

By early 1945, it was clear to Perry that he should be hosting the *Chesterfield Supper Club* in addition to singing on it. This was not a position of arrogance; it was an instinctive and logical conclusion of the kind that would serve him well throughout his career. When Perry expressed his thoughts to the sponsor, they agreed. It didn't make sense to Perry that someone else should be speaking with the guests. Martin Block, however, was not pleased. From his point of view, the announcer did the talking and the singer did the singing. Initially, Martin's disapproval meant that he would not play Perry's records on the air. Eventually though, whatever differences there had been, they were obviously overcome – as Martin continued as master of ceremonies for the shows. Many years later, their paths would cross again when Perry guested on a series of four radio programmes for the National Guard in 1963, hosted by Block.

The *Chesterfield Supper Club* went from strength to strength and welcomed a wide variety of guests across its run, including jazz group the King Cole Trio, pianist Carmen Cavallaro and comedian Alan Reed. Reed is best remembered today for having voiced the character Fred Flintstone in the Hanna-Barbera animated series *The Flintstones,* but in the 1940s, he was famous for playing the character of a fictitious poet by the name of Falstaff Openshaw on *The Fred Allen Show*. It was this character he appeared as on the *Chesterfield Supper Club*. Usually partaking in some comedic dialogue with Perry, Reed (in character throughout) then proceeds to recite one of his latest humorous poems.

Margaret Whiting, one of the many vocal guests from the era, said that Perry reminded her of her father (the composer Richard A. Whiting), who she remembered as a great gentleman and a great golfer. 'He sang with such respect for the song', said Margaret of Perry, 'and such warmth and feeling about a song. A lot of people just would sing the words and get through the melody, and you'd say, "Well . . . that's nice. He's gotta nice voice", but he [Perry] took every song and looked at it and studied it because it came out as a painting'.[8]

The *Chesterfield Supper Club* also had several recurring (often weekly) comedy acts. In addition to Jimmy Savo, there were the Wesson Brothers (Dick and Gene), Jerry Mann (assisted by his wife, Betty Linde) and Pick and Pat (Pick Malone and Pat Padgett). The Wesson Brothers were a double act in which Dick was the comedian and Gene the straight man. One of Dick's catchphrases, usually set up by Gene, was 'You don't put it on . . . You smear it on!'.

Jerry Mann was an actor, writer and comedian. Like Alan Reed, he also had a resume that included animated series. He provided voices for some one-off characters in *The Flintstones* and *Tom and Jerry*. At this stage in his career, though, radio was a regular part of his commitments. His sketches with wife, Betty often included a song sung as an impression of Al Jolson, which nodded back to Mann's vaudevillian roots, where, at the age of nine, he began his career doing impressions of Eddie Cantor.

Pick and Pat were a minstrel-style comedy team who performed in blackface, a tradition that was still prevalent both domestically within the United States and internationally at the time but that would fall out of favour in the coming decades with good reason. Aside from the racial sensitivities, perhaps the most bizarre aspect of their act was that they blacked-up for radio performances. There was a studio audience who would have seen the visual element, but it would have had no benefit for the audience listening on radio. This same peculiarity was true for ventriloquists on radio too. From the audience perspective, a big part of ventriloquism is being able to visually observe the skill of the performer throwing their voice to create the illusion of speech coming from a dummy – this is completely lost on a radio listener. However, it does not detract from the skill of the performer, and it remains necessary for one person to create the audible illusion of a conversation between two.

Musical accompaniment on the *Chesterfield Supper Club* was originally provided by Ted Steele. Ted, who already had a couple of NBC credits to his name, was a host on radio and later television, in addition to his bandleading activities. Ted conducted the orchestra on Perry's first recording session of 1945 – a session which resulted in three songs, one of which would go on to become a gold record, 'Temptation'.

At the height of the recording industry, a gold record was awarded for sales of 1,000,000 copies of a single disc. The first known 'gold record' was an in-house production, consisting of a framed, gold-painted disc with commemorative plaque, presented to Glenn Miller by RCA Victor on 10 February 1942 for his Bluebird label recording of 'Chattanooga Choo Choo.' Many years later, the first independently certified gold record was awarded by the Recording Industry Association of America (RIAA) on 14 March 1958 for Perry Como's recording of 'Catch a Falling Star' and became the benchmark for million-selling disc certification.

Ted Steele provided orchestral accompaniment on *Supper Club* broadcasts until the autumn of 1945, at which point Lloyd Shaffer took over conducting duties on radio. Shaffer would also conduct for Perry on several recording sessions and stayed with him on radio until the summer of 1948. Aside from their conducting talents, Steele and Shaffer co-wrote the song 'Smoke Dreams' along with John Klenner, which would become the theme song of the *Chesterfield Supper Club*.

Throughout the first season, Perry hosted Monday to Friday. Commencing in December 1945, singer Jo Stafford joined the fold, holding the fort on Tuesdays and Thursdays, while Perry maintained Mondays, Wednesdays and Fridays. The exception to this rule was when Perry had filming commitments in Hollywood, during which Perry and Jo swapped rotas. Jo proved an excellent choice to join the *Supper Club* – the pureness of her vocal delivery and her friendly interactions with guests made her a very fitting addition to the *Supper Club* roster. Her future husband, Paul Weston handled orchestral duties on her broadcasts. Another vocalist Peggy Lee joined the club for the 1948–9 season with orchestra led by her first husband Dave Barbour. As well as being a talented vocal artiste, Lee was also an accomplished songwriter, including many collaborations with Barbour, of which 'It's a Good Day' (a favourite of Perry's) and 'Mañana (Is Soon Enough for Me)' are two of the best remembered.

With the AFM dispute resolved on 8 December 1944, Perry was in RCA Victor Studio 1 the same day for his first recordings for the label with orchestral accompaniment, conducted by Lew Martin. The first title slated for recording, composed, no less, by Jerome Kern with lyrics by E. Y. Harburg was 'More and More' from the film *Can't Help Singing*. On disc, 'More and More' was backed with 'I Wish We Didn't Have to Say Goodnight' recorded on the same date and from Perry's first feature film, *Something for the Boys*.

The year 1945 was a year of conflicting emotions. On a national scale, there was the jubilation of the end of the Second World War, but this was preceded by the sudden death of US President Franklin Delano Roosevelt at sixty-three. He never lived to see the victory that was soon to come and for which he played a considerable part. On a personal level, Perry experienced a parallel between sadness and celebration with the death of his father at the age of sixty-eight on 8 July. Just five days earlier, Perry had a recording session that would yield his first multi-million selling No. 1 hit, 'Till the End of Time'. Sadly, Pietro did not get to see the first of his famous son's many major recording milestones.

Upon release, 'Till the End of Time' (based on Frédéric Chopin's 'Polonaise in A-Flat Major') was hardly greeted with a wealth of praise from *Billboard* magazine, who described the song as a 'sombre ballad' that 'holds little melodic charm as a pop song, despite the familiarity of its theme'.[9] The record-buying public, however, clearly knew better. The song resonated greatly with listeners and captured the spirit and sentiments of the time. In the United States alone, the song spent nineteen weeks in the charts, ten of those at No. 1.

The flip-side '(Did You Ever Get) That Feeling in the Moonlight' was met with far greater favour by *Billboard*, who found it reminiscent of Perry's days with Ted Weems 'and with greater effectiveness . . . a real lyrical contagion'. 'Till the End of Time' also found wide international appeal. Surprisingly, however, the song was banned in the UK by the BBC, prohibiting its broadcast on air because of its adaptation from a classical composition. Although a common practice during the era, it was something frowned upon by the BBC at the time. Despite this, the song still achieved prominence throughout the British Isles.

A classic 1940s portrait of Perry.

Most of the recordings that Perry made between 1945 and 1947 were conducted by Russ Case, with whom he made over sixty masters during the period. Of the first ten recordings they made together between May and December 1945, every title was a hit, nine of which were in the top ten, and several achieved gold record status, including 'I'm Gonna Love That Gal (Like She's Never Been Loved Before)', 'Till the End of Time' and 'Prisoner of Love'.

So successful was this period in the blossoming Como career that RCA Victor announced the week of 2–9 September 1946 to be 'Perry Como Week' – during which a reported four million Como discs left the RCA pressing plant in Camden, New Jersey. The following week, Perry was honoured in his hometown when Third Street, Canonsburg, Pennsylvania, was renamed Perry Como Avenue. Among the celebrations was a testimonial banquet held at the State Armoury in Canonsburg to mark the occasion. Como, ever the humble personality later reflected on the occasion, 'Changing the name of a street, that's something you do for a real hero, a guy who's really accomplished something. What did I do big? I'm nobody to yell about. And everybody I knew was acting so stiff. Like Mrs. So and So – she used to smack my behind when I was a kid, and there she was, trying to call me Mr. Como. I wanted to bawl'.[10]

Interspersed between radio and films were further personal appearances. Teenagers swooned over the talented and handsome Italian-American with the rich baritone. These audiences could be boisterous but wildly appreciative. A sea of young, fresh-faced, predominantly pubescent teenagers made up the core audience at the time. One such occasion must have felt like déjà vu for Mr. Como. On 17 August 1947, while appearing again at the Chicago Theatre in Illinois, Perry was mid-song when an audience member threw a jawbreaker (a large piece of hard candy) at him, hitting him on the head.

It was an unfortunate irony, adding insult to injury for Perry, who was already in discomfort, suffering from an abscessed tooth and little sleep consequently. Between performances, the ailing star was back and forth between the theatre and the dentist for pain relief. In a stern response, Perry asked for the house lights to be turned up and invited the likely testosterone-fuelled culprit up onto the stage, along with all his friends. Many years later, Perry joked that he was a 'mean Italian' in those days. 'I challenged the whole theatre!'[11] He waited for a response, but it didn't come, so Mr. Como resumed his performance.

In 1948, a new member was welcomed into the Como family when Perry and Roselle adopted an eleven-month-old baby girl, who they named Therese (Terri for short). Perry described her as the joy of his life. 'She always remembers me on Father's Day', said Perry in 1971 of his daughter, then in her early twenties. He kidded 'Last Father's Day she gave me two neckties – that wide [he gestures about ten inches] yellow and purple, and the other one was pink and green' adding with poignancy, 'but she's a nice girl – she's a delight. I guess she takes after her mother. She's always been so gentle, so kind'. Adding in jest 'I think she's 47 now!'[12]

The Como clan was completed the following year when David joined the fleet, being adopted by Perry and Roselle at the age of three and a half years. David had captured Roselle's heart at an adoption agency. There was, of course, much family discussion before the adoption, but Perry had not seen David until he came home one day to find a little fellow sitting on the front steps of the Como's Long Island home. 'Hi', said Perry, 'What's your name?' David gave his name, adding that his last name was Como. 'Is it?' asked Perry. 'Well, do you know who I am?' he continued. 'Yes', David replied, 'you're my daddy'. Then, Roselle came out of their house. The Comos looked at each other, Roselle nodded, and then they smiled. Perry offered his hand to David and said, 'Come on, son, let's go inside'. And in that moment, the Como household graduated from a quartet to a quintet. Perry had made little David his own.[13]

By the second half of the 1940s, the frequency of Perry's working commitments had increased so much so that Roselle's brother, Dee Belline joined Perry to assist in managing his affairs. 'Perry can't talk to man or child without putting his arm over the guy's shoulder or touching a sleeve', said Dee many years later. 'His warmth is so outgoing that someone once advised us to insulate him from outsiders. Anyway, I think this is what the TV audience feels and says in the letters they write to him'.[14] It was this TV audience which would usher in the next phase in the Como career. Perry Como was well and truly here to stay.

Quintessential Como
Recommended listening 1943–9

Goodbye Sue ★
mw Jimmy Rule, Lou Ricca
and Jules Loman, 1943
20 Jun 1943 - 20-1538
For the Record - 31 Jul 1944
[with Benny Goodman and his
V-Disc All-Star Band] - V-Disc 312

Have I Stayed Away Too Long?
mw Frank Loesser, 1943
1 Dec 1943 - 20-1548

Long Ago (and Far Away)
m Jerome Kern, w Ira Gershwin, 1944
From the film Cover Girl.
8 Feb 1944 - PC Sings Just for You CAL-440

I Love You ★
mw Cole Porter, 1944
From the musical Mexican Hayride.
8 Feb 1944 - PC Sings Just for You CAL-440
CPPC - c. 1944 / PC KMH - 28 Mar 1966

**I Dream of You
(More Than You Dream I Do)**
mw Marjorie Goetschius
and Edna Osser, 1944
8 Dec 1944 - 20-1629

I'm Confessin' (That I Love You) ★
m Doc Daugherty and Ellis Reynolds,
w Al J. Neiburg, 1930
11 Dec 1944 - PC Sings Just for You CAL-440

Temptation ★
m Nacio Herb Brown, w Arthur Freed, 1933
From the film Going Hollywood.
27 Mar 1945 - Como's Golden Records
LPM-1981 / 29 Apr 1974 - Perry CPL1-0585

**I'm Gonna Love That Gal
(Like She's Never Been Loved Before)**
mw Frances Ash, 1945
19 May 1945 - 20-1676

If I Loved You ★
m Richard Rodgers,
w Oscar Hammerstein II, 1945
From the film Carousel.
19 May 1945 - Dream Along with Me CAL-403

**(Did You Ever Get)
That Feeling in the Moonlight**
mw James Cavanaugh, Larry Stock
and Ira Schuster, 1945
3 Jul 1945 - 20-1709

Till the End of Time ★
mw Buddy Kaye and Ted Mossman, 1945
Adapted from Frédéric Chopin's
'Polonaise in A-Flat Major', Op. 53.
3 Jul 1945 - Como's Golden Records
LPM-1981

Dig You Later (A Hubba-Hubba-Hubba) ■
m Jimmy McHugh,
w Harold Adamson, 1945
From the film Doll Face.
13 Oct 1945 - Como's Golden
Records LPM-1981
Doll Face - 1945

Here Comes Heaven Again ■
m Jimmy McHugh,
w Harold Adamson, 1945
From the film Doll Face.
17 Oct 1945 - 20-1750
Doll Face - 1945

I'm Always Chasing Rainbows
m Harry Carroll, w Joseph McCarthy, 1918
Based on Frédéric Chopin's
'Fantasie Impromptu in C-Sharp Minor'.
From the musical Oh, Look!
17 Oct 1945 - A Sentimental Date with
PC LPM-1177

**You Won't Be Satisfied
(Until You Break My Heart)**
mw Teddy Powell and Larry Stock, 1945
17 Oct 1945 - PC Sings Just for You CAL-440

All Through the Day
m Jerome Kern,
w Oscar Hammerstein II, 1946
From the film Centennial Summer.
18 Dec 1945 - PC Wednesday Night
Music Hall CAL-511

Prisoner of Love ★
m Russ Columbo and Clarence Gaskill,
w Leo Robin, 1931
18 Dec 1945 - Como's Golden Records
LPM-1981
25–27 Jun 1970 (Live) - PC in Person at the
International Hotel, Las Vegas LSPX-1001

Blue Skies ★
mw Irving Berlin, 1927
From the musical Betsy.
19 Mar 1946 - Dream Along with Me CAL-403

Surrender
mw Bennie Benjamin
and George David Weiss, 1946
2 Apr 1946 - 20-1877

They Say It's Wonderful
mw Irving Berlin, 1946
From the musical Annie Get Your Gun.
2 Apr 1946 - Dream Along with Me CAL-403

I Want to Thank Your Folks
mw Bennie Benjamin
and George David Weiss, 1947
19 Dec 1946 - 20-2117

Song of Songs ★
m Harold Vicars, w Maurice Vancaire
(Fr.) and Clarence Lucas (Eng.), 1914
23 Jan 1947 - Relaxing with PC LPM-1176

**Chi-Baba, Chi-Baba
(My Bambino Go to Sleep)**
mw Mack David, Jerry Livingston
and Al Hoffman, 1947
10 Apr 1947 - Make Someone Happy
CAL-694

When You Were Sweet Sixteen ★
mw James Thornton, 1898
10 Apr 1947 - Como's Golden Records
LPM-1981

Body and Soul
m John Green, w Edward Heyman,
Robert Sour and Frank Eyton, 1930
11 Jul 1947 - A Sentimental Date with PC
LPM-1177

A Fellow Needs a Girl ★
m Richard Rodgers,
w Oscar Hammerstein II, 1947
From the musical Allegro.
28 Jul 1947 - PC Wednesday Night
Music Hall CAL-511

Love Me or Leave Me
m Walter Donaldson, w Gus Kahn, 1928
From the musical Whoopee.
30 Sep 1947 - A Sentimental Date with PC
LPM-1177

Pianissimo
mw Bennie Benjamin
and George David Weiss, 1948
14 Oct 1947 - 20-2593

Because ★
mw Guy d'Hardelot (Fr.),
w Edward Teschemacher (Eng.), 1902
2 Dec 1947 - Como's Golden Records
LPM-1981

There Must Be a Way
mw Sammy Gallop and David Saxon, 1945
9 Dec 1947 - You Are Never Far Away
CAL-2201

Haunted Heart
m Arthur Schwartz, w Howard Dietz, 1948
From the revue Inside U.S.A.
9 Dec 1947 - 20-2713

Rambling Rose
m Joe Burke, w Joseph McCarthy Jr., 1948
30 Dec 1947 - 20-2947

Far Away Places
mw Joan Whitney and Alex Kramer, 1949
14 Dec 1948 - Relaxing with PC LPM-1176

Blue Room ■
m Richard Rodgers, w Lorenz Hart, 1926
From the musical The Girl Friend and
featured in the film Words and Music.
17 Dec 1948 - A Sentimental Date with PC
LPM-1177
29 May 1948 - MGM Mx. 27494 / Sc.
2417 (Words and Music - 1948)

With a Song in My Heart ■ ★
m Richard Rodgers, w Lorenz Hart, 1929
From the musical Spring Is Here and
featured in the film Words and Music.
23 Dec 1948 - A Sentimental Date with PC
LPM-1177
10 Jul 1948 - MGM Mx. 27503 / Sc. 2427
(Words and Music - 1948)

I Don't See Me in Your Eyes Anymore
mw Bennie Benjamin
and George David Weiss, 1949
13 Jan 1949 - 20-3347

Forever and Ever
m Franz Winkler, w Malia Rosa, 1949
13 Jan 1949 - PC Sings Just for You CAL-440

'A' – You're Adorable (The Alphabet Song)
with The Fontane Sisters
mw Buddy Kaye, Fred Wise
and Sidney Lippman, 1948
1 Mar 1949 - PC Sings Just for You CAL-440

Some Enchanted Evening ★
m Richard Rodgers,
w Oscar Hammerstein II, 1949
From the musical South Pacific.
1 Mar 1949 - PC Sings Hits from
Broadway Shows LPM-1191

Bali Ha'i
m Richard Rodgers,
w Oscar Hammerstein II, 1949
From the musical South Pacific.
1 Mar 1949 - PC Sings Hits from
Broadway Shows LPM-1191

A Dreamer's Holiday
with The Fontane Sisters
m Mabel Wayne, w Kim Gannon, 1949
11 Aug 1949 - PC Wednesday Night
Music Hall CAL-511

I Wanna Go Home (with You)
with The Fontane Sisters
mw Jack Joyce, 1949
11 Aug 1949 - PC Wednesday Night
Music Hall CAL-511

Hush Little Darlin'
with The Fontane Sisters
m Marty Clarke, w Bob Haymes, 1949
3 Oct 1949 - 20-3586

Bibbidi-Bobbidi-Boo (The Magic Song)
with The Fontane Sisters
mw Mack David, Al Hoffman
and Jerry Livingston, 1950
From the animated film Cinderella.
7 Nov 1949 - 20-3607

3

Some Enchanted Evening

On 24 December 1948, in a radio studio in New York City, the well-established *Chesterfield Supper Club* was about to take a monumental step in a newly developing medium called television. Though Perry and his colleagues probably did not realize it at the time, television history was being made. It was apt that Perry's first complete television broadcast would be at Christmas. Over the coming years and decades, his name would become synonymous with the celebrations of the season. Several experimental broadcasts had led up to the occasion and now here, for the first time live on television was Perry Como at Christmas.

This first show and indeed all that followed over the next six months would be simulcast (i.e. simultaneously broadcast) on radio and television. In principle, they were televised radio broadcasts, not designed strictly for television. There were, however, portions of the program specifically dedicated to the visual, which allowed for further exploration of the newly emerging technology. At the time, those in possession of a television set were in the minority, but within a few years, the television would become as much a part of the home as the furniture. The guests on Perry's television premiere were his son, Ronnie, now approaching nine years old, and the Boys' Choir of St. Peter of Alcantara. It was a landmark year for television, and Perry Como was a pioneering figure of the medium.

1948 had been a landmark year for the recording industry too. On 21 June 1948, Columbia Records introduced the first long-playing (LP) vinyl record. These records played at a much slower speed than the standard 78 rpm discs –

running at 33 1/3 rpm and capable of containing up to a total of 20–25 minutes per side on a 12-inch disc and up to 16 minutes per side on a 10-inch disc – several times the capacity of a 78. This was achieved through two key factors. The first was the much slower speed, which meant it would take longer for the stylus to journey across the disc playing surface. The second was a greatly reduced output level at the mastering stage, resulting in a much smaller and finer waveform embossed in the material (now a type of plastic, with vastly lower surface noise), allowing for a far greater amount of recorded data to be contained within a single disc.

The small output signal within the vinyl record was compensated for by a phono preamplifier within the listener's audio setup. This boosted the signal to a level that could be reproduced properly through an amplifier. The increase in running time per side was particularly exciting for the classical music market. It meant that no longer would many classical works need to be split up midway through a piece or movement. In the pre-LP days, a movement from a symphony, for example, would commonly require two sides of a 12-inch 78 rpm disc. It might even be abridged or sped up in passages to avoid running onto a third side. The LP eliminated this problem. The new format was equally beneficial in terms of surface noise (particularly noticeable during quiet passages), which was vastly reduced compared with conventional shellac-pressed 78 rpm discs.

The year had started more problematically for the music industry. In November 1947, the AFM announced another strike from recording, as of 1 January 1948, preventing instrumentalists from recording. This time, however, with Perry now a well-established RCA Victor artist, a heavier recording schedule was arranged prior to the strike to cover the release of new material throughout.

Perry made only one recording during the 1948 ban on 2 December with a female harmony group called the Fontane Sisters. Marge, Bea, and Geri Rosse from New Milford, New Jersey, had just joined the *Chesterfield Supper Club*, performing together as a trio and in collaboration with Perry. Although the song 'N'yot N'yow (The Pussycat Song)' was their first commercial recording with Como, they had all worked together before. Firstly, on the second series of *Columbia Presents Perry Como*, when the ladies went by the name of the

Three Sisters and subsequently, as guests on the *Chesterfield Supper Club* where they guested with Perry twice in 1945 – teaming up on Frank Loesser's 'Have I Stayed Away Too Long?' in April and on the Gordon Jenkins composition 'Ev'ry Time (Ev'ry Time I Fall in Love)' in May. The Fontane Sisters joined Perry in the transition to television with great success, and together they achieved over a dozen hit recordings.

Less than two weeks following Perry's first recording with the Fontane Sisters, the AFM ban was over, and Perry was scheduled for an afternoon session of expedient priority but not before attending a special presentation in honour of recently elected US President Harry S. Truman. Proceedings were headed by AFM union boss James C. Petrillo, who read 'Christmas Greetings to the President'. This was followed by a group of artists, including Perry, Fran Warren and nine headliners from the Metropolitan Opera House, gathering around a piano to sing a chorus of the Noble Sissle and Eubie Blake standard 'I'm Just Wild About Harry'.

The event was captured on film and the story was covered in *Time* Magazine on 27 December that year. 'Everyone was in high spirits; both the record companies and Petrillo were happy that they had found a way around the law so that Petrillo could once again fatten his union's welfare fund with record royalties'. With the presentation complete, the race was on for the first post-ban recording.

> Perry Como rushed into Studio Two, where an all-string orchestra awaited him. A few moments later they were lurching through the 'Missouri Waltz', a Truman inauguration special which was Victor's first commercial disc. The green baize turntables whirled far into the night. Tommy Dorsey and his orchestra hopped over from the Café Rouge at 2 am. Phlegm-voiced Vaughn Monroe, who had been among the last to record last December, tried desperately to get back from Ohio to be the first, but arrived too late. By noon the next day, Como's 'Missouri Waltz' was on sale on Broadway.[1]

The session was conducted by Henri René, and the A-side of the disc was 'Far Away Places', which proved to be another international hit for Como.

A few days later, Perry was back in the studio for the first of two recording sessions to comprise a single of 'Blue Room' and 'With a Song in My Heart' (both from Perry's last film, *Words and Music*). Como was again supported by Henri René, but this would be the first session with one of Perry's longest-standing colleagues, Ray Charles. Not to be confused with the rhythm and blues singer of the same name, this Ray Charles (born Charles Raymond Offenberg) was a choral director, among his many musical talents. He had first worked with Perry in December 1944 during the beginnings of the *Chesterfield Supper Club* when the WAVES (Women Accepted for Volunteer Emergency Service) singing platoon (directed by Ray) were guests on the first Christmas edition of the show, almost four years to the day earlier. December 1948, however, was the beginning of a regular working relationship that would endure for more than thirty five years.

Another new and prominent figure in the Como collaborative who joined Perry during this period was Mitchell Ayres. Ayres, another highly accomplished musician best known as an orchestra leader and arranger began working with Perry on the *Chesterfield Supper Club* in September 1948. Como and Ayres made their first studio recordings together in January 1949. At the time, Mitchell was working with another popular vocalist Buddy Clark. Born the same year as Mr. Como, Clark was a successful singer in his own right, recording for Columbia Records. His hits include 'Linda', 'How Are Things in Glocca Morra?' and 'Love Somebody' (duetting with Doris Day). Clark's career was cut tragically short at the age of thirty-seven when he died in a plane crash in October 1949.

The first Como and Ayres session took place on 13 January 1949 and resulted in the single 'Forever and Ever' backed with 'I Don't See Me in Your Eyes Anymore'. It was the first of several major hits during the year that included 'Some Enchanted Evening' plus 'A – You're Adorable (The Alphabet Song)' and 'A Dreamer's Holiday' (both with the Fontane Sisters). Together they would provide a fitting conclusion to the 1940s.

That same year, RCA Victor unveiled its response to Columbia's new long-playing 10- and 12-inch 33 1/3 rpm records – the 7-inch 45 rpm single. Thus began the 'Battle of the Speeds'. Whereas the Columbia format usually contained all of an album's material on two sides of one disc, RCA Victor's approach was box sets of singles, following on from the 78 rpm folio albums, which for pop music typically contained four discs in separate envelopes, all attached to the inside spine of a cardboard cover. For 45 rpm discs, this changed to a tray/box with either a taped hinge or a removable lid.

RCA's approach emphasized the convenience of being more compact and the benefit of predefined song selection, achieved through the means of RCA 45 rpm disc changers, within which records could be stacked in a particular order by the listener – a precursor to the playlist of the digital era. This also led to the introduction of the 45 rpm extended play (EP) record – usually containing approximately half the content of a 10-inch LP within the size of a 7-inch disc. The emphasis again was on the convenience of a smaller disc and that they were great for parties, which the label plugged within their 1955 10-disc EP box set *The RCA Victor Platter Party* – containing two songs each by twenty of the label's artists for a total of forty recordings, including selections from the Ames Brothers, Harry Belafonte, Eddie Fisher, Freddy Martin and, of course, Perry.

The *Platter Party* set has the distinguishing feature of being the only US release on which Perry's recording of 'The Ruby and the Pearl' originally appeared. Recorded three years earlier, Perry's recording of the song was never originally released as a single in the United States but had made its way to the UK on 78 and subsequently 45 rpm. Of equal distinction is the second selection, which offers the listener an opportunity to hear an early Como version of 'When You Come to the End of the Day'. Perry would return to this composition as the title song for his classic 1958 album of songs of faith and inspiration.

On RCA Victor's part, there was no need to develop their own format to compete with Columbia. The LP was not patented in a bid to encourage wide acceptance of the new format. Columbia wanted RCA Victor to join them in promoting it. This had been the hope of William Paley (chairman of CBS, owner of Columbia) when he demonstrated the new format to Robert Sarnoff (president of NBC, owner of RCA Victor). However, according to a member of Columbia staff, Howard 'Scotty' Scott 'When Sarnoff heard the demonstration, he was furious and chewed out his entire staff in front of Paley and (Bill) Wallerstein (the true inventor of the LP). Sarnoff left in a huff'.[2] Consequently, it was concluded that the 45 rpm single was introduced out of spite rather than necessity. Incidentally, the speed of 45 was reportedly arrived at by subtracting 33 from 78.

The second season of the televised *Chesterfield Supper Club* began on 16 October 1949. Now no longer a simulcast, the television show was a separate entity airing live on Sunday evenings, especially for television. A separate radio broadcast continued with different content and guests, airing for a final season on Thursdays. The show was now in an extended format, running for 30 minutes on both radio and television. This extended time allowed amply for more than one guest (if desired) and comedy sketches of a longer duration. On radio, this allowed Perry to partake in humorous skits with such stars as Cary Grant, Dorothy Lamour and Mae West. One particularly memorable programme on 2 March 1950 featured Kirk Douglas, performing a satire with Perry of his current boxing film *Champion*. The rapport between these two gentlemen is a joy to hear, and the audience has no hesitation in expressing their delight in the proceedings that unfold. The ability to send himself up was something that Perry would increasingly draw upon as his public persona developed.

Over on television, the Sunday evening broadcasts were steadily developing into a warm, family-friendly variety programme with guests from the worlds of music, comedy, and theatre. Sets and props started to become a feature, which was well demonstrated on the pre-Christmas 1949 edition, during which Perry and the Fontane Sisters are pictured in-situ about to embark on a motor car trip as the basis for a performance of their hit 'A Dreamer's Holiday'. They open the show with similar attention to visual elements. With the Fontanes dressed as witches, surrounding a cauldron, Perry (wielding a magic wand) joins them in a rendition of 'Bibbidi-Bobbidi-Boo (The Magic Song)' (another hit for them) with guest Johnny Puleo popping his head through the top of the magic box in front of them as a surprise to the audience at the end of the song.

'Bibbidi-Bobbidi-Boo' came from the forthcoming Walt Disney animated film *Cinderella*. Walt happened to hear Perry's recording of 'Chi-Baba, Chi-Baba (My Bambino Go to Sleep)' on the radio and was particularly struck by both the song written by Mack David, Jerry Livingston and Al Hoffman and by Perry's delivery of the lyrics. Disney hired the songwriting trio to compose the music for the film and was keen for Perry to introduce selections from it.

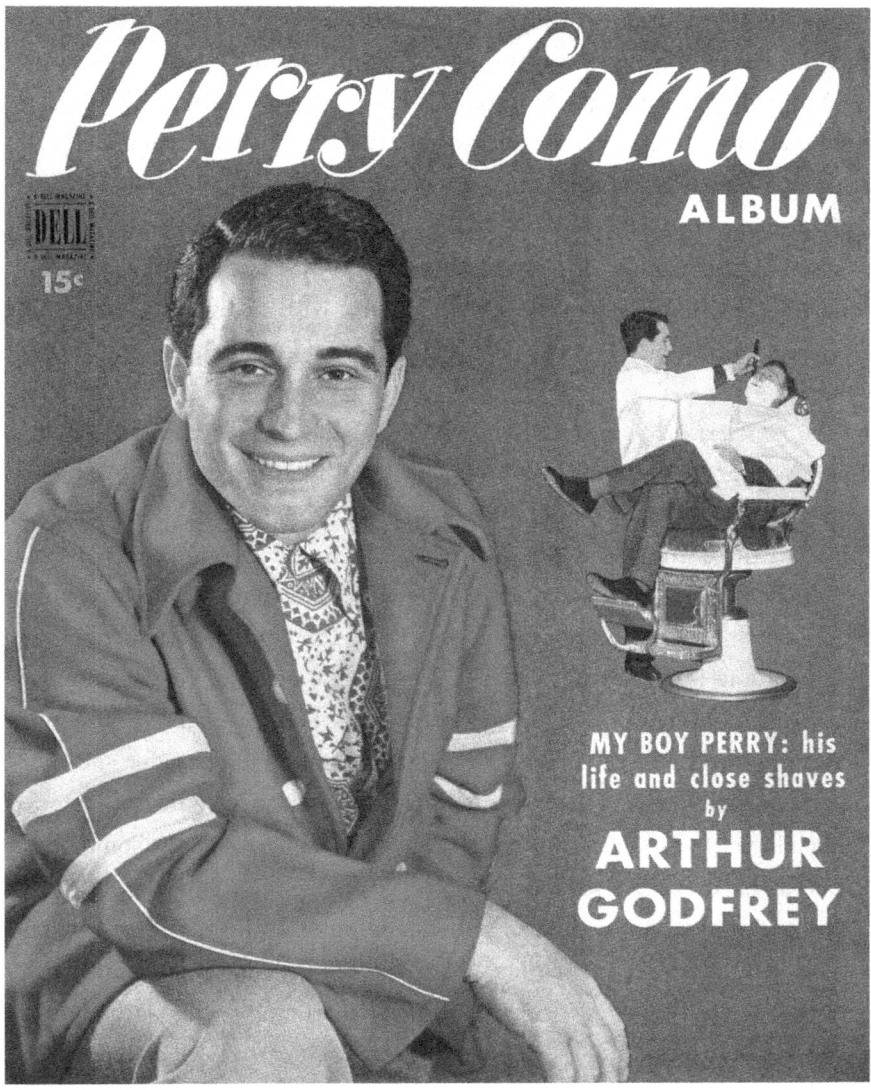

A Perry Como magazine published by Dell in 1950.

On 12 February 1950, three days before the movie's release, the *Chesterfield Supper Club* presented a preview feature for the forthcoming film. Ilene Woods (the voice of Cinderella) guested on the show, along with a cameo appearance by Clarence Nash (the voice of the Disney character Donald Duck). Perry narrates the story of Cinderella complete with animated stills and interspersed with songs from the film performed by Ilene Woods and the Fontane Sisters, concluding with a full company performance of 'Bibbidi-Bobbidi-Boo'. The feature is a charming example of the kind of presentation that would later form the structure of Perry's telling of 'The Story of the First Christmas' and a testament to Perry's influence at the time. Al Hoffman would go on to write further hit songs for Perry with songwriting partner Dick Manning. Together they wrote five hit songs for Perry during the 1950s, including 'Papa Loves Mambo' (also with Bix Reichner) and 'Hot Diggity (Dog Ziggity Boom)' (adapted from the first theme of Emmanuel Chabrier's 'España'.

The *Chesterfield Supper Club* came to an end in the summer of 1950 to make way for a new Como venture, still with the same sponsor, but on the CBS Television Network and titled *The Perry Como Show* – airing for 15 minutes, three times a week (Mondays, Wednesdays and Fridays). The 15-minute running time was carried over from radio and became a common practice in the United States during the 1950s. The Fontane Sisters, now very much coming into their own, joined Perry in the move to CBS. Announcer Martin Block, however, was succeeded by Dick Stark, and the programmes were produced by Lee Cooley. Set designs became much broader and more elaborate, as did many of the musical numbers. Consequently, the show gained a much larger feel than the *Supper Club*. It was here where Perry Como began to perfect his on-screen persona.

Perry exhibited an instinctive understanding of both the immediacy and intimacy of the television medium. He performed for not only the ears but the eyes as well. The energy of live television particularly appealed to Perry and his shows were broadcast live long after many others were routinely pre-recorded. The discipline required to handle the benefits and indeed the challenges of a live broadcast were seen to glorious effect. If there was a delay, a missed cue, bumping of stage scenery or any number of other complications – Perry dealt with them calmly with quick wit and good humour, and audiences clearly loved him for it. It was during this period that the famous cue-card boys came to be. Cue cards were the predecessors of the auto-cue/television prompter – in Perry's case, they were for dialogue and song lyrics.

The show's length and frequency proved to be an excellent platform for the blossoming sales of television sets in the United States. Over five million televisions were sold in 1950 alone. This, combined with figures from previous years, equated to nearly 20 per cent of American households having a television set. By the end of the decade, this number was close to 90 per cent. Television had revolutionized the entertainment industry in a way that radio had done thirty years earlier.

With a bigger set came a bigger audience, which at times could prove challenging for Perry. Perry had entered the world of the solo singer at the beginning of the era of the bobby-soxers in the 1940s, during which the teenagers of the day would scream and shout for their music idols – just like the teenagers of the 1950s would do a decade later for rock n roll and indeed a decade after that for the pop bands. Perry disliked this response from an audience, which was still common for pop vocalists at the time of his show on CBS – especially when he was trying to sing or make an announcement. Perry reflected on the era, saying, 'You walk out there, and you feel like an idiot. I did anyway'. Perry said to fans, 'Listen to what I gotta tell ya and then do whatever you like' and some fans said, 'Well, they do it for him, they do it for so-and-so, why can't we do it for you?' to which Perry responded, 'Because you're not paying attention. How can you scream and listen at the same time?' So, Perry noted, '. . . On our shows you very seldom hear that [screaming] and they [the fans] were very nice about it, which, of course, I appreciated'.[3]

Between 1950 and 1955, *The Perry Como Show* ran on CBS Television for five seasons and over 500 episodes. During the first season, Perry welcomed such distinguished guests as band leaders Artie Shaw, Jimmy Dorsey and Lionel Hampton, plus singer-pianist and composer Hoagy Carmichael, as well as providing an outlet for new singing talents such as Mindy Carson and Teresa Brewer.

The first season concluded on 29 June 1951, after which Peggy Lee and Mel Tormé hosted for the summer season while Perry was on vacation. In an interview forty years later, Mel remarked that to him, Perry was 'the epitome of what I like to see in a singer. He's very laid-back, he's very calm, very cool – his singing reflects that . . . I don't think that Perry . . . is the most "exciting singer" that I've ever seen but he sings so beautifully in tune, he has such gorgeous tonal quality, and he's wonderfully pleasant to listen to'.[4] Praise indeed from the musically astute Tormé.

The stellar guest list continued in the second season, including an appearance by country singer-songwriter Hank Williams (making his television debut) singing one of his signature songs, 'Hey, Good Lookin'. Another of country music's finest and a label mate of Perry's, Hank Snow appeared later that season and sang one of his many hits, 'Music Makin' Mama from Memphis'. When recording his biography in audio form for RCA in the 1960s, Hank recalled the occasion as one of the big steps in his career.[5] Snow made a return appearance in 1954.

The Christmas Eve edition of *The Perry Como Show* in 1952 saw the introduction of a recurring feature of Perry's Christmas programmes. 'The Story of the First Christmas' is an adaptation by John A. Richards of the nativity story as recorded in the Holy Bible. Perry narrates the story of the birth of Jesus Christ, with musical arrangements written by Mitchell Ayres. The music provides ongoing background while the story is told, with pauses in the story at key moments, punctuated with a chorus of a Christmas carol. Perry recorded the story for RCA Victor twice, first in mono in 1950 and again in stereo in 1959. On television, Perry would usually be seated in a chair holding a large prop book containing the story. Seated around him were children whose parents were members of the cast and crew, and on occasion Perry's own children, such as in 1953 when Ronnie assisted his father in the telling of the story. The story was accompanied on television by acted scenes portraying the parts of the story as they were described. The conclusion of the story was almost always followed by a hymn, most commonly 'Ave Maria' as in 1952.

The year 1953 brought a new opportunity for Mr Como. On Saturday 14 February, Perry hosted the *All-Star Revue* with guests including actress Joan Blondell, singer Patti Page and comedian Ben Blue. This programme would provide Perry with his first taste of hosting a prime-time Saturday night variety show and proved a successful endeavour. 1953 also saw Perry's tenth anniversary with RCA. A party was thrown for him at the Stork Club in New York City on 10 January that year in honour of the occasion, and part of the proceedings televised on CBS. Accompanying Perry as guests from RCA Victor were Sales Vice President Larry Kanaga and Pop Recording Manager Dave Kapp, in addition to Perry's regular team.

A few months earlier, Perry had recorded one of his biggest international hits. The session took place at Manhattan Center in New York City on 4 November 1952, conducted by Hugo Winterhalter. It was the first of several recording sessions over the next year with Winterhalter, which together resulted in further major hits, including 'Say You're Mine Again', 'You Alone (Solo tu)' and 'Wanted'.

The first session was not without its difficulties, though. The song that had been brought to Perry's attention was 'Don't Let the Stars Get in Your Eyes' – a country song with a driving rhythm, first popularized earlier that year by the song's composer Slim Willet. Perry had an initial disliking of the song because of its unusual, out-of-meter tempo. 'I sing when I enjoy singing, and sometimes that isn't necessarily the most commercial tune you could do', reflected Perry in 1975. 'We have 17 gold records [as of 1975] and I'm proud of every one of those tunes now, but I'd say half of 'em—I wasn't forced to do, but I was asked to do. Firmly!' When Perry first heard 'Don't Let the Stars Get in Your Eyes' he said, 'I think you guys are flippin' – this is terrible!'[6]

It's a popularly held myth that Perry recorded many of his biggest hits in one take. While it's a story that was often indulged by Perry himself, it was not true. It was probably Perry's inclination to play down his own achievements which encouraged this kind of commentary. It's also possible that Perry may not have remembered specifics about all of these sessions. At his peak, Perry was a very busy man – recording sessions were fitted between his radio and television commitments, which took up most of his weekly schedule.

It would be a gross misconception to say that Perry would record any material brought to him. This wasn't true at all. In fact, he was very selective about the material he recorded for commercial release. Perry explained, 'I went through a period there where people would come up, whether it would be Jack Kapp or Eli Oberstein or whoever was the A&R [Artists and Repertoire] man – they bring up a song, and the first thing I'd say would be "no"—for some reason, I don't know why. But they'd kind of talk to me a little, and they'd say "Well look now, you gotta do this one". It was Dave Kapp who brought 'Don't Let the Stars Get in Your Eyes' to Perry. Dave said, 'Here's one ya gotta do, it's a hit' and Perry said, 'Forget it!'.

Perry eventually came around to the idea, albeit with some reservations, and a recording session was scheduled. 'Ray [Charles] used to have to stand in front of me and point . . .' said Perry. 'He used to say, "Now!" But it was terrible

– it had nine bars and one phrase . . .'.[7] Lead trombonist Warren Covington recalled playing on the session:

> I came in and Hugo said, 'Warren, we want it very brassy – bop bop bop by-ah – bold!' And then Perry came over and he said 'Warren, when you play loud, I have to sing loud. I don't wanna sing loud'. So, here I'm caught in the middle – which one do I listen to? . . . Then I played it soft and Hugo said, 'No, Warren! Pound it out!' So finally, I went towards Hugo's way, because I worked for him more directly than I did for Perry.[8] Definitely not a one-take recording!

With the recording finished and the first discs pressed, 'Don't Let the Stars Get in Your Eyes' backed with a revival of the 1930 song 'Lies' was in US record stores by mid-November on its ascent to the top of the charts. It made a seismic impact in the UK too (also reaching the No. 1 spot) with the different pairing of 'To Know You (Is to Love You)' the last of Perry's collaborations on disc with the Fontane Sisters, who were seeking to spread their wings together on their own. Despite Perry's reservations, 'Don't Let the Stars Get in Your Eyes' became both a transatlantic and intercontinental hit, neatly opening 1953 and selling millions of copies around the world. It remained in his repertoire right through to the 1990s.

Perry had a group of people who would seek out new material for him, including an A&R man, and together they would decide what to record. People like Irving Berlin, Richard Rodgers, Johnny Mercer, Harold Arlen and Sammy Cahn could be found sitting in Perry's office discussing a new song they were seeking Perry to record or broadcast. '. . . you have to be careful', said Perry.

> [Mack] Gordon – he could sell you anything! You know, he'd sit down – make it sound so good . . . and he'd laugh and he'd smile all the way through some of the worse songs you ever heard – he was one I had to be very careful with! Normally, they would come up and they knew the kind of stuff I like to sing. I'm not a jazz singer so to speak. I can beat my foot on something like 'I Believe in Music' but other than that, vocally it sounds like I'm singing the same song; but my forte, or whatever you want to call it, happens to be ballads – the 'Prisoner of Love's . . . kept me from cutting hair.[9]

A hand-signed classic publicity photo of Perry, c. early 1950s.

Perry concluded that if he were to be the picker of songs, he would be back in the barber business. In his view, the right approach was to liaise with A&R staff and song pluggers to find the right songs. Mickey Glass was one such person. Mickey was a song plugger and publisher whose involvement with Perry's company Roncom developed organically over a long period. He started by simply having a presence – helping with anything that needed doing. Time passed, then one day Perry's brother-in-law and manager Dee Belline said, 'Don't you think you oughtta start paying Mickey?' Perry responded, 'Why, does he work here?' 'Well, he's always here' came Dee's response. 'Well, pay him!' said Perry. And Mickey remained a member of Perry's core staff from then on. Reflecting on the arrangement, Perry teased that, if Mickey ever got a little short with him, he'd remind him, 'You know, I never did hire you!' which usually remedied any disagreement or at least dispelled the tension![10]

From an artistic standpoint, *The Perry Como Show* on CBS was a variety show in miniature. It's what led to Perry becoming a mainstay of prime-time television and offered him the vehicle to showcase his own recordings, promote new songs, and be host to many stars of the day. It was a family-friendly, thrice-weekly musical treat – acclaimed by critics and adored by audiences. The show's sponsor, however, was not without controversy. Liggett and Myers as a tobacco manufacturer were keen to dismiss the growing health concerns over the use of their products. In 1950, the British Medical Journal published a research document by Richard Doll, illustrating the close link between smoking and lung cancer; Reader's Digest and many others were to follow in the coming years.

Chesterfield cigarette advertising was a prominent, recurring part of proceedings across the 15-minute shows. The promotions were handled with insistence and assurance by Dick Stark, the show's announcer – and often claimed to be supported by medical professionals. For example, on the 2 May 1952 edition of the show, Stark's dialogue included the following: 'Chesterfields are kept tasty and fresh with tried and tested moistening agents, pure natural sugars; chemically pure, harmless, costly glycerol . . . proved by over 40 years of continuous use in tobacco products to be entirely safe for use in the mouth; and your Chesterfield is wrapped in cigarette paper of the highest purity – the best money can buy . . . NOTHING ELSE!'[11] This is a claim that would appear scandalous in time to come, but in the 1950s, the culture of smoking was a very different one to which it would be by the turn of the twenty-first century.

In 1954, the legendary compilation *Como's Golden Records* appeared in its first form as a 10-inch LP containing eight gold discs recorded between 1945 and 1953. Accompanying the collection is a now legendary and prophetic quote from one of the twentieth century's most enduring songwriters, Irving Berlin:

> A singer, like a songwriter, must be judged by his staying power. You can't point to one or two hit records that he made. You must ask 'how good has his average been over the years?' Perry Como's record (no pun intended) will show that he's been up there on top for a good many years and I know he will remain there for a good many more.[12]

This perceptive observation from Berlin is all the more remarkable considering it was written comparatively early in Como's career and before 'Hot Diggity (Dog Ziggity Boom)', 'Round and Round', 'Magic Moments' and 'Catch a Falling Star' were recorded, later in the same decade. *Como's Golden Records* was expanded in 1958 to fourteen tracks (within which the four aforementioned songs are featured) and would stay in the current RCA Victor catalogue for decades to come.

1954 also saw Perry's first recordings at Webster Hall in New York City – the venue for most of Como's New York recordings over the next fourteen years. The first session on 2 January resulted in two songs, 'Door of Dreams' which would be re-recorded in 1955 and 'There Never Was a Night So Beautiful' which would be coupled with 'Hit and Run Affair' recorded on New Year's Eve 1953 at Manhattan Center. The biggest Como hits of the year, though, were 'Wanted' (recorded at the end of 1953) and 'Papa Loves Mambo' both of which achieved gold record status.

The fifth and final series of *The Perry Como Show* on CBS commenced on 23 August 1954. Perry's vocal backing was now provided solely by the Ray Charles Chorus, soon to be christened the Ray Charles Singers by Perry himself. The chorus had appeared under several names and configurations in previous seasons with varying degrees of involvement but came to prominence in the fourth season, at the end of which the Fontane Sisters left the show.

With their own increasing popularity as a vocal harmony group, it was thought that the Fontane Sisters wanted to take a chance at pastures new. They signed with Dot Records in 1954 and took a different direction in line with the growing popularity of rock 'n' roll music. They had several successful years at

Dot, accruing a total of eighteen *Billboard*-charted singles during their tenure with the label before retiring in the early 1960s. They came out of retirement briefly to fulfil a recording project resulting in the album and single 'The Tips of My Fingers' before departing the industry for good.

Perry himself would also explore the burgeoning rock 'n' roll genre. In January 1955, he recorded what was the first release in the genre by RCA Victor, 'Ko Ko Mo (I Love You So)' which became a huge success, peaking at No. 2 on the US charts. Many further titles with an emphasis on the rhythmic desires of the jukebox-playing teenagers were to follow, including 'Juke Box Baby', 'Just Born (to Be Your Baby)', 'Love Makes the World Go 'Round' and 'Tomboy' all of which were hits domestically. The former two achieved their biggest success in the United States, while the latter two achieved far greater success in the UK. Como handles them all with confidence, good humour and integrity. Observing the musical trend in 1957, Como said:

> There's no such thing as bad music. I mean music that has a bad influence. Sure, some rock 'n' roll numbers have racy lyrics. But, usually, the way they are sung, you can't understand them, anyway. In my day, we had the Miller and Goodman bands to dance to. They had a beat. That's what the kids want and get in rock 'n' roll. That's all it is.[13]

Critics on occasion over the years have fallen into the trap of music snobbery, dismissing Perry Como from the ranks of first-rate vocalist, because of his prolific run of hit singles in the 1950s, particularly catered to the jukebox market and commonly referred to as 'novelty' songs. This viewpoint, however, fails to acknowledge the achievement of these recordings artistically, technically and financially.

For one thing, it's seldom appreciated how astute Perry Como was in his business dealings. He was interested in selling records and to some degree, this requires an artist to be versatile – certainly if longevity is a goal. An artist in a sustained slump of sales might easily be dropped by a major label. Perry's ability to adapt to the rhythmic stylings of the 1950s, such as the mambo and rock 'n' roll, gave him a chameleon-like commercial edge that bridged a generational gap. His artistic integrity and that of his colleagues added authenticity to material that might have been considered throwaway in less capable hands.

He didn't just go through the motions to churn out something for a quick buck – he worked at it, and a recording wasn't approved until he was satisfied. A good example of this is 'Moon Talk', which developed over two sessions in March 1958. No less than twenty-two takes of the song were recorded, of which the twenty-second take was the commercially issued one. But there was more to it than that. Even with a high number of takes and experimentation, a recording might still be rejected, thus were Perry's standards of excellence.

Depending on the definition of what qualifies as an unreleased recording, there are in the region of ninety Perry Como recordings that were not issued within their original time and context for numerous reasons. Some were picked up later, but most have been issued posthumously as bonus content to primary albums. In some cases, it is not difficult to understand why the recordings might have been rejected. In many more instances, however, it would be difficult to tell without knowing specifically that the recordings were not originally released.

There are a similar number of alternative takes that have appeared either through carelessness or accident – but rarely intended. From an artistic standpoint, this presents a considerable problem, certainly for an artist of Perry's calibre. These mistakes have occurred within releases from both the original and third-party labels. An alternative take not stated as such can misrepresent the quality of a product. For example – accidentally publishing an early draft of a manuscript or a preliminary sketch of a painting. The whole purpose of recording multiple takes is to establish and acquire an optimal performance.

Take 'Ko Ko Mo (I Love You So)' for instance. The song was issued accidentally from an alternative take within a Reader's Digest compilation in 1998. When listening to the take, it is immediately apparent that this is not the end product. First, the balance between the instrumentation and vocals is not quite in place, and secondly, Perry is feeling his way through the song. It's not a bad recording – it's a work in progress. To release such a take without explanation or context, however, is a disservice to the final recording. The take officially issued is without question the definitive rendering.

Television proved an excellent vehicle for promoting these recordings. It was only ever a press agent's pitch that Perry was a lethargic, easy-going character. The calm he so easily exuded may have been instinctive, but it was rooted in a confidence in his craft. He knew exactly what he was doing.

When it came to business, Perry maintained a level of control over everything he did, and he was well known to study a contract thoroughly before agreeing to its terms. He also owned a thriving publishing company called Roncom and was keen to acquire music. As a vocal interpreter, exclusivity was important to him. Within Perry's generation, as with those before him in the sphere of popular music, songwriters and singers were not usually one and the same. Songwriters wrote the music and lyrics, and singers sang the songs. In Al Jolson's heyday, he was able to negotiate a songwriting credit on certain songs that he popularized, on the basis that it was his interpretation of some songs that sold them. One might interpret this theory as a precursor to the concept of exclusivity in popular music recordings. A desire to protect one's work efforts is an indicator of the savvy artist.

A song might easily be dropped were such an agreement breached – for instance, if the song was made available for other artists to record at the time of the original release. This could well have been the case for songs such as 'Idle Gossip' which was a major hit in the United Kingdom but never originally released in the United States. The song's release in the UK may have simply been by chance or perhaps because of a contractual loophole concerning non-domestic releases. At the time, RCA did not have offices in the UK, and their recordings were released through the His Master's Voice (HMV) label.

To protect interests of exclusivity made perfect business sense. If one is to invest time, effort and money in promoting something, they want to be assured of an appropriate return. Otherwise, they might just as well be giving free promotion to a song without it equating to sales of the recording.

Perry was able to handle these matters effectively, whether in discussions with company executives or the public. Had he been popular in Rudyard Kipling's time, Kipling's words 'If you can walk with kings nor lose the common touch'[14] might easily have been written just for Perry. Perry's sensitivities to the human touch were legendary. He was always on the level with a person.

True to his roots and humble at heart, the qualities he possessed were precisely attuned with Kipling's poem 'If'.

Despite his calm exterior, Perry was as competitive in the recording studio as he was on the golf courses. Success was the aim – a hit, a win. He took what he did very seriously and did not take kindly to those who didn't share this attitude. A fundamental part of Perry's astuteness was his desire to surround himself with top people in their fields, both in the spotlight and behind the scenes. His philosophy aligned with the view that it is better to pay well than pay twice. None of this was rooted in greed though – it was just good business sense. Perry was able to use his influence to ensure the fair treatment of his colleagues. He was known for his generosity both as an employer and as a person.

Charity was also very important to Perry – equally important was not talking about what he did. When disc jockey William B. Williams brought up the subject in a 1976 interview and thanked him for his work, Perry went quiet and after an extended pause said, 'Those are the kind of things I like to be left unsaid'.[15] Perry had the same view about matters of belief, saying in 1953 that 'Faith is a word for doing, not talking'.[16] In all his years on radio, television and in live performances, he very rarely ever claimed to be religious, nor specifically went into any detail about what he did or did not believe. When Phil Donahue broached the subject in 1979, Perry said:

> I don't really like to discuss religion . . . I think religion is what you have inside. My talking about it [to] tell you how good a Catholic I am is not fair, because I'm what you would call the ordinary Christian. We go to mass. If I feel troubled about something, I go to my confessor. I may do the same thing over again, but I think it relieves me. The people who don't understand what I'm talking about [say] 'Why do you go to him?' – I think a minute's peace is worth a lot. A lot of people don't believe in confession but if I have something to say or something I think I should tell somebody – I go to somebody! 'That might not be everyone's philosophy', he added with a smile 'but that's your problem!'[17]

Perry was tolerant and respectful of the religious beliefs of others, perhaps best exemplified in his album *I Believe*, which combined songs of Protestant,

Catholic and Jewish origins. The reverence with which Perry approaches each of the recordings within the album is awe-inspiring. He sang one of the selections, the Hebrew declaration 'Kol Nidrei', several times on television on the closest date to Yom Kippur.

Initially with Hugo Winterhalter conducting, Mitchell Ayres took over from the second session for the duration. The album features Perry Como performing pristine, traditionally arranged hymns with impeccable taste. The opening recording 'I Believe' (a pop song) receives an arrangement and interpretation of divine beauty. This sense of the divine is replicated throughout the entirety of the album.

In addition to 'Kol Nidrei', Perry recorded another Jewish hymn, 'Eli, Eli'. In both cases, he was keen to ensure that his pronunciation of the Yiddish words was correct. To achieve this, he studied with a friend who was a rabbi and was also assisted by some members of the orchestra and chorus who were Jewish.

Perry was surprised to learn that some people who wanted to hear Christian hymns did not desire to hear Jewish ones or vice versa, which goes a considerable way to demonstrating Perry's openness to interfaith respect. He had expected the album to be the biggest hit he'd ever had – he loved the material and was pleased with his performance, but he retrospectively considered it a commercial failure.[18] This is surprising because the album enjoyed several reissues over more than twenty years, which is almost certainly indicative of a recording's success. Beginning life as an eight-track, 10-inch LP in 1953–4, it was expanded in 1956 to twelve tracks with different artwork in the 12-inch LP format. In the 1960s it was reissued in electronic stereo with the same cover, and again at the beginning of the 1970s. The album was once more reissued in its expanded form with different artwork as part of RCA's Pure Gold series in 1975.

Electronic stereo is a term used to refer to recordings which have been electronically reprocessed from mono sources. More specifically, they are 'fake stereo'. There were various techniques used in the process with different branding for different labels. One technique was to line up two linear copies of the mono recording – reducing the bass frequencies on one copy and increasing the treble frequencies on the other. Another technique was to have the two mono copies separated by a fraction of a second (i.e. one channel is heard slightly earlier than the other).

The approach was introduced on the premise that stereo equalled better, whether real or artificially created. The results were almost unanimously criticized as some of the worst-sounding releases of the era. They were a step back in fidelity terms. Some sounded as if they had been recorded through a tin can in a gymnasium, others sounded grossly out of phase – making it difficult to place the music in the listening environment. The audio results achieved varied vastly, entirely dependent on the skill of the engineer, but more often than not the results were no comparison to the original mono. Ironically, they probably sounded better on crude equipment, which contradicted the apparent mission behind the releases. *I Believe* faired fractionally better than some (such as the electronic stereo version of *Como's Golden Records*), but this was in no small part due to the nature of the recorded material, which lent itself to the large space of a church or cathedral. Nevertheless, the original mono is still undoubtedly the definitive sound.

One of Perry's greatest assets was the ability to infuse a song with emotion without excessive affectation. He didn't act the words, he felt them. He could bring power or subtlety to a performance in equal measure as he felt the composition required it – something that aligned with his instinctive sense of good taste, which made him a perfect candidate for the recording and performance of songs of faith and inspiration.

RCA finally conceded to the power and relevance of the LP in the mid-1950s, although they continued to offer EP variations from their catalogue for some years beyond. In January 1955, Perry commenced recording for his first full-length album, *So Smooth*, the sessions for which were completed by mid-February. The album is a collection of standards, mostly from stage and screen, which certainly lives up to its name.

So Smooth was an opportunity for Perry to record some legendary songs of the kind that were his favourite to sing, such as 'It's the Talk of the Town' which he'd been singing since the days of his CBS radio show and one which was clearly a favourite. In complete contrast but delivered with equal effect is 'For Me and My Gal' (also sung by Perry on CBS). These two recordings, side by side, illustrate two entirely different circumstances of love. One of loss and sadness, the other of jubilation and celebration. Perry gives both songs the treatment they deserve. The sensitive melancholy feeling that Perry infuses into his recording of 'It's the Talk of the Town' demonstrates the perfect balance of subtle tenderness combined with the pain and disbelief of a love lost. In an entirely different vein, Perry glides beautifully along with the up-tempo joy of 'For Me and My Gal' accompanied with pizzicato-like precision by the male voices of the Ray Charles Singers. These two examples represent love from both ends of the spectrum, and Perry is completely in tune with them both – melodically and conceptually.

By this point, it was clear that the 'Battle of the Speeds' had ended. While the 45 rpm record would remain the dominant format for single releases up until the introduction of the compact disc (CD) single, there was no doubt that the LP was the preferred format for albums.

The final season of *The Perry Como Show* on CBS began on 23 August 1954. As was a common trend, the opening show was well received by *Variety* magazine, which said, 'As usual, these 15-minute stanzas run off with unusual swiftness. There's time for three numbers, some easy gab by the stars and a couple of plugs, with everything paced with absolute smoothness'.[19] Richard Heller of *TV Stage* magazine who sat in on a rehearsal in May 1955 observed that:

> Everyone who has ever watched a television show should see a Perry Como rehearsal. As wonderful as the actual show is, the rehearsal is far more wonderful, full of fun and excitement. Perry stepped up to the camera and instead of enunciating carefully, sort of mumbled his way through the introduction. Then, his unfailing sense of humour took over. As he finished the introduction, he said, 'Maybe you people want to know why we're here.' He stopped for a moment, then said, with a face that began solemn and ended smiling, 'Well, we're here to pay the rent.' The rehearsal rolled on, with Perry singing three songs and the Ray Charles Chorus doing one. Throughout the entire run-through, the singer followed his director's directions, grinned, kidded around and sang as only he can. But even when singing, his vibrant sense of humour asserted itself. To one song, he made up a hilarious set of lyrics. Everyone at the rehearsal laughed so hard and so

long that he had to stop. The second run-through began and Perry mumbled his way through the introduction again. When he came to the line, 'Maybe you people want to know why we're here,' he stopped again and finished with this: 'Well, we need the money.' His own joke tickled him so Perry added, grinning at Lee Cooley [the producer], 'Hey, that's good. Think we'll keep that in.' An hour later, when the show went on the air, Perry, speaking clearly, did the introduction straight. His asides at the rehearsal had served the single purpose of relaxing the tension.[20]

The series finale came on 24 June 1955. Perry was in a celebratory mood, looking ahead to the autumn and a brand-new prime time, hour-long musical variety series on NBC. Perry clowns with the staff tries his hand at running a camera and generally has a ball, opening aptly with 'It's a Big Wide Wonderful World'. By request, Perry then sings 'Goodbye Sue' – just over twelve years to the day since his studio recording of the song at his first solo session. Roselle Como even makes a surprise cameo appearance at the end of the show. It all combines as a heartfelt and joyful curtain call for Perry's CBS TV series.

Perry had come a long way since those early days at RCA, and he was now approaching the very pinnacle of his artistry. With the exciting prospect of a new chapter ahead, viewers awaited 'Saturday Night with Mr. C'!

Quintessential Como
Recommended listening 1950–4

Hoop-Dee-Doo ★
with The Fontane Sisters
m Milton DeLugg, w Frank Loesser, 1950
16 Mar 1950 - 47-3747

Patricia
mw Benny Davis, 1950
10 Aug 1950 - 47-3905

A Bushel and a Peck
with Betty Hutton
mw Frank Loesser, 1950
From the musical Guys and Dolls.
12 Sep 1950 - PC Sings Hits from
Broadway Shows LPM-1191

It's a Lovely Day Today ★
with The Fontane Sisters
mw Irving Berlin, 1950
From the musical Call Me Madam.
26 Sep 1950 - PC Sings Hits from
Broadway Shows LPM-1191

You're Just in Love (I Wonder Why) ★
with The Fontane Sisters
mw Irving Berlin, 1950
From the musical Call Me Madam.
26 Sep 1950 - PC Sings Hits from
Broadway Shows LPM-1191

If
m Tolchard Evans, w Robert Hargreaves
and Stanley Damerell, 1951
28 Nov 1950 - Relaxing with PC LPM-1176

More Than You Know ★
m Vincent Youmans, w Edward Eliscu
and Billy Rose, 1929
From the musical Great Day!
11 Jan 1951 - Dream Along with Me
CAL-403

We Kiss in a Shadow
m Richard Rodgers,
w Oscar Hammerstein II, 1951
From the musical The King and I.
27 Mar 1951 - PC Sings Hits from
Broadway Shows LPM-1191

There's No Boat Like a Rowboat
with The Fontane Sisters
mw Irving Gordon, 1950
15 May 1951 - 47-4158

Here's to My Lady ★
m Rube Bloom, w Johnny Mercer, 1951
18 Sep 1951 - Somebody Loves Me
CAS-858 (e)

Tulips and Heather
mw Milton Carson, 1952
18 Dec 1951 - 47-4453

Please Mr. Sun
m Ray Getzov, w Sid Frank, 1952
18 Dec 1951 - 47-4453

One Little Candle ★
m George Mysels,
w Joseph Maloy Roach, 1952
31 Jan 1952 - 47-4631

I Concentrate on You ★
mw Cole Porter, 1940
From the film Broadway Melody of 1940.
4 Mar 1952 - TV Favourites
LPM-3013 (10")

Maybe
with Eddie Fisher
mw Allan Flynn and Frank Madden, 1940
13 May 1952 - 47-4744

My Love and Devotion
mw Milton Carson, 1952
17 July 1952 - Dreamer's Holiday
CAL-582

To Know You (Is to Love You) ★
with The Fontane Sisters
m Robert Allen, w Allan Roberts, 1952
9 Sep 1952 - Dreamer's Holiday CAL-582

Don't Let the Stars Get in Your Eyes ★
mw Slim Willet, 1952
4 Nov 1952 - Como's Golden Records
LPM-1981

Wild Horses
mw Johnny Burke
(under pseud. K. C. Rogan), 1953
Adapted from Robert Schumann's
'The Wild Horseman', Op. 68, No. 8.
6 Jan 1953 - 47-5152

Say You're Mine Again
mw Charles Nathan and Dave Heisler, 1953
28 Mar 1953 - 47-5277

No Other Love ★
m Richard Rodgers,
w Oscar Hammerstein II, 1953
From the musical Me and Juliet.
19 May 1953 - A Sentimental Date with
PC LPM-1177

Idle Gossip
m Joseph Meyer, w Floyd
Huddleston, 1953
19 Aug 1953 - His Master's Voice
B.10667 (UK)

You Alone (Solo tu) ★
m Robert Allen, w Al Stillman, 1953
19 Aug 1953 - PC Sings Just for You
CAL-440

I Believe ★
mw Ervin Drake, Irvin Graham,
Jimmy Shirl and Al Stillman, 1952
23 Nov 1953 - I Believe LPM-1172

Wanted
mw Jack Fulton and Lois Steele, 1954
29 Dec 1953 - Como's Golden Records LPM-1981

Hit and Run Affair
mw Don Roseland, Ray Cormier and Mel Van, 1954
29 Dec 1953 - 47-5749

There Never Was a Night So Beautiful
mw John Rox, 1954
2 Jan 1954 - PC Sings Just for You CAL-440

Papa Loves Mambo
mw Al Hoffman, Dick Manning and Bix Reichner, 1954
31 Aug 1954 - Como's Golden Records LPM-1981

4

Magic Moments

At 8.00 pm on Saturday, 17 September 1955, *The Perry Como Show* debuted on NBC television. The show had now evolved from its 15-minute time frame into an hour-long, prime-time variety series. The opening show originated from the Century Theatre in New York with musical direction by Mitchell Ayres, vocal accompaniment from the Ray Charles Singers and featuring the Louis DaPron Dancers plus announcer Frank Gallop.

A wealth of guests appeared that night, including singers Julius La Rosa, Rosemary Clooney, and Frankie Laine, and comedian Sid Caesar – all of whom would be returning guests of Perry's. La Rosa and Clooney had also guested and deputized for Perry during the fifteen-minute era. Of the premiere show, *Variety* magazine said, 'The Como showmanship, is there in abundance, from his opening themer to his "Tina Marie" and "Abide with Me" coupling for a finale that was as surefire as it was offbeat. His studied casualness and affable qualities registered as potently as ever'.[1] This was the beginning of what would become known as 'Saturday Night with Mr. C.'

Perry's shows were no longer sponsored by Chesterfield. The sponsors now came from various companies – usually with an emphasis on household appliances, beauty products and everyday essentials. Kleenex, Noxzema and the American Dairy Association were among the regular sponsors throughout the Saturday night years. The shows opened with Perry singing an excerpt of his new theme song 'Dream Along with Me (I'm on My Way to a Star)'. The song was written by Carl Sigman, whose later writing credits would include English lyrics for 'Arrivederci Roma (Goodbye to Rome)' and 'Where

Do I Begin?' (the theme from the film *Love Story*). 'Dream Along with Me' quickly became synonymous with Perry and he recorded the song for RCA the following year, paired with 'Somebody up There Likes Me', which he sang on the soundtrack of the MGM film of the same title – a biopic of the boxer Rocky Graziano starring Paul Newman.

The shows usually featured multiple guests, often partaking in a duet with Perry. A request segment where Perry answered viewer requests in a medley became a key feature. The medleys usually comprised three (or sometimes two) classic standards of varying tempos over a six-to-ten-minute duration. The medley opened with another theme, 'We Get Letters', aka 'Dear Perry', composed for the show by Ray Charles, who wrote the vocal arrangements and special material for the series. The requests segment was an opportunity for Perry to sing many of the songs he loved to sing and further connect with his audience. Through the creation of this segment and the many opportunities to sing throughout the show, Perry performed hundreds of songs that he never recorded commercially and very often from the Great American Songbook. Among them, 'All or Nothing at All', 'Love Is Here to Stay', 'Night and Day', 'Autumn in New York', 'Beyond the Sea' and 'Moonlight Becomes You' – all arranged by Joe Lipman and Jack Andrews.

The Perry Como Show quickly settled into its Saturday night slot and attracted guests from all areas of show business. In the first season alone, the guest list included such stars as singer Julie London, actress Joan Collins, actors Henry Fonda and Rock Hudson, dancer Ginger Rogers, and singer-trumpeter Louis Armstrong. Kirk Douglas who made an appearance in December 1955, was even the recipient of a shave from Perry live on air. 'Perry! Perry! Not too close!'[2] Douglas exclaimed as Como shaved near to his famous dimple.

It was during this era that the legendary battle for the 'King of Saturday Night' originated between Perry and comedian Jackie Gleason, whose situation comedy series *The Honeymooners* aired on Saturday night from 8.30 to 9.00 pm on CBS. The press made much of the competition between Como and Gleason, including *Time* Magazine which said:

> Naturally, he [Perry] is distressed that his high-rated *Perry Como Show* (Sat. 8 pm, NBC) is clobbering its CBS rivals, Jackie Gleason's *Stage Show* and

The Honeymooners. Gleason is not only a nice guy but a good friend of Perry's. In the latest Nielsen Top Ten, the Como show is No. 7 and Gleason is nowhere in sight. Says Perry: 'I'd rather go on at 2 o'clock in the morning when there's no trouble. I don't want to fight anybody.'[3]

The weekly hour show was a six- or sometimes seven-days-a-week endeavour. It required a great deal of thought and instinct. As soon as one show was complete, it was on to the next. Ray Charles explained that they never thought what they were doing was anything special – they were 'just' working to deadlines.[4] Ray described Perry as a 'very cautious man'. Continuing, he said:

> We used to rehearse on Sixth Avenue – there's a six-story building and rehearsal halls, and a little elevator, and little corridor, and then you go into the rehearsal room. I never saw him [Perry] come in without stopping at the threshold, get off the elevator, walked the little corridor, kinda look around and see who's in the room, and then come in – sit down, take off his coat. . . he didn't run into anything, he didn't jump into anything – very cautious. I guess you don't trip if you don't run![5]

By February 1956, the battle of the ratings reached its pinnacle. Gleason said, 'The mistake was to let Perry Como get a half-hour head start on us. Como is a very tough man for anyone to beat'.[6] Consequently, the Gleason offerings were brought forward for an 8.00 pm start in a live, direct head-to-head between the two stars. Perry insisted that it was a friendly rivalry.

> Sunday morning, if the telephone rang – I knew it was Jack. He'd say 'Well er, silver throat, we knocked your socks off last night!' so if we would beat him by half a point or something I'd call him. 'Well, big fella, we did it to ya!' It was kind of a wonderful, friendly thing . . .[7]

That April, Perry and Jackie shared the prestigious Peabody Award for the best radio and television programmes of 1955. The 1955–6 end-of-season ratings saw both the Como and Gleason shows in the top twenty, ranking in nineteenth and twentieth place, respectively. By the end of the following season, Perry was ranked in nineth place in the Nielsen ratings, with Jackie having fallen to the twenty-nineth position.

Perry and Jackie were also neighbours at Sands Point, Long Island in New York. Perry spoke of Jackie with much fondness, and one story involving a game of pool was a favourite instance.

> 'They tell me you're a pool man,' Jackie hollered. 'Well, I'm a pool man, too, and I wanna prove to you that a good big pool man can lick a good little pool man any day in the week.' So they shot six games of pool and the good little pool man won. They haven't played together since.[8]

The writers on *The Perry Como Show* were headed by Goodman Ace. Ace, who Perry described as 'the daddy of all writers',[9] had previously written for comedian Milton Berle. During his first meeting with Ace, Como said:

> I am not a comedian. I can't make with the gags. I will fall flat on my face if I try it. You've got to let me be myself. I can handle introductions of guest stars and I can engage in a little patter with 'em, but if I try anything else I will lay the biggest egg this side of an ostrich farm.

Ace was impressed with Como's attitude, remarking that 'He's the first performer I've ever known, who would admit to limitations. It's great to work with a guy like that.'[10] 'It's in one way a little tough to write for Perry,' observed Ace '. . . because you can't give Perry a wise-crack line, because first of all, Perry . . . is such a good editor for himself of what is right for him; and then the people just wouldn't take Perry doing a Don Rickles type of put down.'[11]

Perry understood the importance of a good script. He was dissatisfied with the material he had to work with when making movies in Hollywood and consequently would settle for nothing less than the best. Como's theory was simple and logical: 'in the final analysis, a $200 suit is better economy than a $40 suit. The same applies to anything. You can't replace quality'.[12]

Also on the writing team were Mort Green, George Foster and Jay Burton. Producing the show during its first season was Lee Cooley (who had produced Perry's 15-minute series on CBS), and the shows were directed by Grey Lockwood. Bob Finkel took over the production and staging mantle for the second and third seasons, with Clark Jones becoming director-producer for the fourth and final Saturday night season.

Series two marked the beginning of colour broadcasts of *The Perry Como Show* and a new performance venue, the Ziegfeld Theatre. From here on, the

Perry hugs his friend and golfing buddy, boxer Rocky Marciano, c. mid-1950s.

show with some exceptions would be broadcast consistently in colour. It was a major leap forward and would begin to encourage the homes of America to invest in colour television sets. In 1959, there were even experiments with stereo sound. A stereo transmission was achieved via two separate audio channel feeds from the broadcast – one of which accompanied the visual on television, the other via tuning into a local radio station in New York. With television and radio suitably positioned within the listening and viewing area, a stereo image could be achieved. It was a marvellous feat for the time and highly innovative. It would be over thirty years before stereo sound became common place within television broadcasts.

The show met with the approval of critics and peers alike. Perry won Emmy awards across three consecutive years – twice for Best Male Singer in 1955 and 1956, followed by Best Male Personality in a Continuing Performance in 1957. The show also reached international acclaim. In January 1958, *The Perry Como Show* began airing on BBC Television in the UK. It was the first show of its kind to be bought in by the BBC and was the start of a highly successful three-year run. Producer Yvonne Littlewood was employed with the task of editing the shows so that they were suitable for broadcast on the BBC, a non-commercial corporation. This meant not only removing commercials but also any references to commercial products throughout. It could prove rather challenging at times, especially if a product was referred to in either a running gag or the opening scene of a show.

Littlewood's labours were well worth the effort, and Wednesday evenings became a regular transatlantic treat for British viewers. Other countries would also welcome the Como Show during this period, including Italy, Germany and Australia, and soon Wednesday and Thursday nights became a regular date with Mr. C., in addition to Saturdays back in the United States.

Perry's new regular slot on British television worked wonders for his record sales in the UK. He scored no less than 10 hit singles and several hit albums during the period. One of which, *Dear Perry,* was a retitling of a newly recorded album, *Saturday Night with Mr. C.* Recorded across February and March 1958, the album tied in with Perry's television success and was the first Como album to be recorded in stereo.

Saturday Night with Mr. C. is a superb blend of romantic ballads and swing numbers plus a couple of songs of inspiration. The selections are woven together in a format that nods to the structure of *The Perry Como Show*. Within the album, Perry offers definitive renderings of such songs as 'It Had to Be You' and 'Red Sails in the Sunset'. Perry's recording of 'Come Rain or Come Shine' combines the beauty of the ballad with the pulse of swing to magnificent effect. The song was omitted from stereo pressings of the album in its original form, presumably owing to space limitations at the time. The song was reinstated within the album in stereo for the first time more than forty years later, on compact disc.

Despite his success, Perry was never interested in the music charts. His choral arranger Ray Charles described them as 'the best of the bad'. Perry was seldom aware of a song charting, typically, he would have to be told. It was at Como's behest that the label stopped counting his record sales. He was presented with several gold discs on television over the years, but it was orchestrated by his staff without his prior knowledge. Perry found such displays of public commendation embarrassing. He didn't like anything which might be construed as showing off. For this reason, he seldom danced on television – if he did, it was played down, usually with comedic effect. According to Dinah Shore, Perry was a wonderful dancer, he just didn't like to dance.[13]

The music charts had always been the subject of hyperbole – no different than political polls. For one thing, record sales were usually based on record shipments from the factory, which didn't necessarily equate to actual sales. Bulk sales to record stores were based on a prediction of success but did not guarantee that the disc was a big seller. Similarly, with in-store promotions – it was typically the records that weren't selling that were given the promotional push as the 'big sellers', whereas the actual leading records sold themselves.

The understated approach was part of Perry's formula for success, combining records and television. A performance of a new song on Perry's show would almost guarantee a chart position the following week. It was the perfect combination which served as a forerunner to the music video. Of course, Perry had been doing this from the beginning of his television days. It was only enhanced during this period with bigger sets and larger productions, although a simple set (or even no set at all) proved equally effective for Perry's personal approach to a song and to the camera.

Corruption within the charts, however, was rife – the Payola scandal being one of the biggest examples of this. Record airtime given by disc jockeys was often awarded in exchange for financial incentives or even sexual favours. Record labels could even buy a position in the charts, in the hope that it would encourage sales. A good example of the nonsensical measurements was the differing chart positions of songs on either side of the same physical disc. While this measurement corresponds to jukebox play where the side is selected manually by the operator, it's an impossibility for physical disc sales.

In addition, chart positioning was something easily subject to misinterpretation. It was quite possible, for instance, for a record to chart outside the Top 20 with sustained sales and be more financially successful than a record that briefly reached No. 1. Chart data, even at its best, is not necessarily a true reflection of a record's success. If comparing actual sales data for records over a given period, a record that reached No. 1 in one chart period might have equated to less sales than a record at No. 10 in a more lucrative month. Compare this with sales since the digital revolution at the beginning of the twenty-first century, and a No. 1 might have sold less than a 1950s top 40!

While music charts are always enjoyable to observe, they should certainly be taken with a pinch of salt as a marker of a song's chart presence, rather than supplemented as a religion. As composer Ervin Drake once wrote, 'We are not entitled to our illusions'.[14]

Finances were always a considerable factor in the success of a record – it needed to be promoted, which was why Perry's previewing of a song on television was so important. When the RCA Camden budget label was formed in 1957, however, the financial situation was reversed. Producer Ethel Gabriel, who assembled most of Perry's Camden album compilations, explained that the decision over the inclusion or omission of a song was made based on cents rather than dollars.[15]

When it came to contractual matters within the industry, there was no standard royalty – this could vary depending on the composer and the publisher and their arrangements with each other. Some songwriters would sell their songs outright to a publisher for a set fee. In this case, they might maintain a credit but would receive no further financial reimbursement. In some cases, there would be no credit either. An example of this is the song 'Mood Indigo'. Originally composed as an instrumental under the title 'Dreamy Blues' by Duke Ellington and Barney Bigard, it was introduced by the Ellington Orchestra in 1930. The following year, lyrics were written by Mitchell Parish and the piece was retitled 'Mood Indigo'. However, because Parish was under a 'for hire' contract at the time with composer Irving Mills' publishing company Mills Music, he did not receive credit or royalties for his contributions to the song.

Perry was always keen to ensure that matters of royalties were properly handled and that his colleagues were appropriately compensated for their efforts. He would stop and eat a sandwich or blow a take to ensure that a recording session overran so that the musicians would get paid for extra time.

Perry was known to have paid his musical director Nick Perito more than Frank Sinatra would pay an entire orchestra![16]

In the spring and early summer of 1958, Perry recorded his second album in stereophonic sound. This time, however, the theme was purely inspirational. *When You Come to the End of the Day* is a beautiful example of musicianship paired with faith, without so much as a whisper of self-righteousness within its content. Simply put, it is a heartfelt collection of inspirational songs, sung with precision and sincerity. The title song was composed by Frank Westphal with lyrics by Gus Kahn in 1929 and became anthemic within the Como repertoire, being sung as the sign-off to many of Perry's television shows during the era. The song had previously been recorded by artists including the Ink Spots, but in Como's capable hands, it receives a treatment that gets to the very root of the lyrics.

Throughout the late 1950s, Perry continued to welcome a wealth of stars from stage, screen, music, comedy and sport, and the guest list of his television shows began to read like a 'who's who' of American entertainment. The show was also a platform for many young and up-and-coming acts, such as Brenda Lee, who on 27 October 1956 made her first of five appearances at the tender age of eleven, singing a duet of 'Swinging on a Star' with Perry.

During the first rehearsal for that week's show, Como and another of his guests, singer Frankie Laine, were in awe of Brenda's talent. Millicent Morton recalled the occasion:

> At the first rehearsal it was Brenda's turn to run through her number. She walked over to Perry quietly and, with few gestures, stood there like a good little girl reciting her piece – which happened to be a mighty rock-'n'-roll blockbuster. Then she went back to her comics. Laine, Como, everyone in the rehearsal hall was 'knocked out!' In three minutes Brenda had been accepted as an equal by two of the top old pros in the land. For three minutes they forgot she was a little girl. But then, as the fascinated men talked with the prodigy, they remembered. As always Brenda's earnest charm, with no putting-on, absolutely floored the adults. Perry and Frankie ended by borrowing a couple of Brenda's spare comic books, and the three singing stars sat in a row, busily reading.[17]

The following month, Brenda returned to the Como show; this time, however, in addition to Perry, she joined contemporary child prodigy, organist Glenn Derringer for a performance of 'Life Is Just a Bowl of Cherries'.

The Everly Brothers were another young act who made their debut on *The Perry Como Show*, appearing four times with Perry between 1957 and 1959. In their March 1959 appearance, the versatile, real-life brothers Don and Phil were able to turn their hands to songbook standards. During a cast medley saluting composer Billy Rose, they performed excellent renditions of 'Me and My Shadow' and 'Tonight You Belong to Me' – the latter could easily have been a hit single for them.

Numerous international stars guested on the show throughout its Saturday night run, particularly British acts including comedian and singer Max Bygraves, who joined Perry for a parody of 'I Wonder Who's Kissing Her Now' in 1959. Actress Sally Ann Howes, best known for her portrayal of Truly Scrumptious in the film *Chitty Chitty Bang Bang*, appeared in 1958, duetting with Perry on 'Let's Call the Whole Thing Off', and singer-songwriter Lonnie Donegan, a pioneering figure of Skiffle music, guested in 1956.

From Italy, actress Gina Lollobrigida appeared, joining Perry for a duet of the Italian love song 'Oh Marie' also in 1956. Then there were performers who were naturalized Americans, having their cultural roots outside of the United States, such as Irish American actress Maureen O'Hara, who was a guest of Perry's four times. Thirty five years after her final appearance with Perry, she was in the audience of Perry's Irish Christmas concert in Dublin – the city in which she was born.

Series four of *The Perry Como Show* on NBC brought a new regular feature, which spotlighted a top American songwriter or songwriting team. The feature was first explored during episode two of series three when lyricist Johnny Mercer guested, again with the songs of Irving Berlin midway through the season, and once more during the final show of the series, with the music of Richard Rodgers in the spotlight. Extensive medleys of each composer's songs were arranged, and there were usually special guest appearances by the songwriters themselves.

The first episode of series four featured the songs of Jimmy Van Heusen, who, although delighted by the concept of a songwriter spotlight, said to Perry, 'I wish you would have done it twenty years ago when I had some hair!'.[18] Across the season, further songwriting legends including Jule Styne, Jimmy McHugh, Oscar Hammerstein II, Dorothy Fields and Nacio Herb Brown all took to the Como stage, and along with guests joined in a rousing cornucopia of Great American Songbook standards. It was a golden era of musical variety television.

The shows were not without their challenges, but that all added to the spark. Perry recalled one incident with his trademark self-deprecation concerning the use of cue cards.

> Nobody wanted people to know that they used cue cards, because actually you'd be considered an idiot . . . but there's no way I could learn ten songs [a week] and script, so, we used to have prompting boards like they have even in theatres. I was singing a song, and it was 'Night and Day' and the cue card boy put up . . . the second chorus first, and I sang it, but until I got to the second chorus I says 'Oh my God . . . we did the wrong thing!' At the end I said 'Now you folks know that was all screwed up a little . . . but I'm gonna tell you what happened. 'course I look in the control booth and Bob Finkel's [saying] 'What is he doing? What's he doing?' So it took me five minutes to explain this. Now you know what happened, two commercials went down the drain and I heard gun shots . . . I says 'come out here' and I called the cue card boy and I said 'you better tell them what happened, 'cause I'm not the only idiot on this show.' And I think we got more mail on that show than any show we've ever done.[19]

Perry's calm disposition became the subject of many jokes, directed at his 'relaxed' on-screen persona. This would become a recurring theme throughout his career from then on, and Perry was happy to send himself up, although it did wear thin at times. Speaking in 1977, he said:

> I like to rehearse, 'cause I don't do anything strenuous, as far as I'm concerned I sit around a lot but it gives me a feeling of knowing what's gonna happen, and that's kind of important. I think that's where all that relaxed nonsense that you hear about, that I'm supposedly relaxed [comes from]. Well, I kind of figure, if I rehearse for two weeks and don't know what I'm doing, then I don't belong in the business. Now some people misunderstand that for not caring – that attitude – but I assure you I care.[20]

In the recording studio, Perry had now settled into two distinctly different artistic approaches for his recordings – one for singles and one for albums, as with many artists of the era. Singles were more likely to be brought to him and were aimed from a commercial, jukebox perspective. Albums, on the other hand, were Perry's opportunity to sing the songs he most loved to sing, and 1959 brought two more stellar works to the Como catalogue. The first was *Como Swings*, a phenomenal collection of twelve songs recorded in April and May 1959.

Como Swings is a feast of superbly swinging arrangements, which Perry approaches with great confidence and ease – defying any claims to the contrary. The quality of the recording really emphasizes the wide dynamic range and richness of high-fidelity sound and provides a solid benchmark by which to audition a Hi-Fi system. Musically, the song selections are a perfect blend – from the sunny optimism of 'Let a Smile Be Your Umbrella' to the sultry blues of 'You Came a Long Way from St. Louis'. Also, compare Perry's recording of '*Honey, Honey (Bless Your Heart)*' from this album with his first recording of the song, featured in the album *We Get Letters*. The two recordings side by side provide an excellent example of the versatility of song and singer.

The *We Get Letters* album, recorded by Perry between 1956 and 1957, has the rare distinction of being the only Como album recorded completely with a small ensemble, consisting of a section of Mitchell Ayres' orchestra affectionately referred to during the sessions as Como's Little Combo. It was Perry's only thematic venture into the world of vocal jazz but stands as a testament to his ability within the genre, which he more commonly exhibited on television. The album was both a commercial and critical success, domestically and internationally.

Perry's journey through jazz opens with a fittingly brisk reading of 'Swingin' down the Lane' before easing into a smooth as silk interpretation of 'It's Easy to Remember'. Of the fourteen songs recorded, twelve made the final album cut including favourites of Perry's such as 'Angry', 'S'posin" and "Deed I Do". Interestingly, another favourite 'It's Been a Long, Long Time' was never issued in Perry's lifetime. The remaining unreleased session recording, however, 'If I Could Be with You (One Hour Tonight)' was picked up in 1971. A top-notch recording, every bit the equal of the primary dozen, it was included within the RCA Camden compilation *Door of Dreams*.

Less than two months after the *Como Swings* sessions, *Season's Greetings from Perry Como* was recorded, across three consecutive days in July 1959. The album is made up of mostly Christmas music that Perry had recorded previously but with the advantages of stereo sound and further maturing of the Como vocal style. Hear how Perry combines vocal precision with a smooth and even timbre to produce a more intimate presentation in his second recording of 'The Christmas Song (Merry Christmas to You)'. The arrangement is virtually identical to his 1953 recording but sung with much greater freedom. The same effect is achieved with 'God Rest Ye Merry, Gentlemen', which Perry delivers with further reverence, leading the verses of the arrangement out of tempo. What this period represents is the fully evolved and secured Perry Como vocal style.

'(There's No Place Like) Home for the Holidays' gets a complete overhaul. The song had first been recorded by Perry in 1954 and published by Roncom, but it was with this 1959 arrangement that the song truly secured its place in the pantheon of all-time greatest Christmas songs. The song's origins, though, actually began with the Thanksgiving holiday. The concept of going home for dinner and pumpkin pie is very much rooted in the spirit of the celebration. The song 'always sort of brings a lump in my throat,' said Nick Perito in 2004, 'because of what it says, and well, "Big Daddy" owned it as far as I'm concerned—and he meant it. The lyric is very touching. What's the holidays without family and home?'[21]

'Winter Wonderland' also receives a completely new arrangement. The jazz setting and gently paced rhythm perfectly complement the song's lyrical depictions. Perry had recorded the song with equal effect in a swing arrangement in 1946 for his first album, *Perry Como Sings Merry Christmas Music*. Perry's 1946 recording of 'Winter Wonderland' enjoyed a brief visit to the US top ten, but the album it came from became a million seller.

Perry Como Sings Merry Christmas Music is also one of the first examples of a specifically recorded studio album. Whereas folios up to this point often combined singles recorded at separate times, the *Merry Christmas Music* sessions were specifically recorded for collective release. The original album of eight titles contained a combination of traditional Christmas carols and popular Christmas songs. The album was reissued the following year with one substitution, swapping 'O, Little Town of Bethlehem' with 'White Christmas' which Perry had just then recorded.

The album stayed in its 1947 form through the transition to the 10-inch LP and the full-length 12-inch LP where the album was combined with Perry's second Christmas album, *Around the Christmas Tree*. In 1961 the album was repackaged for the Camden label with one further adjustment, omitting Perry's 1946 recording of 'Santa Claus Is Comin' to Town'. The album remained in this form for decades to come. 'O, Little Town of Bethlehem' was never reinstated, and as such, the original 1946 release of *Perry Como Sings Merry Christmas Music* retains an added collector's value.

It would be unfair to make a direct comparison between the recordings made in 1946 and those re-recorded in 1959. By the close of the 1950s, audio technology had changed vastly from the methods of the 1940s. This difference in recording technology, however, does not in any way detract from the quality and enjoyment of the earlier recordings. In both cases, Perry's love for the Christmas season is abundantly clear, and his performances are pure and heartfelt. It is for precisely this reason that the recordings of artists such as Enrico Caruso are still greatly admired so many years after they were recorded.

The hits continued to flow in the late 1950s, with the back-to-back mega international success of 'Magic Moments' backed with 'Catch a Falling Star'. 'Magic Moments' was an early composition by the legendary songwriting team of Burt Bacharach and Hal David. The song remains one of the most instantly recognisable songs in popular music. For Bacharach, it was one of his first steps into stratospheric success. David, on the other hand, had been writing lyrics for many years by this time. In fact, he wrote another song recorded by Como 'I Wish I Had a Record (of the Promises You Made)' in 1949.

'Catch a Falling Star' was composed by Lee Pockriss and Paul Vance. Together the duo later wrote 'Itsy Bitsy Teeny Weeny Yellow Polka Dot Bikini'. With other collaborators, Vance also brought several ballads to Perry in the

1960s, including the gorgeous Western-themed 'One More Mountain' which could've easily been the title and theme for a film in the genre.

Both 'Magic Moments' and 'Catch a Falling Star' were hugely successful on both sides of the Atlantic, with the former reaching No. 1 in the UK and the latter in the United States. 'Catch a Falling Star' also holds the title of being the first Gold Record certified by the Recording Industry Association of America (RIAA) and also earned Perry a Grammy Award for Best Vocal Performance at the First Annual Grammy Awards for 1958 (held in November 1959). This classic disc has stood the test of time, becoming one of the most legendary double A-side singles in pop music history.

Surprisingly perhaps, Pockriss and Vance did not attempt to repeat their success with Perry – but then, replicating the success of 'Catch a Falling Star' would have been a tall order by any measurement, and less is very often more.

The hit singles for the remainder of the decade continued with a mostly rock 'n' roll feel, each handled as only Perry Como could and notching up further international hits for the Como cannon. The sales of one song 'Kewpie Doll' plateaued around the 750,000 mark. As Ray Charles had harmonized with Perry on the chorus, Perry presented a gold record to Ray with a quarter missing. To be able to consider a record that had sold three-quarters of a million as missing the mark, you know you've really hit the big time!

Perry capped off the decade with a recording session on 28 December 1959 which resulted in the single 'I Know What God Is' paired with 'Delaware' released in early 1960 and billed by RCA Victor as the 'Two Sides of Como'. A recording session between Christmas and New Year was an occasional tradition for Perry, and several recordings over the years were made during the festive period. The two recordings released from this session could not be much further apart artistically, but both are outstanding – exhibiting the key ingredients that make a first-class popular vocalist: clarity in enunciation, sincerity in performance and precision in delivery. The recordings also demonstrate the exceptional quality and flexibility of the Como voice. Perry Como was now at the absolute peak of his craft.

Quintessential Como
Recommended listening 1955–9

Ko Ko Mo (I Love You So)
*mw Forest Wilson, Jake Porter
and Eunice Levy, 1955
4 Jan 1955 - Make Someone Happy
CAL-694*

You Do Something to Me ★
*mw Cole Porter, 1929
From the musical Fifty
Million Frenchmen.
20 Jan 1955 - So Smooth LPM-1085*

It's a Good Day ★
*mw Peggy Lee and Dave Barbour, 1947
8 Feb 1955 - So Smooth LPM-1085*

For Me and My Gal ★
*m George W. Meyer, w Edgar Leslie
and Edward Ray Goetz, 1917
8 Feb 1955 - So Smooth LPM-1085*

In the Still of the Night ★
*mw Cole Porter, 1937
17 Feb 1955 - So Smooth LPM-1085*

It's the Talk of the Town ★
*m Jerry Livingston, w Marty Symes
and AI J. Neiburg, 1933
17 Feb 1955 - So Smooth LPM-1085*

**Chee Chee-oo Chee
(Sang the Little Bird)**
*with Jaye P. Morgan
m Saverio Seracini, w Ettore
Minoretti (It.),
w John Turner and Geoffrey Parsons
(Eng.), 1955
28 Apr 1955 - 47-6137*

Fooled
*m Doris Tauber, w Mann Curtis, 1955
Adapted from 'Come to the
Little Arbor Here' from Franz Lehár's
operetta The Merry Widow.
21 Jun 1955 - 47-6192*

The Rose Tattoo
*m Harry Warren, w Jack Brooks, 1955
27 Sep 1955 - Dreamer's Holiday CAL-582*

Tina Marie
*mw Bob Merrill, 1955
21 Jun 1955 - Love Makes the World
Go 'Round CAS-805 (e)*

All at Once You Love Her
*m Richard Rodgers,
w Oscar Hammerstein II, 1955
From the musical Pipe Dream.
27 Sep 1955 - PC Sings Hits
from Broadway Shows LPM-1191*

Juke Box Baby
m Joe Sherman, w Noel Sherman, 1956
2 Feb 1956 - Somebody Loves Me
CAS-858 (e)

Hot Diggity (Dog Ziggity Boom) ★
mw Al Hoffman and Dick Manning, 1956
Adapted from the first theme of
Emmanuel Chabrier's 'España'.
2 Feb 1956 - Como's Golden Records
LPM-1981

More
m Alex Alstone, w Tom Glazer, 1956
8 May 1956 - Love Makes the World Go
'Round CAS-805 (e)

Glendora
mw Ray Stanley, 1956
8 May 1956 - Love Makes the World
Go 'Round CAS-805 (e)

Somebody Loves Me ★
m George Gershwin, w Ballard
MacDonald and B. G. DeSylva, 1924
From the revue George White's
Scandals of 1924.
18 Jun 1956 - We Get Letters LPM-1463

They Can't Take That Away From Me ★
m George Gershwin, w Ira Gershwin, 1937
From the film Shall We Dance.
18 Jun 1956 - We Get Letters LPM-1463
PC Music from Hollywood - 28 Mar 1977

Mi casa, su casa
(My House Is Your House)
mw Al Hoffman and Dick Manning, 1957
8 Jan 1957 - Como's Golden Records
LPM-1981

Round and Round ★
mw Lou Stallman and Joe Shapiro, 1957
15 Jan 1957 - Como's Golden Records
LPM-1981

That's What I Like ★
m Jule Styne, w Bob Hilliard, 1954
From the film Living It Up.
12 Feb 1957 - We Get Letters LPM-1463

'Deed I Do ★
m Fred Rose, w Walter Hirsch, 1926
19 Feb 1957 - We Get Letters LPM-1463

Just Born (to Be Your Baby)
mw Luther Dixon and
Billy Dawn Smith, 1957
1 Jul 1957 - Dreamer's Holiday CAL-582

Dancin'
mw Jerry Leiber and Mike Stoller, 1957
1 Jul 1957 - 47-6991

Catch a Falling Star ★
mw Paul Vance and Lee Pockriss, 1957
9 Oct 1957 - Como's Golden Records
LPM-1981

Magic Moments ★
m Burt Bacharach, w Hal David, 1958
3 Dec 1957 - Como's Golden Records
LPM-1981

Almost Like Being in Love ★
m Frederick Loewe, w Alan Jay
Lerner, 1947
From the musical Brigadoon.
12–13 Feb 1958 - Saturday Night
with Mr. C. LSP-1971 /
PC KMH - 13 Feb 1964
Duke Children's Classic - 20 May 1995

Love Letters ★
m Victor Young, w Edward Heyman, 1945
The theme from the film Love Letters.
13 Feb 1958 - Saturday Night with Mr. C.
LSP-1971 / CSC - c. Oct 1945 - V-Disc 594

It Had to Be You ★
m Isham Jones, w Gus Kahn, 1924
19 Feb 1958 - Saturday Night with Mr. C.
LSP-1971 / PC KMH - 10 Feb 1960

Ac-cent-tchu-ate the Positive ★
m Harold Arlen, w Johnny Mercer, 1944
From the film Here Come the Waves.
19 Feb 1958 - Saturday Night with Mr. C.
LSP-1971

Red Sails in the Sunset
m Will Grosz (under pseud. Hugh
Williams), w Jimmy Kennedy, 1935
20 Feb 1958 - Saturday Night with Mr. C.
LSP-1971

Little Man You've Had a Busy Day ★
m Mabel Wayne, w Maurice Sigler
and Al Hoffman, 1934
20 Feb 1958 - Saturday Night with Mr. C.
LSP-1971

Moon Talk
mw Al Hoffman and Dick Manning, 1958
6 Mar 1958 - Love Makes the World
Go 'Round CAS-805 (e)

Kewpie Doll
mw Sid Tepper and Roy C. Bennett, 1958
11 Mar 1958 - Dreamer's Holiday CAL-582

Come Rain or Come Shine ★
m Harold Arlen, w Johnny Mercer, 1946
From the musical St. Louis Woman.
12 Mar 1958 - Saturday Night with Mr. C.
LOP-1004 [omitted from stereo pressings]
PC NBC - 23 Feb 1957

I May Never Pass This Way Again
mw Murray Wizell and Irving Melsher, 1957
1 May 1958 - When You Come
to the End of the Day LSP-1885

Prayer for Peace
m Nick Acquaviva, w Norman Gimbel, 1955
1 May 1958 - When You Come
to the End of the Day LSP-1885

No Well on Earth ★
m David Mann, w Bob Hilliard, 1950
18 Jun 1958 - When You Come
to the End of the Day LSP-1885

Scarlet Ribbons
m Evelyn Danzig, w Jack Segal, 1949
19 Jun 1958 - When You Come
to the End of the Day LSP-1885

Love Makes the World Go 'Round
mw Ollie Jones, 1958
16 Sep 1958 - Love Makes the World
Go 'Round CAS-805 (e)

Mandolins in the Moonlight
mw George David Weiss
and Aaron Schroeder, 1958
16 Sep 1958 - Somebody Loves Me
CAS-858 (e)

Tomboy
mw Joe Farrell and Jim Conway, 1959
29 Jan 1959 - Hello, Young Lovers
CAS-2122

**Kiss Me and Kiss Me and Kiss Me
(Tre volte baciami)**
m Arturo Casadei, w Luciano Beretta
(It.), 1958, w Al Hoffman
and Dick Manning (Eng.), 1959
29 Jan 1959 - Somebody Loves Me
CDN-5126 (UK)

I've Got You under My Skin ★
mw Cole Porter, 1936
From the film Born to Dance.
9 Apr 1959 - Como Swings LSP-2010
25–27 Jun 1970 (Live) - PC in Person at the
International Hotel, Las Vegas LSPX-1001

Honey, Honey (Bless Your Heart)
m Larry Stock, w Dominick Belline, 1954
16 Apr 1959 - Como Swings LSP-2010

Dear Hearts and Gentle People ★
m Sammy Fain, w Bob Hilliard, 1949
23 Apr 1959 - Como Swings LSP-2010

I Know
mw Carl Stutz and Edith Lindeman, 1959
14 May 1959 - Somebody Loves Me
CAS-858 (e)

You Are in Love
mw Bart Howard, 1959
14 May 1959 - Make Someone Happy
CAL-694

Begin the Beguine ★
mw Cole Porter, 1935
From the musical Jubilee.
21 May 1959 - Como Swings LSP-2010

I Know What God Is
mw Don Raye, John G. Bowen
and Ned Freeman, 1960
28 Dec 1959 - The Lord's Prayer
CAS-2299 (e)

Delaware
mw Irving Gordon, 1960
28 Dec 1959 - An Evening with PC CAL-742

5

The Sweetest Sounds

Saturday nights at eight became Wednesday nights at nine in the autumn of 1959. In March of that year Perry had signed a contract with Kraft Foods to produce 66-colour television shows. The contract worth $25 million was reported to be the biggest in show business history. The story was covered widely in the national press, including within a legendary issue of *Look* magazine. There were supporters and sceptics of the deal at the time – some celebrating the figure, others questioning what it entailed, hence the article title 'Perry Como: How Much Is His $25,000,000 Worth?'. The reality was that the contract involved Perry's production company, Roncom (a combination of his son Ronald's name and the family last name), covering all costs to produce sixty-six shows. Media sensationalism and exaggeration were by no means a new thing, even in 1959, neither was the perpetuation and proliferation of press agent pitches and diatribes.

Look Magazine explained that in the weeks after the story broke:

Comments expressing every emotion from admiration to envy to disgust were recorded. Walter Winchell reported that, when asked whether the agreement would change Como, a patron at Lindy's replied, 'Why should all that money change him? All that success never did.' Sidney Skolsky noted that the singer seemed even more relaxed after the announcement and concluded that the pact must be worth its weight in tranquilizers. Jack Paar said on his show that actually, Como 'could have made $35 million, but he fell asleep during negotiations.' And a serious-minded student sent a letter to a New York newspaper saying that her 'blood boiled' at the thought of a man who already had so much being given such a large salary. Like many others, she assumed that a major part of the money, rather than a small percentage of it, would go directly to Como.[1]

Thus, illustrating the potential danger of mass media where misinformation is concerned – again, not a new problem.

The article ends, however, on a more positive note, concluding that:

> Como's low-pressure approach on each show leaves the viewer feeling that he has spent an hour with an easy-going friend. The choice of songs leans toward the sweet and sentimental. The production numbers are casual. The repartee (written by top TV wits) is pleasant, but not so clever as to make a viewer feel inferior. In explaining why they like him, a high percentage of his admirers use the word 'sincere.' But what happens to this image now? Won't Como's production numbers have to be flashier, his jokes funnier, his guest stars more glamorous? Won't even the host have to become high-powered? If so, there could be trouble ahead. But Como's admirers are sure the old image will stick, and that the move out of his old Saturday spot will help him.[2]

A Perry Como programme could ensure viewers of certain guarantees. These were: family-suitable viewing, timeless music, high production values and a star-studded guest line-up. There was very little in the way of controversy, even when viewed retrospectively after decades; and the show's presentation was always sincere. British journalist and television chat show host Michael Parkinson observed that Perry was

> one of that handful of entertainers who created a singing style, which many copied, and none surpassed. Similarly, on television – where for a time he was the world's highest-paid and most popular performer – he invented an image and a technique which again set new standards for fellow performers to attain.[3]

One such singer who was inspired by the 'Como way' in the United States was Andy Williams.

One of the things that I use that Perry taught me is taking time. I come out after there's been a big production number and a lot of loud music and things, and I take a stool and sit down (which is actually Perry's thing, what he used to do, sit on a stool). And then take time with the audience as far as not rushing into the song and doing the verse of a song ad-lib with no piano and no guitar or anything and just sing the verse a cappella and it really works; and it wouldn't work as well if I hadn't grown up seeing Perry take his time doing that.[4]

Similarly in the UK, Irish-born singer-musician Val Doonican utilized a rocking chair in his shows, which directly descended from Perry's stool.

Of course, then – *The Perry Como Shows* on television were so popular back in the fifties, all black and white shows, but they were the musical show in the world of that time and that's what started the type of show that I tried to do for so many years, you see. *The Perry Como [Show]* was the milestone – that's when it all started to happen, because he had world guests on and he sang duets with people and that had never been done before on television and it became the accepted way to do a television show if you're a singer. So, naturally, whether sort of purposely or not, when the time came for me to make my own television shows, naturally that was the template I used – what Como used to do in the old days. So, he inspired a lot of people.[5]

The newly titled show *Perry Como's Kraft Music Hall* (still often referred to vernacularly as *The Perry Como Show*) premiered on Wednesday, 30 September 1959. The show provides an opportunity for both introductions and reflections. In an early scene, Perry nods to one of his radio predecessors at the *Kraft Music Hall*, Bing Crosby, with whom he sings an affectionate duet via a Crosby record of 'Somebody Else Is Taking My Place' – ending sensitively with the adapted line 'For nobody's taking your place'. This is the kind of touch which was classic Como. On the one hand, a wink of humour, on the other, a sincere gesture of respect for another performer – two of the factors that were key to Perry's enduring popularity on television.

Over the course of its first season, *Perry Como's Kraft Music Hall* welcomed such guests as singer-bandleader Phil Harris, bandleader Benny Goodman, actor José Ferrer, actress Anne Bancroft, and comedian-host Johnny Carson. The St. Patrick's Day show aptly featured Bing Crosby, who was returning the favour for Perry's appearance on *The Bing Crosby Show* a couple of weeks earlier. Across the reciprocal guest appearances, the two song stylists charged their way through several dozen Songbook standards to 'record' their 'first LP'.

During an Irish medley with the cast on Perry's show, the whole company had just finished a rousing rendition of 'MacNamara's Band' after which Como and Crosby were to share solos on 'Too-Ra-Loo-Ra-Loo-Ral (an Irish lullaby)' with Perry singing the verse and Bing the chorus. As Perry tenderly sings the verse, a crashing sound is heard in the background, resemblant of a tin bucket hitting a hard floor. Perry, who is seen in a close-up camera shot leaning over a bar within the set of an Irish pub, purposely rolls his eyes with a cheeky grin and says, 'You couldn't do it in the other song, right?'[6] to a burst of laughter from the audience. Where some stars would be irritated by such mishaps, Perry took them in his stride. In fact, they only added to the enjoyment of the programme – and Perry understood this completely.

On 16 April 1960, Perry arrived in London to tape a landmark production for the series – an on-location edition. It was the first of what would later become a mainstay of Como television specials. Over the course of the next week Perry rehearsed and taped his show with actor Sir Ralph Richardson, singer-comedian Harry Secombe, ballet dancer Dame Margot Fonteyn, pianist Russ Conway, and actress Fenella Fielding, even being invited for a visit with John Robert Russell (The 13th Duke of Bedford).

To compensate for the travel and extended production time, there was no Wednesday night broadcast in the United States on 20 April. The show from London, which aired the following Wednesday, was well received, being described as 'a travelog with style and taste'[7] by *Variety* magazine. Perry sings some of his favourite songs including 'I Love You' and 'Where or When' and partakes in a nostalgic rendering of 'Cruising down the River' with some of his guests – capturing the essence of a British pub sing-along. Soon after, Perry returned to New York to resume his weekly schedule for the remainder of the season – appearing on set with coat and golf bag as he had done in England, to symbolize his return to the United States.

The show, referred to by BBC personnel as 'Operation Como' was a major endeavour for the broadcaster. At the time, BBC television technology in the UK was significantly behind the advancements in the United States. Consequently, the corporation had to hire various pieces of televisual equipment to bring the resolution standard up to a level that would be acceptable for audiences in the United States. Even with these advancements, the show was still only shot in black and white. This was the normal mode of operation in the UK, but Perry's shows had been broadcast in the United States in compatible colour for four years by this time.

Compatible colour was NBC/RCA's invention. Whereas CBS had been first off the mark with a colour television format, their version was not compatible with black-and-white television, which meant that none of their colour broadcasts could be seen by viewers with a black-and-white set (which made up a millions-strong share of the American viewership of the time). Consequently, CBS were forced to abandon their technology to maintain comprehensive viewer coverage.

An equivalent scenario was encountered in the recording industry, where stereo records were being plugged while most homes still had mono equipment. The solution was two-fold – the first aspect was continuing to press mono mixes of stereo albums (which is why most albums from the 1950s and 1960s are available in either format). The second was introducing a suitable turntable cartridge and stylus combination that was backward and forward compatible. This meant that stereo records could be reproduced on mono equipment with mono sound, and the stereo benefits revealed should the listener upgrade to a stereo system. Listeners already in possession of a stereo system could continue to enjoy their mono records with a stereo pick-up, but to reduce surface noise, integrated amplifiers would commonly be fitted with a mono switch, which, when activated, summed the information of both channels into a single channel. This was then output through both loudspeakers.

Perry Como's Kraft Music Hall in London was produced by Yvonne Littlewood, who had previously been tasked with the editing of Perry's shows, so that they were suitable for non-commercial broadcast. Yvonne worked with Perry on numerous projects for the BBC over the years and spoke thoughtfully of their association:

'He knew very much what he liked and he didn't like, and he would say so. He didn't, I think, suffer fools gladly at all,' recalled Littlewood. 'I think if something didn't please him too much, he let people know in a very subtle way that he wasn't too happy with it afterwards – but it was nothing that was a problem in the working relationship we had.'[8]

It was decided by the end of season one that a change of production would be beneficial to bring a new feel to the *Kraft Music Hall*. The first change came with the hiring of Nick Vanoff as producer. Vanoff began his career as a dancer before moving into television in the 1950s, producing shows most notably for Steve Allen. His connection with Perry began as a cue-card boy.[9] Nick's wife Felisa reflected on her husband's connection with Perry:

> I get tears in my eyes because the relationship between Perry and my husband and me and my family and his family was so close. He did anything for Nick, and more importantly, my husband would do anything on Earth for Perry. Perry generated that kind of love.[10]

Vanoff invited his friend and colleague Dwight Hemion to come and meet Perry, along with a few other potential members of personnel, including set designer Gary Smith, who was responsible for creating the iconic set for Perry's new request segment 'Sing to Me, Mr. C.' Together they became three core members of the new behind-the-scenes team of the *Kraft Music Hall*.

Both Vanoff and Hemion were only in their thirties at the time. Hemion had worked with Vanoff on *The Tonight Show* (as hosted by Steve Allen) and had a similar CV of television credits to his name. He described Perry as one of the kindest men he'd known and very professional. 'Television misses Perry Como . . .' lamented Hemion in 2001. 'Perry was so terribly important', he added. The 'number one show for many years. I can only say that my respect for him was and is more than I can suggest . . . He was just a kind, kind guy, who sang better than anybody, in those days . . . to me he was always "just Perry" – [he] never tried to be anything other than who he was.'[11] Nick Vanoff, Dwight Hemion and Gary Smith would work with Perry on television for the next three seasons, with Dwight continuing beyond the fourth season.

Season two opened in fine form with singer and actress Ethel Merman. Merman, already a recurring guest, was poised with Perry in script and song to highlight the distinct differences in their vocal approach, with mutual affection. The show opens cleverly with a medley of parodies, including 'Taking a Chance on Love', during which Perry introduces viewers to some of his team both in front of and behind the cameras.

For a solo spot in the season's autumnal premiere, Perry gives a stunning performance of one of his television perennials. The scene opens at ground level, while leaves blow, and the camera gently pans upward to the top of a scaffolding set. The set simulates the appearance of an apartment block and alludes to the 'canyons of steel' referred to in the forthcoming song's lyrics. The opening is underscored beautifully by an a cappella excerpt of 'Autumn Leaves' sung by the Ray Charles Singers, with Perry brought steadily into focus as he sings the opening bars of 'Autumn in New York'. After a few moments focused atop the structure on which Perry stands in a checked coat, he calmly descends the steps leading to the stage floor. His voice is rich and reassuring – his presentation confident, but unassuming. The whole segment is handled by a single camera following Perry. Its beauty is in its simplicity, and it is a technique that would be implemented time and again across the series to superb effect.

Other highlights from the season include the annual Christmas show with child performer Ginny Tiu among the guests. Ginny sings 'Do-Re-Mi' in a charming duet with Perry, preceded by some cute dialogue and interaction between them. In the nineteenth episode of the season, Perry joins Anne Bancroft and Jimmy Durante in a combination of medleys and sketches surrounding the subject of marriage for a post-Valentine's Day-themed show. 'Stop the music! Wait a minute, stop the music! That's no way to say goodnight!' shouts Durante at the end of the show interrupting Perry's closing theme, 'You Are Never Far Away'. 'How then?' asks Perry, leading to a rendition of Jimmy's own signing off theme, the 'Good Night Song', aka 'Goodnight, Mrs. Calabash Wherever You Are'.[12]

Season three saw the gradual introduction of a supporting cast who would become known as the Kraft Music Hall Players. Paul Lynde was one such performer who first appeared regularly towards the end of season two.

Perry between rehearsals for his television show, c. 1961.

Lynde, known for his flamboyant on-screen persona would go on to star in the television comedy series *Bewitched* and the game show *The Hollywood Squares*. He was also a distinctive voice actor – becoming the voice of animated characters such as Sylvester Sneekly (aka the Hooded Claw) in the William Hanna and Joseph Barbera cartoon series *The Perils of Penelope Pitstop*.

Another member of the Kraft Music Hall Players was Kaye Ballard. Her career began in the 1940s as a musical comedian with a touring revue headed by Spike Jones. Making her television debut in the early 1950s, she enjoyed success on stage and screen. Also featured was singer Sandy Stewart, who during her time on the *Kraft Music Hall* had a top 20 hit with her recording of 'My Colouring Book'. Together, Ballard and Stewart recorded an album with Como, *The Best of Irving Berlin's Songs from Mr. President* – Berlin's final and short-lived Broadway production. Completing the company was comedian Don Adams, who went on to star in the television sitcom *Get Smart*, for which he is perhaps best known. The quartet of talent brought a change of pace to the Como hour, and along with Perry, they combined for numerous sketches and features.

Lena Horne and George Burns were among the guests that season. It became common during this period to typically have one or two big names who had a recurring involvement throughout the show, for instance, Janet Blair, Don Ameche and Frances Langford, Alice Faye, and Martha Raye. The trio of Como, Horne and Burns made for an inspired combo. Originally aired on 31 January 1962, the show (which was taped six months in advance) even saw a repeat airing in 1963. Lena, who guested with Perry many times, reflected in 1979 that it always made her happy to be invited to appear with him, saying that singing with Perry anytime was 'almost the most fun a woman can have!'[13] Como and Horne reprised a Birdland medley they had performed two years earlier, this time interjected with humorous melodic bursts from Burns.

It was now becoming more common for Perry's Kraft shows to be pre-recorded, but Perry still preferred the spontaneity and energy of a live broadcast. The show opened with a suitably swinging version of 'On the Street Where You Live' a song that would later become the subject of some mystery for Como fans when referred to in the film *Blast from the Past* starring Brendan Fraser and Alicia Silverstone. During a romantic moment towards the end of the film, Fraser's character says to Silverstone's 'There is a song that Mr. Como sings called "On the Street Where You Live". Do you know it?' 'Sing it to me!'[14] responds Silverstone's character softly, and Frasier's character proceeds to sing part of the lyrics to the classic song from the musical *My Fair Lady*. True, Perry did sing the song (at least four times on television), but the dialogue seemed to imply that he was known for singing it, leading some fans to the conclusion that Perry had recorded the song, which he did not.

Earlier in the season, a historic reunion of Perry and members of the Ted Weems Orchestra came to fruition. Appearing with Ted were Country Washburn, Red Ingle, Parker Gibbs and Elmo Tanner, and together they recreated some happy moments from the 1930s and 1940s. It's a heartfelt and joyous show, with some amusing banter between Weems and Como, beginning on a tour bus. 'I never got to sing any of the real popular songs', says Perry, to which Ted replies 'well, you'd never learn the words. You'd walk out to the mike with a sheet of music in your hand, and as I look at these [cue] cards, things haven't changed any!' Perry later jests that he doesn't have to give his new boss (at Kraft Foods) a haircut, to which Ted says, 'Well, you weren't such a hot barber, Perry'. The audience laughs, Perry pauses and then replies to Weems (now balding) 'I don't know, the last haircut I gave you seems to have lasted a long time!'[15] There is a great sense of affection between these two gentlemen on camera, and the musical segment that follows serves as a fitting tribute to those early days on the road.

As Ted Weems' theme music 'Out of the Night' fills the air, followed by the whistling of Elmo Tanner, Ted enters the stage to introduce his featured stars performing songs they made famous with the band. The running gag with each of Ted's introductions is Perry's assumption that Weems is introducing him. The first offering comes from Country Washburn, playing bass and singing 'Oh! Mo'nah' (which he and Weems wrote together). Parker Gibbs is up next to sing 'Piccolo Pete' followed by some virtuosic violin comedy from Red Ingle. Elmo Tanner then takes to the stage to whistle 'Heartaches' with Perry providing percussion accompaniment on the guiro. The segment concludes with a rendition of 'I Wonder Who's Kissing Her Now' by Como, backed by Tanner, Ingle and Gibbs.

Another new feature was introduced in series three of *Perry Como's Kraft Music Hall*. Beginning with episode five and becoming a regular segment, Perry and company honoured the history and contributions of a state within the United States of America. Perry provided narrations and shared the spotlight with his guests and the Kraft Music Hall Players. The first state to be saluted, naturally, was Pennsylvania. The following week was Missouri, and as the season progressed, the Como team dotted their way around the US map, honouring states including Florida, Texas, Maine, California, Minnesota, and Arizona – two dozen states in all, across the next two seasons. The theme to the segments 'Fifty Nifty United States' as with most of the show's special material was composed by Ray Charles.

In the recording studio, 1962 saw the creation of what is considered by many to be one of the finest albums of Perry Como's career – *By Request*. The album was produced by the team of Hugo Peretti and Luigi Creatore, also known for their work with Sam Cooke and Elvis Presley. *By Request* was their fourth album with Perry Como in two years – each of which is a classic. The album, which was recorded in June 1962, contains a dozen standards, old and new, many from the worlds of stage and screen, each fitting perfectly with the Como voice. For instance, 'Can't Help Falling in Love' sounds as if it could've been written just for Perry. The song was co-written by George Weiss and the album's producers and introduced by Elvis Presley in the film *Blue Hawaii*. From *West Side Story*, observe the breath control in Perry's interpretation of 'Maria' – the recording is a masterclass in vocal balance, which Perry demonstrates with serenity and command in equal measure. The warm and lush arrangements provide the perfect accompaniment to Como's sincere, authoritative, and controlled delivery. The rear cover of the album said it best – 'A superbly performed, beautiful collection – By Request'[16]. This album should be in every serious music collection.

Outside of albums, Perry's recording partnership with Hugo and Luigi yielded several classic singles. In one instance, Perry returned once more to the rock 'n' roll genre, with a new song titled 'You're Following Me', which, as with 'Magic Moments' before it, was composed by Burt Bacharach. This time, however, lyrics were written by Bob Hilliard, whose writing credits include 'Dear Hearts and Gentle People' and 'In the Wee Small Hours of the Morning'. Surprisingly, the song made only a modest impact, despite possessing all of the ingredients that had worked so well commercially only a few years before. Regardless of this, the song remains a superb example of Perry's versatility, and the confidence of the performance is a testament to his musicianship. Perry would have far greater success the following year with 'Caterina' and again the year after with '(I Love You) Don't You Forget It' – both of which have become all-time Como classics.

Burt would compose once more for Perry in the second half of the decade. This time, with Hal David again in the lyricist role. The song they came up with was titled 'He Who Loves'. For one reason or another, it was never originally released but stands out as one of the best of the unissued recordings from the period, which clearly involved a lot of experimentation.

Back on television, *Perry Como's Kraft Music Hall* opened for its fourth season in October 1962. The season premiere partly originated from Sands Point Golf Club, Long Island, New York, at which Perry was a long-standing member. The guests were golfing legends Arnold Palmer, Gary Player, and Jack Nicklaus, all friends of Perry's and with whom he spends time on the course during the show. Also on the show, a new member is welcomed to the Kraft Music Hall Players, Pierre Olaf. Olaf was a French actor with a background in Parisian musical revues. At this point in his career, Pierre had recently enjoyed great success playing Jacquot in the original Broadway production of Bob Merrill's *Carnival!* in which he was joined by co-star and fellow Kraft Music Hall Player Kaye Ballard in the role of Rosalie.

The close of the fourth season would be the last of Perry's weekly television duties. At this time, Perry had a desire for a change of pace and direction. He had indicated on several occasions that the weekly schedule was becoming a grind and that he had desires to do a smaller number of bigger shows. He was also concerned about repetition and who they could seek out as new guests. The change came in 1963. Perry had an idea in mind – to take the *Kraft Music Hall* series on the road. And so, plans began for a series of monthly shows commencing in the autumn from different parts of the United States. Episode one of season five aired on 3 October 1964 and originated from Pittsburgh Civic Arena in Pennsylvania. From there the show headed to San Francisco, then on to Dallas and further locales before concluding the season in Chicago. Season six took on the same form, opening in Detroit and once again closing in Chicago.

While the idea of touring the *Kraft Music Hall* was, in principle, an appealing one, Perry was to later describe it as one of his most expensive mistakes.

> I took it [the show] all over the states, we went to . . . the big cities, the marketing cities . . . I don't make too many deals, but that was one of 'em. And that was one of my most expensive mistakes, because I undertook all costs, and I didn't realise. For an example – the first show we did on the road was in Pittsburgh. It's near my hometown but now we had to have

our own stages and we had to construct stages, 'cause they weren't for television. And we brought our camera trucks and it was just ridiculous . . . We did eight shows and the first show we did, I think it cost me about $400,000 to do . . . but it was my idea and I was going to stick to it, 'cause I think we were getting $300,000, but it cost $700,000 to do the show, and I underwrote everything. I says, 'I'm not a very good businessman!' I says 'we ain't gonna do that anymore!' But I was stuck with eight shows, 'course it got less and less, because the first show is always the most expensive. But I know that my lawyer says, 'don't make any more deals – stick to your singing!'[17]

Over the course of the next two series and a total of fourteen shows on the road, *Perry Como's Kraft Music Hall* continued to bring the best in musical variety to television screens across the United States. The fifth season premiere in Pittsburgh opened aptly with 'Back in Your Own Back Yard' and the guest list included two of Perry's co-stars from *Words and Music* – June Allyson and Cyd Charisse, with Como and Allyson duetting on a medley of songs nodding to the fact. In November, the *Kraft Music Hall* was in San Francisco with Victor Borge among the guests. It was Borge's first appearance with Perry since his visits to the *Chesterfield Supper Club* in the 1940s. With Victor at the piano, Perry sings 'No Other Love'. Victor returned to the *Kraft Music Hall* once more for the opening show of series six from Detroit.

Lena Horne was again a guest of Perry's during the season when the show opened its doors at NBC's Studio 4 in Burbank, California for a pre-Valentine's Day edition. Also on the bill was Dean Martin, who was a Como guest several times over the years. As in 1962, when Horne guested with George Burns, the trio of Como, Horne and Martin made for another superb combination of talents. Dean pokes gentle fun at the Como image and vice versa in what had become a customary repartee between the two singers. As Perry moves into camera view singing 'Sentimental Journey' pushing along a map on wheels, Dean says, 'I hate to see you rushing in like this Per'. When Dean asks what it is that Perry has wheeled in, Perry pauses for a moment to study the squiggled lines across the map and then remarks that it 'looks like a blown-up picture of one of your eyeballs' – referring to the Martin persona's drinking habits. In reality, Perry was never lethargic on stage and Dean's whisky glass contained apple juice, not bourbon.

In March 1964, the Como Kraft ensemble was at the Municipal Auditorium in New Orleans with another of Perry's co-stars from *Words and Music* guesting – Mickey Rooney. Como and Rooney sing Cole Porter's 'Brush Up Your Shakespeare' from the musical *Kiss Me Kate* to mark the 400th anniversary of the birth of English playwright William Shakespeare. Also featured is the honeyed horn of trumpeter Al Hirt, who accompanies Perry on the soulful Southern lullaby 'When It's Sleepy Time Down South'.

After an absence from the recording studio of more than a year-and-a-half, at least partly owing to his touring schedule with the *Kraft Music Hall*, Perry returned to the studio in 1965 at the encouragement of RCA Victor A&R man Steve Sholes. Instead of recording in New York, however, these sessions took place in Nashville, Tennessee, with legendary guitarist and producer Chet Atkins in the production role.

The recordings, made across four days in February 1965, resulted in the album *The Scene Changes*. Perry was backed vocally by the exceptionally talented Anita Kerr Quartet. Anita also wrote the arrangements. Among the legendary Nashville musicians providing instrumental colour were pianist Floyd Cramer (whose hits include 'On the Rebound' and 'Last Date') and saxophonist Boots Randolph (whose 'Yakety Sax' would become synonymous with British comedian Benny Hill).

Anita recalled her time working with Perry in Nashville:

He was a very nice, quiet person, but still very friendly. During the session my singers and myself, [SATB] [soprano, alto, tenor, and bass] were standing behind tall wooden slabs in order to not leak into Perry's microphone and also to keep the band, who were recording simultaneously with us, from leaking into our microphone. Perry sang so soft, we could hardly hear him. There were lines where we would have to phrase a lyric line with him and we had to have the wooden screen moved just enough so that we could watch his lips to be sure to phrase the line with him. He liked to tease a little bit, but as a whole, the session was very concentrated but relaxed. We all liked him instantly.[18]

The song selection on *The Scene Changes* includes compositions from country royalty such as Willie Nelson, Cindy Walker, and Don Gibson. 'Dream On Little Dreamer' became the hit single from the album and was anthemic in its connection with Perry's Nashville recordings. Perry's singing style was a perfect fit with country music. He quickly adapted to the new recording environment and blended seamlessly into the genre, while maintaining his own unique vocal approach. Over the next ten years, Perry would record more than seventy songs in Nashville, resulting in three albums and several singles – each with their own distinctive sound.

Follow-up sessions to *The Scene Changes* took place in the summer of 1965 but unfortunately did not materialize in another album. Two tracks were, however, released at the time as a single 'Oowee, Oowee' and 'Summer Wind' – the latter being one of the first recordings of the song and undoubtedly one of the best. The pathos in Perry's delivery of the song gets to the root of melancholy within the lyrics, and his inclusion of the variation of the last verse 'Now I'm alone, I might have known, but who can guess?' makes Como's rendition all the more special, complemented further by the understated accompaniment with shimmering percussion, which creates an entrancing image of wind caressing a sandy shoreline.

Further changes of scene would occur that year too. Having recently become Perry's musical director, Nick Perito was at the helm for his first recording session, conducting for Perry in November 1965. The two songs recorded 'Meet Me at the Altar' and 'Bye Bye Little Girl' were both picked up from Perry's summer sessions in Nashville and released together as a single, with new arrangements by Perito. Nick had first worked with Perry in the early 1950s on Perry's 15-minute CBS series as an accordionist. '"Hoop-Dee-Doo" was my big number,' recalled Nick. 'During the course of the season, they would do "Hoop-Dee-Doo" three or four times, and that was my moment to shine. It was in D-flat, I didn't like that so much! But I did "Hoop-Dee-Doo" and I got to see Perry and [of] course Ray [Charles] and all the people that I loved'.[19]

Nick's first ongoing work with Perry began in the autumn of 1964 with the departure of Mitchell Ayres. Ayres had moved to Hollywood to become musical director of the *Hollywood Palace* television series, where he stayed until his untimely death at 58 in 1969. Mitchell was killed when he and a colleague, violinist Betty Phillips, were hit by a car while crossing a street in Las Vegas near the Riviera Hotel. Only days after Mitchell's death, his wife Georgianna died of a heart attack. Ayres' death was a tragic end for a supremely talented man who left behind a wealth of recordings and arrangements.

Also joining the Como collaborative in late 1965 was producer Andy Wiswell. Wiswell, alongside Nick Perito and Ray Charles, worked together over the next three years on four albums, each with its own distinctive sound and brilliance in execution. Of the four, *Look to Your Heart* has been rated by industry professionals as an outstanding achievement artistically and technically – the best in its field. It was also a personal favourite of both Nick's and Ray's. Andy's son Hank, who was present at some of the sessions for the album, was impressed by Perry's sense of excellence.[20]

Perry's attention to detail at a recording session was legendary. He would typically study a song and arrangement there in the studio, make suggestions, try different approaches and not settle until he was happy with the result. Once that point was reached – he stopped. Nick recalled how once, during an afternoon recording session, he (Perito) wanted one more take just before the end of the session. 'Oh, Perry – one more!' called Nick, then proceeding to talk to the musicians. Ready and set, Nick tapped off the orchestra only to see confetti coming up over the top of Perry's booth – consisting of his vocal part, which he'd torn up. 'Oh, Perry!' cried Nick 'I just needed one more!', and Perry answered 'Nah . . . that last one was my record!'[21]

The first of Perry's albums produced by Wiswell was *Lightly Latin*, which as the rear cover confirms is 'A perfect matching of man to music'.[22] The ease and assurance of Perry's vocal performances, supported by the smooth, flowing feel of the arrangements, makes for quintessential Como listening. Perry had previously explored the bossa nova within his 1963 album *The Songs I Love*, when he recorded 'Slightly out of Tune (Desafinado)' and 'Carnival (Manhã de carnaval)'. The latter was re-recorded for *Lightly Latin*, where it receives a larger orchestral arrangement by Perito with the vocal accompaniment of the Ray Charles Singers, in contrast to the stripped-back arrangement from *The Songs I Love*. While the two recordings are notably different, they share equal merit.

This pairing of man and music was equally evident when Perry visited the home of his ancestors to record *Perry Como in Italy*. His vocals throughout combine the Italian and English language across a dozen songs, both traditional and contemporary. From the crisp precision of 'Forget Domani' through the haunting intimacy of 'Un giorno dopo l'altro (One Day Is Like Another)' to the romantic plea of the 'Love Theme from *La Strada* (Travelling down a Lonely Road)' – once again, Mr. Como is right on the mark. The recordings were made in RCA's Italiana Studios in Rome in May 1966, with the Alessandro Alessandroni Singers directed by Ray Charles adding charm and further cultural authenticity to the project.

After a period of considerable experimentation in 1967, resulting in such classic singles as 'Stop! And Think It Over' and 'You Made It That Way (Watermelon Summer)', Perry closed the year with another pre-New Year recording session on 29 December, consisting of three songs – 'How to Handle a Woman' which would be re-recorded in 1968, and 'Somebody Makes It So' which would be coupled as a single with the leading song of the session 'The Father of Girls' written by Ervin Drake.

It has been assumed in the past that the single version of 'The Father of Girls' is the same as employed within the *Look to Your Heart* album, when in fact, Perry re-recorded the vocal for the album to the existing orchestral accompaniment. This was done purposely to address a difference in diction from what was desired for the album. For instance, the re-pronunciation of the word 'you' in place of 'ya' on the single [e.g. 'ya worry' revised to 'you worry']. This attention to detail is an example of the intricacies of quality that Perry and his colleagues aspired to. It could be argued, however, that the single version of 'The Father of Girls' is more poignant. The elongated hold of the end of the line 'Boys come 'round when they want a date' on the album version is far more restrained and less natural than the single, which effectively utilizes the single syllable of the word 'date' with far greater freedom. The phrasing on the single was clearly more natural to Perry and was exhibited to great effect numerous times on television and in live performance.

'The Father of Girls' was autobiographical in nature for Perry. He understood first-hand the joys and worries of having a daughter. 'Family to him is number one', observed Vic Damone. 'First priority – his wife, children – then comes his work, his singing – after that golf, fishing and so on; but first his family – first priority'.[23]

The *Look to Your Heart* album was recorded in June 1968 and represents, again to many fans and professionals alike, a hallmark example of Perry Como at his pinnacle. It is a beautiful collection of love songs, completely in tune with the Como philosophy. The songs are of love and reflection with a definite sense of autumnal maturity. The title song of the album was composed by Jimmy Van Heusen with lyrics by Sammy Cahn for an episode of the television series Producers' Showcase ('Our Town') where it was introduced by Frank Sinatra in 1955. Como's vocal, paired with Nick Perito's accompaniment, however, eclipses the Sinatra recording by a considerable margin. The notably slower tempo and sensitivity of the orchestral arrangement far more effectively lends itself to the depth of the lyrics. The gentle easings in and out of tempo only add to the sincerity of Como's interpretation of the song.

Of the album, Canadian music critic Gene Lees wrote:

> I have of necessity given a good deal of thought and study to the art of singing, and Como's work consistently astonishes me. He is a fantastic technician. Listen in this album to the perfection of his intonation, the beauty of the sound he produces, the constant comfortable breath control. And take notice of his high notes. Laymen are often impressed by the high note you can hear for five blocks. Professionals know that it is far more difficult to hit a high note quietly. Como lights on a C or D at the top of a tune as softly as a bird on a branch, not even shaking it[24] – praise indeed.

At his best, Perry Como was peerless. He was in a category of his own, and the *Look to Your Heart* album stands as a defining example of this. One of the key ingredients to Perry's genius was his distinctly personal approach to a song. He took recordings very seriously and performed exclusively for the ears. On television, his approach was more casual – he was performing for the eyes as well as the ears. In this respect, his vocal delivery took on a more conversational approach at times – as if to remove any distance between viewer and performer. This instinctive understanding of the differences between recordings and television was fundamental to Perry's paralleled success in both mediums.

Perry was a distinctly different character from both Bing Crosby and Frank Sinatra. This is probably a factor in why their paths (in the broader sense) rarely crossed. One thing that both Crosby and Sinatra exhibited at times within their presentation, certainly on television, was an element of self-importance, both in terms of their dialogue and body language – a kind of assumed superiority. Crosby tended at times to speak in an overly studious manner, like Rudy Vallée. For both Vallée and Crosby, this was perhaps due in part to their academic backgrounds, but it resulted in less on-screen warmth.

Perry, by contrast, was from much humbler beginnings, but it would be foolish to suggest he was not intelligent. The reality was quite the opposite. A person does not get to a position such as Perry's by being lazy or laidback. Perry was simply secure enough within himself that he did not require that kind of validation. He avoided the trappings that many entertainers have succumbed to through a life rooted in the traditional values of his upbringing. He lived with humility and was able to go about his life without fanfare.

Perry might have been embarrassed to hear such an observation, but this is a worthy point of commentary. This isn't just about Perry Como; this is true for anyone who possesses such qualities. Such people serve as an example for future generations, and there is something deeply meaningful in that. In Perry's case, it's a legacy that even transcends his music. As with Gene Lees' description of the laymen, it is often those who speak less who have more to say.

The final Andy Wiswell produced album to be recorded, but the third to be released, was *The Perry Como Christmas Album*. It is an abundantly festive album which is every bit the equal of Perry's previous Christmas recordings, with its own unique sound and an all-female collaborative of the Ray Charles Singers. The sessions commenced in the blazing heat of July 1968 at Webster Hall in New York City with recording engineers Ed Begley and Ray Hall. Despite the less-than-optimal humidity, most of the scheduled recordings for the album were laid down, although with apparent difficulty. During one of the sessions, though, a few members of the Ray Charles Singers were overcome by the heat, leading to the postponement of the sessions.

Recording recommenced in the cooler environment of RCA's Studio A in August. With Bob Simpson engineering, all previously recorded titles were remade. Despite this, he did not receive credit within the original release nor the 1976 reissue. The labours of all involved, however, had been worth it, and the album stands as an excellent finale to the combined efforts of Como, Perito, Charles and Wiswell.

Perry's recordings from the 1960s represent to many the very peak of his artistic achievements, and auditioning any of these albums, it is very easy to see why. One of the factors behind this is a relaxing in the necessity of hit singles, which had been a dominating factor throughout the 1950s. Perry afforded himself the opportunity to sing more of the songs that were dearest to him. The songs he loved, to paraphrase the title of his 1963 album. The hit singles were still a presence, but the album format was more emphasized. The decade had begun with a distinct change of production. Charlie Grean, who had worked with Perry for more than a decade, was succeeded by Hugo and Luigi with equally successful artistic achievement.

Perry had also perhaps psychologically reached a point in his career where there was no longer a need to prove himself artistically or commercially. He'd already long proven he had the musical chops to handle a wide range of music, and he had the financial rewards for his many hit singles to prove his commercial powers. The comfort Perry exhibited within his own skin was clearly audible and visible. This sense of confidence is evident throughout all of his 1960s album recordings, whether he is approaching a showstopping ballad, a tender love song, or a rhythm number. With a new decade nearing, though, further triumphs lay ahead.

Quintessential Como
Recommended listening 1960–8

Make Someone Happy
m Jule Styne, w Betty Comden
and Adolph Green, 1960
From the film Do Re Mi.
13 Oct 1960 - Make Someone
Happy CAL-694

You Make Me Feel So Young
m Josef Myrow, w Mack Gordon, 1946
From the film Three Little Girls in Blue.
25 Oct 1960 - For the Young at
Heart LSP-2343

Hello, Young Lovers ★
m Richard Rodgers,
w Oscar Hammerstein II, 1951
From the musical The King and I.
26 Oct 1960 - For the Young at Heart
LSP-2343
25–27 Jun 1970 (Live) - PC in Person
at the International Hotel, Las Vegas
LSPX-1001

Young at Heart
m Johnny Richards, w Carolyn
Leigh, 1954
26 Oct 1960 - For the Young at
Heart LSP-2343

Especially for the Young
m Ben Weisman, w Mann Curtis, 1960
2 Nov 1960 - For the Young at Heart
LSP-2343

Say It Isn't So ★
mw Irving Berlin, 1932
15 May 1961 - Sing to Me, Mr. C.
LSP-2390

Here's That Rainy Day ★
m Jimmy Van Heusen, w Johnny
Burke, 1953
From the musical Carnival in Flanders.
15 May 1961 - Sing to Me, Mr. C.
LSP-2390

All by Myself
mw Irving Berlin, 1921
15 May 1961 - Sing to Me, Mr. C.
LSP-2390

The Way You Look Tonight ★
m Jerome Kern, w Dorothy Fields, 1936
From the film Swing Time.
17 May 1961 - Sing to Me, Mr. C. LSP-2390
The Royal Variety Performance - 24 Nov 1974

You're Following Me
m Burt Bacharach, w Bob Hilliard, 1961
18 Oct 1961 - Love Makes the World
Go 'Round CAS-805 (e)

The Island of Forgotten Lovers
mw Dick Manning and Kay Twomey, 1962
14 Feb 1962 - Somebody Loves Me
CAS-858 (e)

Caterina
mw Earl Shuman and Bugs Bower, 1962
14 Feb 1962 - An Evening with PC
CAL-742

Moonglow and Theme from Picnic
mw Will Hudson, Eddie DeLange and
Irving Mills, 1934 / m George Duning, w
Steve Allen, 1956
8 Jun 1962 - By Request LSP-2567

The Sweetest Sounds
mw Richard Rodgers, 1962
From the musical No Strings.
8 Jun 1962 - By Request LSP-2567

I'll Remember April
m Gene De Paul, w Don Raye
and Patricia Johnston, 1942
From the film Ride 'Em Cowboy.
21 Jun 1962 - By Request LSP-2567

What's New?
m Bob Haggart, w Johnny Burke, 1939
26 Jun 1962 - By Request LSP-2567

Can't Help Falling in Love
mw George David Weiss, Hugo Peretti
and Luigi Creatore, 1961
From the film Blue Hawaii.
26 Jun 1962 - By Request LSP-2567

Is She the Only Girl in the World
mw Irving Berlin, 1962
From the musical Mr. President.
1 Oct 1962 - The Best of Irving Berlin's
Songs from Mr. President LSP-2630

Empty Pockets Filled with Love
mw Irving Berlin, 1962
From the musical Mr. President.
2 Oct 1962 - The Best of Irving Berlin's
Songs from Mr. President LSP-2630

When I Lost You
mw Irving Berlin, 1912
18 Mar 1963 - The Songs I Love LSP-2708

I Left My Heart in San Francisco
m George Cory, w Douglass Cross, 1954
18 Mar 1963 - The Songs I Love LSP-2708

Days of Wine and Roses
m Henry Mancini, w Johnny Mercer, 1962
From the film Days of Wine and Roses.
19 Mar 1963 - The Songs I Love LSP-2708

This Is All I Ask
mw Gordon Jenkins, 1963
19 Mar 1963 - The Songs I Love LSP-2708

Slightly out of Tune (Desafinado)
m Antônio Carlos Jobim, w Newton
Mendonça (Port.), 1958, w Jon Hendricks
and Howard S. Richmond (under pseud.
Jessie Cavanaugh) (Eng.), 1962
25 Mar 1963 - The Songs I Love LSP-2708

What Kind of Fool Am I?
mw Leslie Bricusse
and Anthony Newley, 1962
From the musical Stop the World –
I Want to Get Off.
26 Mar 1963 - The Songs I Love LSP-2708

(I Love You) Don't You Forget It
m Henry Mancini, w Al Stillman, 1963
1 May 1963 - Love Makes the World
Go 'Round CAS-805 (e)

A Hatchet, a Hammer, a Bucket of Nails
mw Eddie Snyder, Richard Ahlert
and Sarah Graham, 1965
11 Feb 1965 - The Scene Changes
LSP-3396

Dream on Little Dreamer
mw Jan Crutchfield and Fred Burch, 1965
11 Feb 1965 - The Scene Changes
LSP-3396

Stand Beside Me
mw Tompall Glaser, 1965
12 Feb 1965 - The Scene Changes
LSP-3396

Here Comes My Baby
mw Bill West and Dottie West, 1964
12 Feb 1965 - The Scene Changes
LSP-3396

Quiet Nights of Quiet Stars (Corcovado)
mw Antônio Carlos Jobim (Port.), 1960,
w Buddy Kaye (Eng.), 1962
30 Dec 1965 - Lightly Latin LSP-3552

The Shadow of Your Smile
m Johnny Mandel,
w Paul Francis Webster, 1965
The theme from the film The Sandpiper.
30 Dec 1965 - Lightly Latin LSP-3552

Carnival (Manhã de carnaval)
m Luis Bonfá, w Antônio Mariz (Port.),
1959, w George David Weiss, Hugo Peretti
and Luigi Creatore (Eng.), 1960
From the film Black Orpheus.
28 Feb 1966 - Lightly Latin LSP-3552

Yesterday
mw John Lennon and Paul McCartney, 1965
28 Feb 1966 - Lightly Latin LSP-3552

Forget Domani
m Riz Ortolani, w Norman Newell, 1965
From the film The Yellow Rolls Royce.
9 May 1966 - PC in Italy LSP-3608

O marenariello
m Salvatore Gambardella,
w Gennaro Ottaviano (Nea.), 1893
13 May 1966 - PC in Italy LSP-3608

Oh Marie ★
m Eduardo Di Capua and Alfredo
Mazzucchi, w Vincenzo Russo (Nea.),
1899, mw Ray Charles and Nick Perito
(adapt. and arr.), 1966
18 May 1966 - PC in Italy LSP-3608

Souvenir d'Italie
m Lelio Luttazzi, w Giulio Scarnicci
and Renzo Tarabusi (It.), 1954,
w Carl Sigman (Eng.), 1955
19 May 1966 - PC in Italy LSP-3608

How Beautiful the World Can Be
mw Buddy Zais, 1967
15 Feb 1967 - 47-9165

Stop! And Think It Over
mw Sid Tepper and Roy C. Bennett, 1967
15 Feb 1967 - 47-9165

**You Made It That Way
(Watermelon Summer)**
mw Dwayne Blackwell and Rani
Blackwell, 1967
22 Aug 1967 - 47-9356

The Father of Girls ★
mw Ervin Drake, 1963
29 Dec 1967 - 47-9448
25–27 Jun 1970 (Live) - PC in Person
at the International Hotel, Las Vegas
LSPX-1001

In These Crazy Times
m Sydney Lippman, w Sylvia Dee, 1968
7 Jun 1968 - Look to Your Heart LSP-4052

Try to Remember
m Harvey Schmidt, w Tom Jones, 1960
From the musical The Fantasticks.
12 Jun 1968 - Look to Your Heart LSP-4052

My Cup Runneth Over
m Harvey Schmidt, w Tom Jones, 1966
From the musical I Do! I Do!
12 Jun 1968 - Look to Your Heart LSP-4052

Sunrise, Sunset
m Jerry Bock, w Sheldon Harnick, 1964
From the musical Fiddler on the Roof.
19 Jun 1968 - Look to Your Heart LSP-4052

Sunshine Wine
mw Cindy Walker, 1969
10 Oct 1968 - Seattle LSP-4183

Seattle
mw Jack Keller, Hugo Montenegro
and Ernie Sheldon, 1969
10 Oct 1968 - Seattle LSP-4183

6

How Beautiful the World Can Be

On 22 May 1967, the last edition of *Perry Como's Kraft Music Hall* aired on NBC Television. The show was a salute to the centennial of Canada, with a mostly Canadian guest list, including singer Monique Leyrac and pianist Oscar Peterson. Together with Perry, they perform a standout version of 'Canadian Sunset'. Como and Leyrac harmonize elegantly on the lyrics, while the brisk embellishments and solos of Peterson tie things together. It was a classy end to a wonderful series.

Starting in the autumn of 1967, Perry reduced his television activities to an annual holiday special and a few guest appearances. Perry's focus had transferred more to his recordings. The surprise hit of 'Seattle' at the end of the decade quickly transported Perry back into the top forty, and an album of recordings from the late 1960s was assembled in response to the success.

Perry capped off the decade as guest host of the *Hollywood Palace* Christmas special on ABC television. Perry is host to ballet dancer Edward Villella, comedian Shecky Greene, Burr Tillstrom's puppets Kukla and Ollie, and singer Diahann Carroll. The show combines for a warm and welcoming hour of festive entertainment.

Through his appearance on the *Hollywood Palace*, Perry was reunited with some of his colleagues from the *Kraft Music Hall*, including associate/executive producer Nick Vanoff. 'I kinda feel like I've been here before', remarked Perry in his opening talk. He was especially pleased to be hosting during the holiday season because, he said, 'it's like home to me' – and of course, it was. 'Christmas was very important to Perry', said Nick's wife, Felisa, 'and I think you see that when he sings any of the Christmas songs. You can tell that his heart is in it and his devotion.'[1]

The same warmth that Perry had displayed within his own series was just as evident when he hosted at the *Hollywood Palace*. When it came to hosting guests, Perry was content to gently drift into the background of a scene if desired. He never made a show all about him. Take, for instance, the way Perry handled his duet with Diahann Carroll. They sang a perfect version of 'Silver Bells'. Perry holds his voice lightly harmonising behind Diahann's. This was a technique Perry used many times over the years on television. He wasn't in competition with his guest; he was in collaboration with them. He was happy for his guest to enjoy their moment in the spotlight. Even if a humorous sketch called for him to broadly assert himself, he still played it down. Perry's dislike for anything overly indulgent was legendary.

Before their duet, Perry had calmly made his way down to join Diahann on the steps of the stage where she sat in a dress, having just finished her musical segment. 'It shows Perry's ease and his charm, and his ability to be really *with* the person that he's with', said Felisa. 'Stepping down from the stage to the step that they sat on, especially for Diahann's dress there, was not easy ... he handled it and ad-libbed – and it's all so natural!'[2]

That same year, Perry signed a contract for $5 million to appear in four specials, which earned him an entry into the *Guinness Book of Records* as the highest-paid TV performer per hourly rate.[3]

The year 1970 started off in great form with a special sponsored by Sears on NBC TV. Como with his trademark ease, plays host to comedians Bob Hope and Flip Wilson, plus singer Nancy Sinatra and singer/actor Bobby Sherman who was then starring in the television series *Here Come the Brides*, from which the song 'Seattle' originated. *The Many Moods of Perry Como* has a lot of funny moments but reaches a point of poignancy when Perry performs a version of Bob Hope's theme song 'Thanks for the Memory' with special lyrics, accompanied by a montage of photographs. As Bob enters the stage and shares a few moments of reflection with Perry, there is a genuine sense of respect and friendship expressed between the two gentlemen. Como and Hope worked together no less than a dozen times on television in addition to radio and public benefit appearances.

Three months later, a watershed moment occurred on 5 and 6 May 1970, when Perry Como recorded a new song titled 'It's Impossible'. The sessions were arranged and conducted by Marty Manning, produced by Ernie Altschuler and with Perry's long-standing and trusted recording engineer Bob Simpson. The song was composed by Mexican songwriter Armando Manzanero and originally released by him in 1968 under the title 'Somos novios'. It was adapted with English lyrics by Sid Wayne in 1970 and became an international bestseller for Como. The song's mood and elements of its orchestration nod back to 'Till the End of Time' recorded twenty-five years earlier, which serves as a testament to the timeless quality of the Como voice.

The following month, Perry opened in Las Vegas at the International Hotel (soon to become the Hilton) with his first live nightclub engagement in nearly twenty-five years. Perry had been reluctant to perform in Las Vegas for many years because of the lifestyle it promoted, but by 1970, he was encouraged to appear. Nick Perito observed that if mafia members came and sat by him, 'he [Perry] was a model of courtesy and would simply get up and walk away'.[4]

With his heavy television schedule, concert performances had not been a priority on the Como calendar since the 1940s. He was initially nervous of the idea – concert venues and particularly nightclub audiences were a distinctly different proposition to a television show. However, very quickly, Perry settled into this reinvigorated area of his career. With Nick Perito conducting and Ray Charles writing special material and providing musical supervision, Perry performed for a sell-out three-week season. Opening with a delightfully swinging medley of 'I've Got You under My Skin' and 'Hello, Young Lovers' – Perry Como was on top form.

The set list for Perry's Las Vegas opening included well-established Como standards such as 'Without a Song' and 'Prisoner of Love' alongside newer material, such as the then-current Harry Nilsson hit 'Everybody's Talkin'' from the film *Midnight Cowboy*. Also included was a new song, written especially for Perry by Ray Charles. 'If I Could Almost Read Your Mind' is a send-up of Perry's relaxed image and enquires as to some of the questions that audiences might have. The song was very well received and became a recurring feature of Como's concert performances.

During the first week of Perry's engagement, RCA Victor recorded performances from three successive nights – 25, 26 and 27 June 1970, which resulted in Perry's first album of the new decade, *Perry Como in Person at the International Hotel, Las Vegas*. Of the album, *The Gramophone* magazine said '. . . all the Como magic of yore is still evident, enhanced by his refreshing personality', concluding that 'the LP bears the distinguished hallmark of the complete professional entertainer from beginning to end'. [5]

> 'When I saw him in Las Vegas', recalled Val Doonican 'the thing that surprised me really was having seen so many Las Vegas-type acts who come on and do this crash bang wallop sort of performance, he came on, and I don't think he even said "good evening" for the first fifteen minutes. He just came on and stood there and he just sang song after song after song and brought the house down.'[6]

With the success of 'It's Impossible' came a new album centred around the song. Nine titles were recorded over three days in November 1970 to complement the new hit single. At the time, Perry was fulfilling a return engagement at the International Hotel, and the recordings were made as such using the hotel's facilities. The album is made up entirely of contemporary material as the Como career had entered a new chapter. Perry lends his magic to songs such as the Burt Bacharach and Hal David classic 'A House Is Not a Home' and an awe-inspiring interpretation of Paul Simon's 'El cóndor pasa' based on a Peruvian folk melody adapted by Daniel Alomía Robles. George Harrison's 'Something' also receives an excellent treatment from Perry. From the opening rasps of brass lined with luxurious strings, Don Costa's smooth and classy arrangement has the warmth of an open fire, complementing the rich bouquet of Perry's vocal performance.

In the 1950s, Perry had embraced rock 'n' roll. Now in the 1970s, he was lending his vocal stylings to the lyrics of contemporary pop. As with country music, Perry's vocal style fit hand in glove with the writing of such people as Paul McCartney, David Gates, Jimmy Webb, Paul Williams and, of course, Burt Bacharach.

With new work opportunities building and renewed international interest, Perry returned to the UK to present a television special for the BBC. Loosely based on his current nightclub act, the special gave Perry an opportunity to reconnect with friends and colleagues such as Yvonne Littlewood (who produced the special) and his millions of fans on the other side of the Atlantic. By this time, 'It's Impossible' was already a big hit in the UK and a new single, 'I Think of You' was on its ascent to popularity.

Back home in the United States, Perry's television presence had started to build once again. His Christmas programmes were beginning to edge closer to the holiday, and he made several guest appearances during the era, including with singers Doris Day and Tom Jones. Returning the favour for Flip Wilson, Perry appeared on *Flip* (aka *The Flip Wilson Show*) in October 1970. The show connected Perry with a younger audience and his on-screen banter with Flip is a joy to watch. Perry is in particularly animated form and even partakes in a sketch playing a psychiatrist to Flip's female character Geraldine Jones. The distinct contrast between the two performers only adds to the amusement.

Misfortune struck, however, in October 1971. While taping his *Winter Show* with Art Carney and Mitzi Gaynor, Perry fell off a stage platform. Recalling the incident in an article for the *Associated Press* in 1972[7], Perry said:

> I remember I was to walk up a platform that was to split apart. Something went wrong. The spotlight wasn't on me, and I moved to my left to compensate for it. Meanwhile the set was starting to separate. I fell off the platform, hit the other side with my knee and dropped about five feet. All this with the cameras on me. People started rushing over to see what happened to me.

Perry returned to complete the special with his leg in a cast, disguised using various stage props and camera work from the waist up when necessary, but the whole incident set back his professional activities by eight months. 'I almost went out of my mind', said Perry.

> What the hell can you do for eight months in a cast? I watched television. I mean everything – *Guiding Light, General Hospital, As the World Turns,* all those goodies. I was like that comedian who said he was so hung up on

TV that he watched the test patterns when the station went off the air. I even watched that little dot that disappears when you turn off the set.

Golf, one of his favourite leisure activities, was out of the question for the duration, although another, fishing, was achievable with some difficulty – 'I could swing myself into the boat at normal tide; at low tide, forget it'.[8]

Following the removal of his cast, there began a long period of therapy; however, by the summer of 1972, he was ready and able to complete a new engagement at the Hilton Hotel in Las Vegas from 20 July to 3 August. Perry's recent ailments had in no way diminished his vocal prowess. 'Como, at 60, is something of a phenomenon', wrote John L. Scott of the *Los Angeles Times*, 'Heaven knows, he has never abused his voice, and it pays off at an age when most of his contemporaries are resting on their laurels'.

After completing his engagement at the Hilton, Perry moved on to Lake Tahoe for an eighteen-day season of twice nightly shows at Harrah's. Following some television taping commitments in the autumn, including for his *Winter Show* of 1972, Perry returned to Harrah's for performances in the hotel's South Shore Room. Perry was joined in Tahoe by Roselle, their children and grandchildren to spend Christmas together.

Perry recalled that Christmas with a particular fondness:

'The kids' present was an airline ticket to Tahoe, and it was absolutely the best Christmas we've ever spent, because we were all together. That's the eight grandchildren, and the three [children]. Looked like an Italian army for a while!' Of the weather, he said, 'Oh it was gorgeous! It was cold and unreal, because Christmas morning we had about an inch of snow; and we all had our own houses, we had four houses together there; and the trees and the log fires going. 'Course I was working there at Bill Harrah's and I was having a great time with the little ones – with the noses running and the tears and stuff. I think the last day I cracked up – my back went out, because I was trying to follow a three-year-old – forget it! But it was a delightful year'.[9]

The year 1973 brought even wider international success in the form of a new album recorded in Nashville. Back with his friend and colleague Chet Atkins, Perry set to work on a new album of country-flavoured material, including a song called 'And I Love You So' written by singer-songwriter Don McLean and featured in his 1970 album *Tapestry*. The sessions which took place in January resulted in twelve songs, mostly new or unknown at the time.

'And I Love You So' was first released as a single from the sessions, but the song caught on so quickly and favourably, that Perry returned to Nashville that March to record some alternative songs for inclusion. The direction of the album had now turned to a more pop-oriented collection, with Perry turning in stellar renditions of 'For the Good Times', 'Killing Me Softly with Her Song' and 'Tie a Yellow Ribbon Round the Ole Oak Tree'.

Perry had an exceptional skill for taking songs that had been hits for other artists and making them his own. 'For the Good Times' had previously been a US country hit for Ray Price but achieved much wider international fame through Perry's recording. And, after hearing Perry's version of 'Tie a Yellow Ribbon Round the Ole Oak Tree' (originally a hit for Dawn featuring Tony Orlando), it is difficult to imagine the song had been written for anyone else.

The *And I Love You So* album was tremendously successful and is probably the most widely released and internationally recognisable of Perry's entire career. Two additional songs from the album were released as singles in the UK: 'For the Good Times' and 'I Want to Give', which both became top forty hits, with 'For the Good Times' achieving equal fame to the title song. The album spent two years in the UK charts alone and was released in countries right across the globe, including Australia, South Africa, India, Brazil, Spain and Japan.

Such was the international success of 'And I Love You So' that Perry recorded a Spanish language version under the name 'Yo te quiero asi'. 'I Want to Give', re-recorded for the flip side, already originated as a Spanish song titled 'Ahora que soy libre'. The two songs were issued primarily for the Spanish language market during the same year. These vocal takes added to the existing instrumentals formed part of the follow-up sessions to *And I Love You So* but did not result in a follow-up album.

A single was released from the sessions – 'Love Don't Care (Where It Grows)' – which was backed with 'Walk Right Back', a song originally popularized by the Everly Brothers in the 1960s but with the original second verse (not recorded by the Everlys) reinstated. 'Love Don't Care' was pulled from release

Perry receives awards from the British Phonographic Industry (BPI) in October 1973 for sales of the album And I Love You So *and the singles 'And I Love You So' and 'For the Good Times'. Perry is pictured with British radio DJ Pete Murray (left) and American lyricist Johnny Mercer.*

in the UK, but 'Walk Right Back' became a top 40 hit, enjoying a ten-week stay in the British charts. This, combined with 'And I Love You So' and 'For the Good Times' gave Perry the unique distinction of three simultaneously charting hits in the British singles chart – an achievement celebrated by RCA in *Billboard* magazine.

The remaining titles recorded in June, along with those unused from the original January sessions, remained originally unreleased, surfacing among collectors in the first instance via a reference acetate disc produced at the time. Forty years later, a number of these titles did make their way onto CD. The unreleased recordings from January 1973 are remarkable in their freshness, and it seems clear that they were not omitted due to a lack of artistic or technical quality.

Perry's sustained success and new audience prompted an increase in his television schedule once again. Between 1974 and 1982, Perry hosted at least two specials a year, with 1975–6 seeing a quarterly Como offering. He also made further guest appearances, including a particularly memorable special with Julie Andrews titled *Julie on Sesame Street* recorded at ATV television studios in the UK. Perry's contributions included singing 'And I Love You So' in a 'Sing to Me, Mr. C'. staging with the *Sesame Street* set as its backdrop. A spectacular medley of songs sung with Julie Andrews with 'sing' or 'song' in their title formed a ten-minute cavalcade of music old and new – it was the centrepiece to a delightful hour of family entertainment.

Just ahead of his sixty-second birthday in May 1974, Perry was back in the UK to give his first ever live concert appearance outside of North America. Perry starred as top of the bill in a Gala Midnight Charity concert at the London Palladium. Perry started shortly before 3.00 am and entertained for over an hour with the Jack Parnell Orchestra under the direction of Nick Perito. Tony Mansell's Coffee Set, directed by Ray Charles, provided vocal accompaniment. The roars, cheers and whistles from the crowd as Perry entered the stage and throughout are a wonderful testament to the affection with which the British public regarded him.

During an interlude before his encore, Perry joked with the audience saying, 'I've been in the business a couple of years, playing in front of all kinds of people – some of 'em are very happy, exuberant, some of 'em are [he gestures indifferent] – but you folks aren't well!' adding with affection 'I've never heard such applause – it makes us very happy'.[10] Recalling the event in 1977, Perry said, 'I had a smile on my face for about a week, I couldn't rub it off!'[11]

Writing of Perry's gala performance in *Music Week*, Brian Mulligan said:

> it was the sheer professionalism of his vocal performance that sticks in mind, the impeccable phrasing, the tonal purity contrasted with an unexpected robustness, and the ease and assurance with which he hit and held high notes.[12]

James Green of the *Evening News* concurred, observing that the concert was:

> superbly professional. Show business as it used to be without moan, screech or mumbled lyric. A nice guy singing nice songs and anxious for the words to be heard. It was roses all the way for Mr. C. He might have been a fair barber, but he would never have earned the applause he drew today.

At the show's close and as he waved farewell, he said that if Britain was this good, they could expect him on an extended tour the following year.[13]

In November 1974, Perry returned to the London Palladium to guest on *The Royal Variety Performance* in the presence of the Queen Mother (Mother of Queen Elizabeth II of Great Britain). Perry headlined a star-studded programme of guests which included British entertainers Billy Dainty and Roy Castle, French chanteuse Josephine Baker and the hilarious visual comedy of George Carl.

Perry performed a remarkable thirty-minute set opening with blazing versions of 'The Way You Look Tonight' and 'Where or When' following with a touching rendition of 'For the Good Times' before leading into Nick Perito's cool and complex new arrangement of Perry's 1945 hit 'Temptation' recorded for the 1974 album *Perry*. Perry then reprises his patter from May, proceeding to sit down on a stool, centre stage saying, 'Gee it's good to sit down. You know the legs go first'. Pausing as the audience laughs, he then adds, 'OK, second!'. He then reflects on his May appearance:

> it started at midnight, so I didn't get on till about 3 o'clock in the morning. [He chuckles.] They told me I had a good time. You know I go to bed at ten/eleven o'clock. I'm sure you've heard that somewhere, haven't you? 'Oh he doesn't drink, he doesn't smoke – he doesn't do anything'. Don't believe that friends. You're looking at an Italian tiger![14]

Perry then masterfully leads into a beautiful rendering of 'It's Impossible' with Nick Perito's exquisite piano accompaniment leading the orchestral arrangement. A change of pace follows with a golden records medley backed by the Tony Mansell Singers, which includes 'Magic Moments', 'Catch a Falling Star', 'Round and Round' and 'Don't Let the Stars Get in Your Eyes' – four of the dozens of hit songs that had become immediately recognisable with the Como name. The penultimate number in the performance was the timeless standard 'Without a Song', which Perry performed with his legendary power and control, accompanied again with great effect by the Tony Mansell Singers and concluding in a magnificent crescendo. Taking his bows and leaving the stage to the cheers for more, Perry returns for an encore, singing 'And I Love You So' as a fitting conclusion to what was a masterclass in concert performance. Comfortable and assured throughout, Como wows with his vocal brilliance and warms the heart with his sincerity and self-deprecation. This is a performance that should be studied within the popular music curriculum.

The world-famous London Palladium in Argyll Street. Author's photo.

In January 1975, Perry began recording sessions for his final Nashville outing, which resulted in two releases. The first release was the single 'World of Dreams' backed with 'Wonderful Baby'. The former title was composed by British entertainer Des O'Connor and the latter by Don McLean as a tribute to dancer Fred Astaire. The second release was an album, which developed over a long period of time and was eventually titled *Just out of Reach*.

While in Nashville, Perry taped a television special which celebrated his connection with the legendary music city. *Como Country: Perry and His Nashville Friends* featured guests representing some of the cream of Nashville, including instrumentalists Chet Atkins, Boots Randolph and Floyd Cramer who together formed part of the colloquial 'Nashville A-Team', and Danny Davis and the Nashville Brass, alongside singers Charley Pride, Charlie Rich, Donna Fargo and Loretta Lynn, plus a special guest appearance by comedian Minnie Pearl.

Later that year, *Nashville Sound* magazine ran an article about the making of the special, remarking that 'the behind-the-scenes action turned out to be as good as if not better than the final product'.

> The comedy highlight of the night came with a trio of songs done by Lynn, Fargo and Como. Loretta was at her best that night, ready to handle anything Mr. C. might hand her. 'You all set, Walter,' Como said into the microphone to the producer of the show who was in the tape room behind the stage peering at a panel of television monitors with images from cameras on stage. 'Let's try take one,' came the reply. Fargo then kicked off the number by standing and moving toward the center of the stage as she sang the song's first verse. Lynn was to follow Fargo's lead with the next verse. As Lynn stood up, however, her beige crocheted dress became entangled in the rocking chair. As she began to walk center stage, she dragged the chair along with her. It was too much for Como. He nearly fell out of his rocking chair with laughter. 'We ought to leave that in,' he said between laughs. 'You'd really have gotten a laugh if I'd lost my dress right here on stage,' retorted Loretta. After Como and Lynn were reseated getting ready for the sequence to begin again he leaned over toward her and said into the microphone for everybody to hear, 'You know, Loretta. I just might carry you away with me, tonight, after we've finished.' 'You better watch it,' said Loretta. 'My old man's back stage watching us on the TV monitor.' 'How

big is he,' said Como. 'About as big as me, I guess,' she replied. 'I think I can handle him,' said Como thinking that would be the end of the conversation. 'Yeah, well I know I can and all I have to do is look at him right.' It was the final straw for the usually composed and controlled Como. He laughed freely and admiringly at the wit and charm of the Kentucky lady.[15]

The UK tour that Perry had hinted at came to fruition in the spring of 1975, beginning on 2 April at the Winter Gardens, Bournemouth, then onto Bristol, Manchester, London, Birmingham, Southport, Glasgow, Edinburgh and back to London to complete his tour with two concerts at the Theatre Royal, Drury Lane. The following day, Perry was interviewed by musician and broadcaster Benny Green for the forthcoming BBC documentary *The Barber Comes to Town*, saying of the experience, 'I never dreamed that it would be like this. The people have been an absolute delight to work for; and you could feel it. I've been calling it now just one big love affair.'[16]

'PC 63!' said Perry to his adoring fans, referring to his initials and upcoming 63rd birthday. 'I don't mind being 63 years old . . .' said Perry, 'but when I start to feel it . . . then it's time to do more fishing and more eating and more drinking!'[17]

Recalling a particularly memorable moment on the tour, Perry explained:

> We wound up in Scotland . . . and of course if you've never been to Scotland, that's the wildest bunch of people you've ever seen! But such affection . . . I've never seen anything like it; and finally they started coming up on stage and it scared me for a second, because I didn't know what they were gonna do . . . One of the guys . . . came up to me and he started to hug me and kissing me and I was kind of whispering in his ear I said 'these people are gonna start to talk in a minute' and . . . he says, 'I don't give a damn what they think!' He says, 'I love you and I've loved you for thirty years!' and he went on and on, and I said, 'Well, maybe we should pick out some furniture in the morning!'[18]

Wherever he visited on his tour of the UK, Perry was greeted with an abundance of love and excitement. Many people remarked on the quality of his voice and how the years had done nothing to diminish the beauty

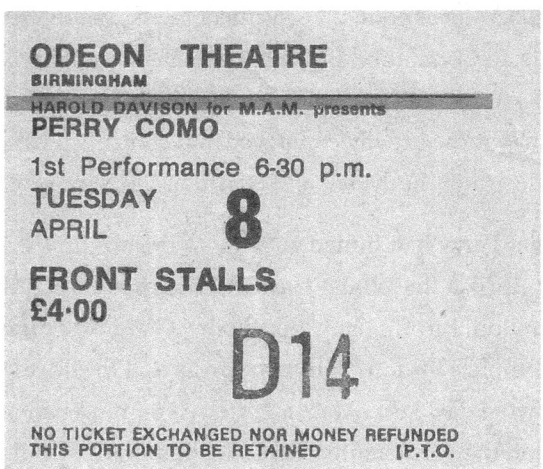

A ticket stub from the first of Perry's two performances at the Odeon Theatre, Birmingham, in 1975. Photo courtesy of Michael Dunnington.

and power of his instrument. 'The type of voice and the type of singing I do isn't something you get up in the morning and start vocalising', said Perry with his trademark self-deprecation. ''cause if I vocalise for half hour, then I've blown the show – it's time to go take a nap again! But if I feel good and have had a good night's sleep, I don't have to worry too much about singing. I love to get out of bed . . . I take a nap before every show and . . . I wake up right in the middle of "Without a Song" – 'cause that's the loudest!'[19]

One night, after a show in London, Perry was escorted out of a different exit to the car awaiting him. As the car drove off, Perry observed in the distance a crowd of people waiting in the dark wet evening at the stage door. 'Are they waiting for me?' he asked. And once he knew, the car was taken down to greet the waiting fans. Perry didn't leave until everyone who wanted to chat or get an autograph had the opportunity.[20]

In terms of its commercial success, Benny Green said it best:

> Financially the tour is a hit before it begins, it's the same story from every town – complete sell-outs, box office records broken everywhere. Theatre managers wishing Como was doing a week instead of a night; and all this, with no advanced advertising or publicity.[21]

Perry signs autographs outside the Odeon Theatre, Birmingham, in 1975. Photo courtesy of Michael Dunnington.

It was a magical tour that touched the hearts of the tens of thousands of people who attended, and the BBC captured the mood wonderfully in its documentary which aired in the run-up to Christmas that year. A 2-LP compilation album, *40 Greatest*, was the Christmas No. 1 and reportedly sold in excess of a million units in the UK, achieving Platinum status.

Further tours were to form part of the remainder of the 1970s, first in Australia, then the United States, and finally Japan. When Perry arrived in Japan, he and Nick Perito were surprised to learn of a Como song that had been popular there for many years – 'The Rose Tattoo'. The song was composed by Harry Warren with lyrics by Jack Brooks for the 1955 film of the same name but not used in the film. Perry had no recollection of the song or having recorded it. The song had been the flip side to 'All at Once You Love Her' but had never been performed by Perry on television or in concert up to that point. The song went on to become a recurring feature of Perry's subsequent Japanese tours, performed rubato with Nick on piano.

Back in the United States in September 1975, Perry performed another concert season at Harrah's hotel and casino in Lake Tahoe. While there, he taped a television special, *Perry Como's Lake Tahoe Holiday*. The special combines the beauty of Lake Tahoe with a celebration of outdoor sports. Bob Hope provided his classic brand of comedy, while Anne Murray contributed perfectly to the musical proceedings. From the sporting world were guests including tennis champion Billie Jean King and golfing champion Sandra Palmer. Anne was particularly struck by both the warmth of Perry's personality and the power of his voice. Having admired Perry since she was a child, watching him on television with her father, she described the opportunity to duet with him as something she never dreamed of.

That October, Perry arrived in Mexico to tape his Christmas special. It was the first outside of the United States since his visit to Rome in 1964 and the first of a long run of internationally and domestically recorded on-location Christmas specials over the next decade. The special, a co-production between Roncom, Bob Banner Associates and Televisa was directed by Sterling Johnson. This was Bob's second television special with Perry, having co-produced the Lake Tahoe special that September. Banner was already a long-established producer by the time of his association with Perry. He had produced long-running variety programmes featuring Dinah Shore, Garry Moore, and Carol Burnett, among many others.

The template of the Banner-produced Como seasonal specials was a musical travelogue with Perry as friendly and gracious host – singing numerous solo numbers, duets with guest stars, and experiencing local customs and traditions. Perry was such a good person to do this because of the sincerity of his approach and the warmth of his personality. The specials became must-see television for millions in the United States and internationally.

In addition to fine music and an array of talented guests, the cinematography of the specials was exceptional. This was perhaps best exhibited in *Perry Como's Christmas in the Holy Land* from 1980, which won an Emmy for Outstanding Video Tape Editing for a Limited Series or a Special – credited to Marco Zappia for video tape and Branda S. Miller for film. The special is a masterpiece of television, possessing the qualities of a small-screen epic in much of its presentation.

The music selections for *Perry Como's Christmas in the Holy Land* were very appropriate. Perry opens with 'The Holy City' backed by the Singers of Praise, and staged within the glorious setting of the ruins of the Roman colony of Aelia Capitolina. Perry's atmospheric opening dialogue is presented at the Garden Tomb in Jerusalem, beautifully underscored by Nick Perito and leading into a haunting performance of 'I Wonder as I Wander'. Guests on the show include Israeli singer Ilanit and American actor Richard Chamberlain. Perry and Ilanit join for a duet of 'The City of Tradition' composed especially for the show by Ray Charles. The song highlights the religious connections of the Jewish, Muslim, and Christian faiths to the region and is handled with taste and respect, two qualities evident throughout the entire special.

Later in the programme, Perry is honoured to be invited to a Hanukkah celebration with the people of Kibbutz Ginosar and sings a moving rendition of 'Bless This House'. The special concludes with Perry's telling and singing of 'The Story of the First Christmas' followed by another of Perry's signature Christmas offerings, 'Christ Is Born'.

'Christ Is Born' first came to Perry's attention during the taping of his Christmas special in Rome. It was composed by Domenico Bartolucci and performed by the Sistine Chapel Choir on the show. Ray Charles later wrote English lyrics to the song, which Perry recorded for his 1968 Christmas album. Perry sung the song no less than eleven times on television in the years that followed.

Speaking of the impact of television on Christmas in 1984, Perry said:

> I know if I'm having dinner now, and if there isn't any music going on – I think I'm absent! ... You feel you have to say something, and then whatever you say is kinda dumb. I think television has stopped all conversation. I don't think it's hurt Christmas any, I think it's improved it a lot. A lot of people don't know about nativities and things that you can do at Christmas time which are beautiful.[22]

And this desire to spread the message of Christmas was at the heart of Perry's Christmas specials.

By the time Perry taped his French Canadian Christmas special in 1981, his crew were at the very peak of their craft. The magic of Christmas is captured throughout with an ethereal quality that emphasises the joy and peace of the celebration in a timeless manner that is worthy of an annual airing. This special is to musical variety what *A Charlie Brown Christmas* is to animation.

During the special, Perry introduced a song that warmly conveys his feelings for the season. With heartfelt lyrics by Richard Matheson and a lilting melody by Nick Perito, 'I Wish It Could Be Christmas Forever' was recorded in 1982 and became another Como Christmas standard. It was his first new festive song since 'Christmas Dream' in 1974, penned by Andrew Lloyd Webber and Tim Rice, with German lyrics by André Heller, and recorded for the soundtrack of the film *The Odessa File* starring Jon Voight. The sentiments expressed within both songs align perfectly with Perry's fondness for the Yuletide season and have since become firm festive favourites.

Another example of fine cinematography is found within *Perry Como's Christmas in Austria* from 1976. The special sees Perry with guests including comedian Sid Caesar and actress Senta Berger exploring the charm of local streets and the pristine backdrop of the Austrian Alps. The special's finale takes place in the town of Arnsdorf, where Franz Xaver Gruber set the words of a poem by Joseph Mohr to music and in doing so created one of the most beloved Christmas carols 'Silent Night'. Perry sings the carol in keeping with the way it was first performed on Christmas Eve 1818 in German with guitar.

The specials from this era afforded Perry the opportunity to sing further material that he did not record for RCA Victor. For instance, 'Wonderful, Wonderful Day' (which proved a fitting pairing with the Como philosophy), 'I Write the Songs', 'The Happy Wanderer (Val-De-Ri, Val-De-Ra)' and 'Sloop John B' – which all received the Perry Como magic.

In the summer of 1977, Perry was invited to the UK to record an album titled *The Best of British*. The album's title and concept were suggested by RCA UK's Tommy Loftus to tie in with Queen Elizabeth II's silver jubilee. Tommy explained that the title came from the English expression 'the best of British'[23], which means to wish someone luck, although it is often conveyed with irony. The album might best be described as a souvenir to the British public from Perry.

Unfortunately, there appear to have been some difficulties encountered during recording, which are possibly a factor in why the album was never released in the United States. Perry was suffering some vocal difficulties at the time due to some recent dental work. His voice sounds quite hesitant at points and is generally restrained, but most surprisingly, his diction which was usually so clear on recordings is notably less distinct. The most problematic part of the album, however, is the mastering which has a distant, hazy sound throughout. The beautiful arrangements of Nick Perito and Don Costa are covered in a thick audible fog.

There are several factors to be considered here, though, to provide context. Como was not the kind of person to rush a recording session – he was known to go over a vocal many times until he was satisfied. He also worked best around people whom he knew and trusted and in locations he was comfortable with. Three days to record an album in unfamiliar surroundings and in another country was a tall order. There appears to have been no specifically assigned producer at the helm for these sessions either, a role that is often underestimated.

One of the album's most redeeming qualities is the sincerity within Perry's readings of these classic British compositions. He doesn't compromise his artistic integrity despite the difficulties. His 'The Very Thought of You' is dreamy bliss from beginning to end. 'There's a Kind of Hush (All over the World)' works particularly well with its bouncy rhythm and muted trumpets (an attribute exhibited to equal effect within 'My Kind of Girl') and 'Where Is Love?' one of Perry's favourite numbers from the album, receives a heartfelt and sensitive treatment.

Interestingly, two of the strongest selections from the sessions in terms of vocals were not intended for inclusion in the album – 'Where You're Concerned' and 'Girl You Make It Happen' – the first of which would become the title track for the US variation of the album, released the following year. Both Perry's vocals and the greater clarity of the mix seem to suggest a good possibility that these two songs were overdubbed later, back in the United States, prior to the release of the *Where You're Concerned* album.

An overdub is a portion of music added to a recording after the initial content has been laid down. It could be adding further instrumentation to a recording – for example, adding orchestral elements to a smaller ensemble rhythm track, as was a common technique in Nashville; or it might be a vocalist returning to the studio to record further vocal takes to an existing background. In the magnetic tape era, this was all achieved through the utilisation of additional linear tracks across the width of a tape, which could all be mixed together or some elements eliminated completely via the mixing desk – such were the advancements in multi-track recording by the 1970s.

The importance of original master recordings cannot be overstated. Not all recordings are created equal, and a particular format does not guarantee a certain level of fidelity. The skills of the mixing and mastering engineers are integral to this. As with Perry's analogy of the $40 versus the $200 suit, Perry sought the best in their field, one of whom was Bob Simpson. Of equal importance is the selection of correct/suitable takes. For unreleased recordings with no master take number identified, every care should be taken to select an appropriate take for issue. The question should also be asked as to why the recording was not released in the first instance.

Perry was back in the UK to tape his annual Christmas television special in the autumn of 1977. *Perry Como's Olde Englishe Christmas* opens in the picturesque rural village of Chiddingstone in Kent, where Perry has 'spent the night' at a coaching inn (the role of which was accommodated by the village post office). After some opening humour and pleasantries, Perry rides aboard a horse-driven carriage, moving onto the majestic setting of nearby Hever Castle. Joining Perry there are guests Petula Clark, Leo Sayer and Gemma Craven. Together they join in a medley of Christmas carols throughout the castle. They all reunite later in the television studio for a charming segment about the tradition of pantomimes in Britain. With Clark as fairy godmother and subsequently principal boy, Craven as Cinderella, and Sayer as Buttons – Perry indulges his English guests' explanations of this uniquely British entertainment, which culminates in a rousing chorus of 'Hot Diggity (Dog Ziggity Boom)'.

The special concludes with Perry's telling of 'The Story of the First Christmas' in what is one of the most beautiful stagings of the nativity across all of Perry's television specials. The finale takes place at St. Paul's Cathedral in London where Perry sings 'Ave Maria' accompanied by the cathedral choir.

The special was again produced by Yvonne Littlewood, who had nothing but praise for her experiences working with Perry:

> He's really very delightful, he's a very genuine person, very sincere, very professional, and really, when he gets down to it – no problem at all, he's a delight to work with. He has a sort of calming influence, I mean even ourselves – when you work, you work hard all day, but there's never a hassle, because he generates this sort of atmosphere around him – that's great.[24]

When asked if he had any special feelings for Britain, Perry said 'If they ever deport me from the United States for . . . smuggling some Italian mozzarella or something, I assure you you'll have a customer here, 'cause I love it'.[25]

Also during his visit, Perry made his worldwide debut on a television talk show. In conversation with Michael Parkinson, a whole episode of *Parkinson* was dedicated to Perry's appearance. It's an hour of warm reminiscences and good humour, delivered in Perry's trademark understated style, interspersed with selections performed from his newly released album *The Best of British* and an impromptu performance of 'It's Impossible', accompanied on piano by Nick Perito who leads Harry Stoneham's house band. It was fitting that Perry's chat show debut should be in the UK because of the level of love and regard British audiences had long had for him. Perry observed that the level of adulation he received in Britain was even greater than back home in the United States.

> 'He could laugh at himself, you know', recalled Yvonne Littlewood, 'and he always used to say that he was amazed that people were still wanting to queue up and see him. He couldn't believe this, and he used to say something like "Why would I want to do a chat show? I could talk about my whole career in 37 seconds flat. What would there be to say?"'[26]

Perry's 1978 Christmas special continued in a similar mode to the previous year – another traditional, historic Christmas setting. This time though, instead of the backdrop of Chiddingstone and Hever Castle, Perry travelled to Colonial Williamsburg in Virginia for his *Early American Christmas*. Perry's guests included actress Diana Canova, violinist Eugene Fodor, and actor John Wayne.

John Wayne's appearance on Perry's Christmas special would be one of his last television performances. John had been diagnosed with throat cancer, which would take his life the following year. Perry remembered John as a great guy, who came across with a gruffness, but that was his character – inside he was much more childlike (in the nicest sense of the description).

There was one incident, though, that Perry never forgot. One morning during the taping of the special, John had an 8.00 am call to be present for an outdoor games sequence including lawn bowling. The crew had specifically arranged for John to shoot his individual sequences early in the morning because that was when John felt best to perform. Sure enough at 8.00 am, John was there. Perry had a later call time of 9.30 am. Dozens of onlookers were there both to observe and partake in the lawn bowling game and John was entertaining them as well. Then at 9.30, Perry arrived. As soon as John saw Perry, he made a point of grumbling at him for what he thought was an unacceptable lateness of his arrival.

'Well, here he comes now – the star!' said Wayne. 'I come here at eight o'clock, but John Wayne doesn't mean a hell of a lot!' and he proceeded to lay into Perry verbally in front of the whole assembly. While this went on Perry just kept looking at John. He took his time, let Wayne get what he needed to out of his system and said nothing. People began to gather around wondering what was going on. Eventually, John looked at Perry and said 'Well? Aren't you going to say something?' Perry paused, looked up at John ('9 feet tall') and retorted 'Yeh – you're a pain in the ass!' and in that moment the cast and crew (John included) broke up with laughter. John then grabbed Perry as if he were a small child, lifted him up, kissed him and said 'Nobody's ever said that to me before!' – Perry's response had clearly diffused the situation, and the two gentlemen proceeded with their work. [27]

Also starring in the special was actress Diana Canova (daughter of singer and actress Judy Canova and Cuban musician Filberto Rivero). At the time, Canova was starring in the sitcom *Soap* where she stayed until 1980. Her pairing with Perry resulted in yet another perfect on-screen partnership. Their charming interaction and beautiful duets make for delightful festive viewing.

At the end of the decade, Perry received an Award of Merit at the 6th *Annual American Music Awards*, led by Debby Boone with touching testimonials from Bob Hope, Lena Horne, and Hal Linden. Ella Fitzgerald (the previous year's recipient) presented Perry with his award.

That December, Perry's Christmas special originated from New Mexico. Anne Murray was once again among the guests. Recalling the occasion, Anne said, 'it was just like going home to be with him and singing with an old friend ... it was always such a treat for me'.[28]

Perry Como might easily have rested on his laurels at the close of the 1970s. He'd been one of the biggest selling and most enduring personalities on radio, records and television for over thirty-five years. He had enjoyed the rise to superstardom as a solo vocalist in the 1940s, ridden the waves of musical change in the 1950s and 1960s and enjoyed a tremendous comeback in the 1970s. But many more exciting times lay ahead as the 1980s dawned.

Quintessential Como
Recommended listening 1970–7

Long Life, Lots of Happiness •
mw Owen McGovern, 1970
5 May 1970 - 74-0387

It's Impossible ★
mw Armando Manzanero (Sp.), 1968,
w Sid Wayne (Eng.), 1970
5–6 May 1970 - It's Impossible LSP-4473

Without a Song ★
m Vincent Youmans, w Edward Eliscu
and Billy Rose, 1929
From the musical Great Day!
25–27 Jun 1970 (Live) - PC in Person at the
International Hotel, Las Vegas LSPX-1001

If I Could Almost Read Your Mind
mw Ray Charles and Nick Perito, 1970
25–27 Jun 1970 (Live) - PC in Person at the
International Hotel, Las Vegas LSPX-1001
PC Irish Christmas - Dec 1994

Raindrops Keep Fallin' on My Head
m Burt Bacharach, w Hal David, 1969
From the film Butch Cassidy
and the Sundance Kid.
23 Nov 1970 - It's Impossible LSP-4473

Something
mw George Harrison, 1969
23 Nov 1970 - It's Impossible LSP-4473

El cóndor pasa
m Traditional, c. 18th century,
m Daniel Alomía Robles (adapt.), 1913,
w Paul Simon, 1970
24 Nov 1970 - It's Impossible LSP-4473

(They Long to Be) Close to You
m Burt Bacharach, w Hal David, 1963
25 Nov 1970 - It's Impossible LSP-4473

I Think of You
m Francis Lai, w Catherine Desage
(Fr.), 1970, w Rod McKuen (Eng.), 1971
10 Feb 1971 - I Think of You LSP-4539

Yesterday I Heard the Rain
mw Armando Manzanero (Sp.), 1967,
w Gene Lees (Eng.), 1968
26 Apr 1971 - I Think of You LSP-4539

If
mw David Gates, 1971
27 Apr 1971 - I Think of You LSP-4539

Where Do I Begin (Theme from Love Story)
m Francis Lai, w Carl Sigman, 1970
The theme from the film Love Story.
27 Apr 1971 - I Think of You LSP-4539

I Want to Give (Ahora que soy libre)
mw Juan Eduardo and Juan Marcelo
(Sp.), 1971, w Gene Nash (Eng.), 1973
15 Jan 1973 - And I Love You So APL1-0100

And I Love You So ★
mw Don McLean, 1970
17 Jan 1973 - And I Love You So APL1-0100
PC Irish Christmas - Dec 1994

Love Looks So Good on You
*mw Charlie Williams and
Steve Stone, 1969*
17 Jan 1973 - 74-0906

I Thought About You
mw Ronal McCown, 1970
17 Jan 1973 - And I Love You So
APL1-0100

**Tie a Yellow Ribbon
Round the Ole Oak Tree**
*mw Irwin Levine and L. Russell
Brown, 1973*
26 Mar 1973 - And I Love You So
APL1-0100

For the Good Times
mw Kris Kristofferson, 1971
26 Mar 1973 - And I Love You So
APL1-0100

Walk Right Back
mw Sonny Curtis, 1960
7 Aug 1973 - APB0-0096

The Hands of Time (Brian's Song)
*m Michel Legrand, w Alan Bergman
and Marilyn Bergman, 1972
From the film Brian's Song.*
4 Jan 1974 - Perry CPL1-0585

I Don't Know What He Told You
*m Tony Renis, w Alberto Testa
and Giulio Rapetti (Mogol) (It.), 1972,
w Robert I. Allen (Eng.), 1973*
7 Jan 1974 - Perry CPL1-0585

Weave Me the Sunshine
mw Peter Yarrow, 1972
7 Jan 1974 - Perry CPL1-0585

The Way We Were
*m Marvin Hamlisch, w Alan Bergman
and Marilyn Bergman, 1973
From the film The Way We Were.*
1 May 1974 - Perry CPL1-0585

The Most Beautiful Girl
*mw Rory Bourke, Billy Sherrill
and Norro Wilson, 1973*
1 May 1974 - Perry CPL1-0585

World of Dreams
mw Des O'Connor, 1970
7 Jan 1975 - RCA 2541 (UK)

Let's Do It Again
mw Tony Hatch and Jackie Trent, 1974
9 Jan 1975 - Just out of Reach APL1-0863

Here, There and Everywhere
mw John Lennon and Paul McCartney, 1966
9 Jan 1975 - Just out of Reach APL1-0863

Then You Can Tell Me Goodbye
mw John D. Loudermilk, 1967
16 Jan 1975 - Just out of Reach APL1-0863

The Grass Keeps Right On Growin'
mw Gloria Shayne, 1975
16 Jan 1975 - Just out of Reach APL1-0863

The Very Thought of You ★
mw Ray Noble, 1934
6–10 Jun 1977 - The Best of British PL 12373 (UK)

Michelle
mw John Lennon and Paul McCartney, 1966
6–10 Jun 1977 - The Best of British PL 12373 (UK)

Where You're Concerned
mw Nancy Goland, 1977
6–10 Jun 1977 - Where You're Concerned AFL1-2641

Feelings ●
m Louis Gasté, w Albert Simonin and Marie-Hélène Bourquin (Fr.), 1956, mw Morris Albert (Eng.), 1974
5 Oct 1977 - Where You're Concerned AFL1-2641

7

The Best of Times

The 1980s began busily for Perry. He opened the decade with the taping of a new on-location television special in the Bahamas (one of his very best) to be broadcast that May. The special, centred in Nassau, guest starred Loretta Swit (famous for her role as Major Margaret 'Hot Lips' Houlihan in the television comedy-drama series *M*A*S*H*) and returning guests Captain and Tennille, plus an array of Bahamian talent. The special opens with Perry and company dressed in beach attire and making the persuasive argument in song that 'It's Better in the Bahamas'. As always, Perry's chemistry with his on-screen guests is a delight to see and hear.

One of the highlights of *Perry Como's Bahamas Holiday* is a medley of 'When I Fall in Love' and 'It Could Happen to You' sung by Perry with piano accompaniment provided by Nick Perito. This beautiful performance is complemented by a perfectly understated setting of a grand piano with a single rose and glass of wine atop, tucked in a quiet corner of an elegant restaurant. Perry wears a striking white suit with a blue shirt and looks as handsome, if not more so, than he did twenty years earlier, belying his sixty-eighth year by a substantial margin. This template would be returned to with equal effect in future specials from San Francisco and Guadalajara.

With the Bahamas special complete, Perry was soon immersed in a new recording project – his first full album in three years. Titled simply *Perry Como*, the album was recorded at RCA Studios C and D in April 1980, and the album artwork utilized photography from the Bahamas taping. The album hears Perry with a change of A&R, being produced by Mike Berniker and conducted by Byron Olsen. Berniker had worked with Perry briefly before in December 1978 on a session which approached some contemporary pop material of the period, with a partly disco-infused flavour. The resulting single 'When I Wanted You' (also recorded by Barry Manilow) backed with 'Forever' failed to make a commercial impact, but the recordings serve as an interesting example of further diversification within the Como canon.

The 1980 *Perry Como* album was a return, however, to more familiar territory – tender love songs and a couple of current Broadway hits. 'Not While I'm Around' from *Sweeney Todd: The Demon Barber of Fleet Street* takes on a whole new meaning in Perry's interpretation and his recording of 'The Colours of My Life' from *Barnum* is handled with the optimism and warmth that the lyrics deserve. Several familiar names are present among the songwriting credits for the album. Paul Vance, for instance, co-wrote the joyously romantic 'You Are My World' with Bobby London. Also in appearance are the lyrics of Ervin Drake ('Save Me the Dance') and Richard Ahlert ('Someone Is Waiting').

Further recording took place in July, when Perry was captured live in concert at the Mill Run Theatre, Niles, Illinois, during his US summer tour for 1980. *Perry Como Live on Tour*, which was released in 1981 presents Perry on great form – his ease and rapport with the audience is delightful, and the power in his voice on favourites such as 'Where or When' and 'You'll Never Walk Alone' is outstanding.

This new boost in recording activity had been prompted by Perry's signing of a ten-year extension on his recording contract with RCA Victor. This was a remarkable achievement for a major artist in the pop field. Upon signing the extension, in his trademark self-deprecating way, he said to his fellow signatories, 'You must be crazy. I'll be in a wheelchair 10 years from now!'

Perry's opening act on his 1980 summer concert tour, and previously in 1979, was American comedian and host Jay Leno, then in the early stages of his career. Jay described Perry as 'Probably the greatest man I've ever worked with in show business'.

'He was the first guy I ever toured with', Leno said, 'and my mom was never very impressed with show business till I was doing a show once... I opened for Perry – it was a huge place – I told Perry my mom was sitting in the audience, and Perry went down, walked into the audience, took my mom's hand and sang "Always" – my mom's favourite song – right to her. From that point on, I could do no wrong... I got free meatballs for life!' Jay considered Perry to be a man who made show business classy. 'You hear all the terrible things about show business', continued Leno, 'but you meet Perry and it cancels them all out. He's really the nicest, nicest man I've ever met...'[1]

After concerts, people would often gather backstage to enjoy refreshments and meet Perry. Nick Perito recalled one occasion which highlighted the Italian ethnic humour they both shared and loved:

> One night, he [Perry] came out of his dressing room and people were assembled in there, dressed in their finery and sipping wine and so forth. He looked over to me and says, 'Hey Niccolò! Do you have to keep playing all those damn wrong chords all the time?' And I said 'Whatta ya talkin' [about]?' He says 'Nick... They're wrong!' and I said 'Perry, I'm sorry about that but look, could you do me a favour? You're singing a little too loud over my arrangements. Could you... maybe hum a little bit? I wrote all the pretty string parts, and nobody's hearing 'em... could you just hold it down a little bit?' and he says 'Ah, get outta here!' And the people of course were like 'Oh! What the hell's going on here?' They'd mumble and talk a little bit, and several would come over later on and whisper to me 'Gee, I thought you played rather well tonight!' and I'd say 'Well, I did too, thank you – and so did Mr. Como.' 'But he said you played all...' 'No, you see – what he really meant was he *liked* it! That's his way...' 'But he said you...' [and] I said, 'Want some more coffee, ma'am?' And [I'd] pour some more wine. That was it – they couldn't understand this thing. But if you knew Perry... you know that ethnic kind of correspondence and communication, it makes sense.[2]

As Nick explained, in their tradition, a put-down was a compliment.

On 25 March 1982, Perry Como and Frank Sinatra were invited to perform at a White House Dinner in honour of Italian president Sandro Pertini, who was on a state visit to the United States. Perry and Frank entertained for forty minutes, opening with a duet of 'I'm Sitting on Top of the World' then taking it in turns to sing their solo numbers, concluding with a medley of American Songbook standards. Accompanying them instrumentally were Nick Perito and Vincent 'Vinnie' Falcone (Frank's musical director), both leading the ensemble on piano, bassist Gene Cherico, guitarists Tony Mottola and Bucky Pizzarelli and drummer Irving 'Irv' Cottler.

> 'It was so surprising, to see the difference between these two guys who had such a great admiration for one another', recalled Tony Mottola. 'Frank would have a Jack Daniels, have a steak, have a baked potato with all the trimmings and this and that; Perry would have a glass of white wine with a piece of Dover sole with a green salad . . . I never forget one time, Frank was repaying Perry for a favour, we did a benefit for Perry down in Durham for Duke University Hospital [May 1983] that he was interested in, and after the show we were backstage, and Roselle Como . . . said "You have no idea how much my husband admires you, Frank. He would love to be just like you!" and Frank looked in amazement and said "He wants to be like *me*? I should be a little like *him*!" But they were very, very good friends and admired each other greatly. It was a thrill for me when I was doing that show. The realisation came to me that – here I am at the White House, on a stage appearing with the two men that I was mostly associated with during my whole career, from the time I was a kid up until the time I retired'.[3]

Perry and Frank would reprise their Standards medley in February 1983 on the M*A*S*H soundstage at 20th Century-Fox studios in Hollywood, California as part of a dinner entertainment for Queen Elizabeth II who was visiting the United States on a 10-day tour of the West Coast. Also appearing on the bill were George Burns and singer Dionne Warwick.

That summer, Perry Como celebrated his fiftieth anniversary in show business and his fortieth anniversary with RCA Victor Records. It was also the year of his fiftieth wedding anniversary to Roselle. RCA hosted a party for Perry at the Rainbow Grill, Rockefeller Center in New York to mark the historic occasion. It was a classy engagement with members of the press and leading figures from New York in attendance. The wall behind the performance area was adorned with photos and album covers from throughout Perry's career and he was presented with a bronze sculpture of his profile. The rosewood base on which the sculpture was mounted contained a plaque reading 'To Perry Como in appreciation of 40 Golden Years, June 17, 1943, to June 17, 1983', signed by RCA Corporation Chairman and Chief Executive Officer Thornton F. Bradshaw and RCA Records President Robert D. Summer, who together led the events proceedings. The phrase '40 Golden Years' also formed the title of a non-commercial compilation album produced especially to commemorate the occasion and presented to guests. The album collects a selection of Perry's gold-certified records and has the unique feature of an embossed facsimile of Perry's autograph in the LP run-out grooves.

In his opening speech, Bradshaw said that 'He [Perry] is a remarkable man with a remarkable career, not only in records but in two of RCA's other established traditions – radio and television'. Bradshaw went on to say that the label was 'honored by its long association with one of the most gifted gentlemen in the entertainment business'.[4] Summer added that 'Through the years, his music has become part of the fabric of our times, giving us moments that evoke memories of the best times of our lives'.[5]

Congratulations to Perry also came in the form of a letter from President Ronald Reagan in which he wrote, 'On the musical scene, you are virtually an American institution and a source of entertainment and inspiration to all who enjoy a true artist. Your talent and creativity have charmed millions for years'.[6] In response to the tributes, Perry said, 'It's a great day for me and Mrs. Como. You (the media) have been very generous'.[7] He went on to tease, 'Did I REALLY sell 100 million records? Where'd the money go?!'[8]

Also part of the celebrations was a parody song written for Perry by composer Marvin Hamlisch (who performed the song) and lyricist Sheldon Harnick, utilising the titles of some of Como's hits and sending up his on-screen persona. Hamlisch said of Perry, 'I think there were two secrets of his. I think one was he had a wonderful voice, and I think the second secret is he made you feel comfortable'.[9]

Both *Entertainment Tonight* and *The Today Show* in the United States picked up the story of Perry's anniversaries. During a three-part mini-documentary, Brian Gumbel of *The Today Show* asked Perry why he didn't look his age. After kidding that he put it down to a lot of drinking, Perry said that there are three stages in life: adolescence, middle age and 'gee, you look good!' placing himself just about in the third category.

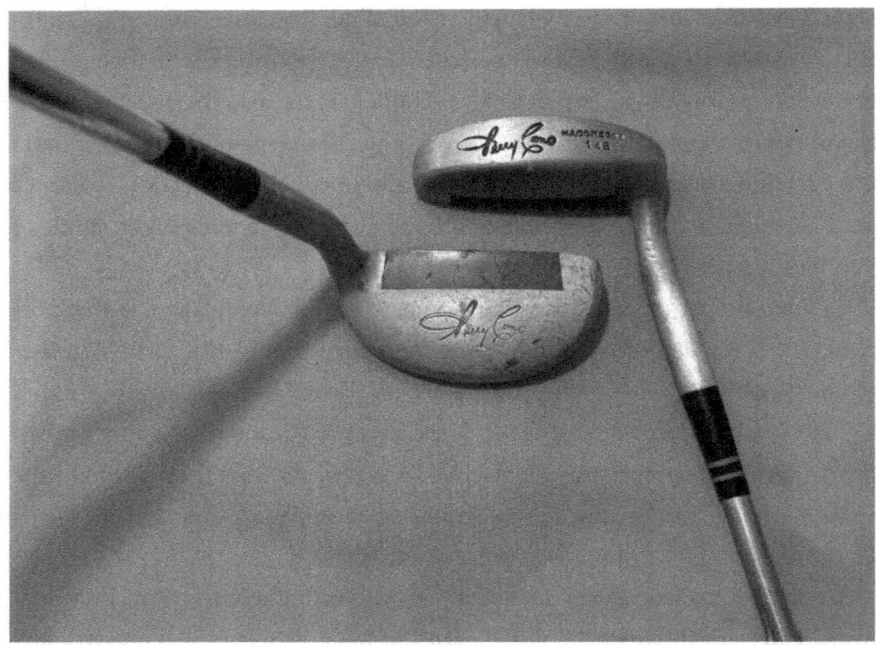

Golf was one of Perry's favourite hobbies. MacGregor issued putters 144 (bottom) and 148 in the 1970s. Author's photo.

In October that year, Perry recorded two songs 'The Best of Times' and 'Song on the Sand (La Da Da Da)' (both from the musical *La Cage aux Folles*) to form a new single release. The positive and reflective mood of the two recordings was a fitting celebration for Perry's triple anniversary year. 'The Best of Times' later prompted a new compilation album in the UK when the British public took to Perry's recording of the song.

Now in his seventy-first year he was just as eager to keep working. The Christmas specials continued, with the 1983 edition originating from New York, linking in nicely with the year's celebrations. Bob Banner Associates had now left the Como television crew with Jeff Margolis producing for the next two years.

Como's guests that year included actress Michele Lee and rising Broadway star Sarah Litzsinger who was just twelve years old at the time. 'It was a really wonderful experience', reflected Litzsinger in 2023. 'Perry Como was such a kind, just wonderful person to be around. He said, "Call me uncle Perry". When we were done with the shoot, he sent me a big bar of chocolate'.[10] The bar of chocolate would remain in the family for around a decade afterwards as a reminder of a special time.

The taping was done in Central Park, Little Italy and numerous other New York tourist spots. Michele joins Perry in a duet of his new single 'The Best of Times' while aboard a horse-drawn carriage, and Sarah visits the F. A. O. Schwarz toy store with Perry to help choose a plush animal, leading to a charming duet of 'Talk to the Animals'. There is even a cameo appearance from New York mayor Ed Koch.

The special culminates in a Christmas dinner gathering with the Balducci family (of Balducci's groceries in Greenwich Village) and closes with a rendition of 'Ave Maria' at St. Patrick's Cathedral. 'Como is a marvel', said *Variety* magazine of the special.

> He doesn't age nor does his voice show signs of time's passage – and the suave gentility of his manner is ever welcome. And nobody catches the true spirit of Christmas as he does in his specials.[11]

'I think it [Christmas] means, being with the family and 'course the true meaning is the birth of the Christ child . . .'[12] said Perry in 1984. It was a heart-warming hour of magical Christmas music and memories with an audience figure of over 17 million.

The following year, Perry embarked on his fiftieth anniversary tour. Unfortunately, the tour had to be temporarily postponed early on when Perry contracted a bronchial virus. Speaking to Regis Philbin in August that year, he explained that 'I think I caught it in Arizona. We went to Phoenix, it was 117°F and you go from that to 65°F air-conditioned . . . back and forth in three days – out'.[13] Consequently, three weeks of performances had to be cancelled, and Perry resumed the US tour on 20 June 1984 at the Carlton Celebrity Room, Minneapolis. The extensive tour covered several states including Michigan, Massachusetts, Ohio, New York, and concluded with nine sold-out performances at the Valley Forge Music Fair in Devon, Pennsylvania.

The year 1985 continued very much in the same vein with another extensive summer tour. That autumn, Perry and his crew had intended to tape the annual Christmas special in Italy, but due to concerns over terrorist activities in the country at that time, the team opted for Hawaii, with returning guest star Marie Osmond and fellow Floridian and actor Burt Reynolds.

Jupiter Lighthouse, close to Perry's home in Florida, where he enjoyed another of his favourite pastimes, fishing. Author's photo.

Perry's last annual Christmas special came in 1986. The special originated from San Antonio, Texas with guests including actress Angie Dickinson, country singer George Strait, and opera singer Julia Migenes-Johnson. The show was not Perry's finest as regards Christmas specials, perhaps most noticeably in terms of production values. In this respect, the show is missing the touches of Bob Banner. Compared to Perry's last special with Banner, from Paris in 1982 (on which Angie Dickinson also appeared), there is a distinct difference in the overall feel. Interestingly, it was the show's producer Bob Wynn who led the crew for *Perry Como's Irish Christmas* eight years later, which proved to be a triumph. The festive heart was still there, though, and Perry sings a nice version of 'Do You Hear What I Hear?' with the Fifth Army Band and Air Force Band of the West, plus there is an opportunity to hear one of the only times that Perry sang 'Ave Maria' as a duet – on this occasion with Julia Migenes-Johnson.

Also appearing on the show were the San Antonio Symphony Orchestra and Master Singers. Lucinda Cummings Kilmer, who along with her husband were members of the Master Singers, recalled the occasion with fond memories. Describing her impression of Perry during the dress rehearsal, Lucinda said that:

He introduced himself to us – didn't ignore us as some soloists do – and it was a collaboration that was fun and happy. He was all those tepid things: nice, pleasant, calm, polite. And he was more – he looked people in the eye, he always smiled, he knew what he was supposed to do, he let people be who they were... In short, he was the gentleman barber singer. He did not betray his roots, he rose above his station (which of course, is the American dream), and he was professional. He also was kind and had a sweet spirit, and left the room shining a bit brighter.[14]

The end of Perry Como's annual Christmas specials came in 1987 after an almost unbroken run of Christmas programmes on television across thirty-eight years. According to an article in the *Orlando Sentinel*:

The singing barber asked ABC for a different time slot, and when the network refused, Como called the whole thing off. 'I hated to do it,' said Perry 'but I just kind of felt that we were throwing our show away Saturday night at 10. That's kind of late, don't you think'. TV critic Ed Bark of Dallas Morning News 'asked his readers to consider the "ugly implications" of Christmas without Perry Como and to write letters of protest that he promised to forward to ABC.' Bark reportedly received 30 letters on the first day and expected hundreds more, adding that 'One woman wrote that Perry was a star atop a mediocre ABC tree'.[15]

It was a bittersweet end to Perry's annual Christmas specials, but all was not lost. On 30 December 1987, Perry was one of the honourees on *The Kennedy Center Honors – A Celebration of the Performing Arts* on CBS Television. Perry received his award on 6 December, presented to him at the White House by President Ronald Reagan – a year to the day after Perry's last annual Christmas special had been broadcast. The show was directed by Dwight Hemion and produced by George Stevens Jr. and Nick Vanoff. Perry received a lovely tribute, introduced by actor Don Ameche. A barbershop group, the Harmonizers, sang a medley of Como hits, and the segment concluded with further Como classics rendered by Diahann Carroll and Vic Damone, including a duet of 'Prisoner of Love'. Sitting proudly behind Perry in the auditorium was Roselle. They'd come a long way together from those heady days on the road with the Ted Weems Orchestra, and it had all been worth it.

Early in the year, Perry made his final recordings for RCA Victor. Perry had become increasingly disenchanted with the recording studio environment, which had changed vastly over the years. Commenting in 1984, he said, 'Sometimes I feel like I'm not even in the business, really'.[16]

A couple of years earlier, Perry had walked out of sessions in RCA Studios C and D for what became the *So It Goes* album. Eight songs had been successfully laid down, and Como sang with confidence, but he was unhappy with the surroundings. The producer on the sessions was Mike Berniker. Ray Charles said, 'Mike Berniker found us [Ray and Nick Perito] irrelevant. We didn't think much of him, either. Or maybe we couldn't figure out what he was doing there'.[17] Ray recalled a dark, gloomy studio (which Perry compared to a morgue) and one of the few times that Perry recorded his vocals to track, without a live orchestra. None of this was Perry's style.

Perry was now more reluctant to make recordings, but with the encouragement of his friend and musical director Nick Perito, Perry made his final recordings for RCA on 2 and 3 February 1987 at Evergreen Studios, Burbank, California. The album has the unique distinction of having been arranged, conducted, and produced by Nick Perito and co-produced by Roncom Productions, Inc. The album was also the first and only studio album of Perry's to be originally released simultaneously on LP and CD. Although still released through the original label, RCA had been sold to Bertelsmann Music Group (BMG) in 1986.

The song selections for the album are a cross-section of genres, mostly with a feel and vibe reminiscent of the pop landscape of the time, with an emphasis on synthesized accompaniment. The opening title 'Making Love to You' was composed by Nick Perito, who reached out to Sammy Cahn for the lyrics. It's a beautiful recording and sets the tone for the album. The Burt Bacharach and Carole Bayer Sager song 'That's What Friends Are For' receives a brilliantly swinging arrangement from Perito – significantly contrasting with the Dionne Warwick and Friends version, but with equal heart.

'The Wind Beneath My Wings' was effectively the hit single that never was from the album and was both autobiographical in nature and sensitively performed. Perry's manager Mickey Glass pleaded with the label to release the song as a single, but it was not to be. It did not, however, stop the song from becoming both a fan favourite and a key inclusion within Perry's concerts from then on.

There is a nod to Perry's novelty songs of the 1950s in 'Sing Along with Me' (also composed by Perito, but with lyrics by Dee Williams) and two Great American Songbook standards by one of Perry's favourite songwriting teams, Richard Rodgers and Lorenz Hart – 'My Heart Stood Still' and 'You're Nearer' – both previously recorded by Perry for RCA (in 1952 and 1968, respectively), which make for a most interesting comparison. Concluding with a revised arrangement of 'The Best of Times', *Perry Como Today* represents an excellent effort which stands as a fine tribute to Como and Perito's enduring friendship.

That summer, Perry embarked on another tour. One night in July, after performing at South Shore Music Circus in Cohasset, Massachusetts, Perry was able to bring a magic moment to a dear lady who was suffering from a debilitating medical condition, which had left her wheelchair bound. The lady's daughter explained that she had purposely declined offers to go out for meals and entertainment because she felt a burden to those around her. Staying home was her way of maintaining dignity. One time, however, her daughter called her up as she often did to extend an invitation to go out. In this instance, she had two tickets to see Perry Como. Without any hesitation, she accepted the invite to the great surprise of her daughter. She was so enthusiastic about the idea that she was quick to put the phone down to arrange to have her hair done!

The night came, and the performance was thoroughly enjoyed by mother and daughter. For the duration of the concert, the lady was transported from the confines of her condition into a dreamy, musical place courtesy of Mr. C. Before the show, the daughter had passed on a request, brought to the attention of Mickey Glass, to see if a song could be dedicated to her mother. Mickey located the two ladies and explained that this wouldn't be possible, but would they like to meet Perry after the show – and so it was arranged.

When the time came, Perry, his manager and a couple of men from the band helped wheel the lady up a steep slope leading into the trailer where the show members got changed. At the top was a huge step, too much for the lady to manage on her own. So, the gentlemen lifted the lady into the living room of the trailer and onto a chair. 'They did it all matter-of-factly, as if it were nothing, when in fact it was everything', said her daughter. 'I thought then that it would have been enough for Perry Como just to have said hello after the show. And it *would* have been enough; but it wouldn't have been as special'.

For nearly an hour, Perry sat and talked with the lady and gave her his attention – not because he had to or as a publicity stunt but because he cared, and he wanted to. Mickey and the members of the band all talked to her too – appreciative of this gentle lady who had come to the show all dressed up and smiling. Before parting, they had a photo together which she treasured. Her daughter later had the photo enlarged, where it hung with pride in her mother's kitchen, where she spent most of her time.

When the lady later moved to a nursing home, the photo was carefully wrapped and brought with her. There it hung, proudly displayed on the wall next to her bed. A lovely reminder of a wonderful evening. The photo made her somewhat of a celebrity in the home. Many a member of staff or visitors would stop and study the photo, asking, 'That's not Perry Como, is it?' and in that moment, the lady would sit a little taller and prouder in her seat and begin to tell the story of how she met Perry Como.[18]

In the summer of 1988, Perry was booked to appear on *Evening at Pops*, a televised concert series with the Boston Pops Orchestra conducted by John Williams. Perry had been booked to perform a tribute to Bing Crosby, in which Perry sang a slightly revised version of his Bing Crosby medley as a tribute to the singer. The medley, which was arranged by Nick Perito, had been a regular part of Perry's concert performances since around 1980 and was re-orchestrated for the Boston Pops by Nick on John Williams' request. Williams introduces Perry's segment by saying 'Ever since I've been here at the Boston Pops, I've looked forward to tonight. That's because tonight's guest is not only one of my favourites, but one for whom the word 'legend' genuinely applies'.[19]

'Strange as it may seem', recalled Nick,

> Perry was a bit apprehensive singing in front of such a large ensemble. He didn't think they could play softly enough for him. They certainly could, and they did, and he was very happy with everything that transpired. As soon as we got back to the hotel after the concert, I was happy to see Perry rush to a phone and call John to thank him for the wonderful musical experience we had all shared.[20]

St. Jude Catholic Church in Tequesta, Florida. Perry was a regular member of the congregation. Author's photo.

Joining Perry that night were a group of female singers, now accompanying him on tours. One member Cassie Miller remembered:

> We were doing a run-through and I was standing in the hallway, looking through the crack in the door into the house (where the people sit) watching

that black and white video of Bing and Perry . . . all of a sudden I felt a hand on my right shoulder. It was Perry. All he said was, 'I sure loved that man', meaning Bing. We both just stood there for a minute and I literally thought to myself, 'I need to remember and cherish this moment.' How special. Perry was a very sweet and generous man. His demeanor was the same offstage and on.[21]

As the 1980s neared its closing, so too did the presidential office of Ronald Reagan, who was succeeded by George H. W. Bush on 20 January 1989. Perry had always maintained a distance from explicit comment on political matters throughout his career, but his friendship with Ronald and Nancy Reagan was apparent. On 22 October 1989, Perry took part in a *Friendship Concert* at the Yokohama Arena in Japan. The concert was a charity gala honouring the relationship between Japan and the United States with former President Reagan and his wife Nancy in attendance. Perry was especially invited to appear at the concert and opens his set with a superb performance of 'And I Love You So', which he dedicates to Nancy. Perry follows aptly with a solid rendition of 'That's What Friends Are For', after which Japanese vocalist Yuzo Kayama joins Perry on stage. Clearly in awe of Perry, he says:

'Oh! Wonderful – just wonderful! Splendid! You're too good. I'm almost crying. Yes! I was waiting for this moment . . . long time. Was my dream – standing centre with you, someone I deeply respect.'[22] 'I'm happy to be here, I really am', Perry responds, adding 'course with the President and Mrs. Reagan here – makes everything right, doesn't it?'.[23] What follows is a moving duet between Perry and Yuzo of 'Sing' written and composed by Joe Raposo.

Also specially invited to appear was opera singer Placido Domingo. When it came to deciding who would close the show, Placido, a fellow Italian and admirer of Como, looked at Perry and commanded, 'He's going to close the show!' 'Come on!' replied Perry. 'You want me to sing after you get through singing? You've gotta be joking!' But Placido was insistent that Perry should close the show. 'I felt like an idiot singing after him!' Perry said, but added that he's 'a wonderful man . . . he's a comic! When you're around him a little bit, he's got all those little funny stories . . . and he laughs himself. He's a delight to be with.'[24]

As a finale to the evening's proceedings, Perry, Placido and the entire cast of the evening join in a rousing performance of 'You Are My Sunshine' in honour of Mr. & Mrs. Reagan, who join in themselves from their seats. After a poignant speech from President Reagan, the cast reprise the song with special lyrics in honour of 'Ron'. It was a wonderful end to another decade in the Como career.

Quintessential Como
Recommended listening 1980–7

The Colours of My Life
m Cy Coleman, w Michael Stewart, 1980
From the musical Barnum.
8–17 Apr 1980 - Perry Como AFL1-3629

Love
mw Gerard Kenny and Drey
Shepperd, 1979
8–17 Apr 1980 - Perry Como AFL1-3629

Not While I'm Around
mw Stephen Sondheim, 1979
From the musical Sweeney Todd:
The Demon Barber of Fleet Street.
8–17 Apr 1980 - Perry Como AFL1-3629

Regrets
mw Barbara Wyrick, 1979
8–17 Apr 1980 - Perry Como AFL1-3629

There'll Never Be Another Night Like This
mw David Reilly and Anthony Bygraves, 1980
8–17 Apr 1980 - Perry Como AFL1-3629

When She Smiles
mw Jerry Liliedahl, 1980
8–17 Apr 1980 - Perry Como AFL1-3629

You Are My World
mw Paul Vance and Bobby London, 1980
8–17 Apr 1980 - Perry Como AFL1-3629

Where or When ★
m Richard Rodgers, w Lorenz Hart, 1937
From the musical Babes in Arms.
29–31 Jul 1980 (Live) - PC Live on Tour
AQL1-3826 / PC NBC - 23 Feb 1957 &
29 Mar 1958 / PC KMH - 17 Feb 1960
The Royal Variety Performance - 24 Nov 1974

You'll Never Walk Alone ★
m Richard Rodgers,
w Oscar Hammerstein II, 1945
From the musical Carousel.
29–31 Jul 1980 (Live) - PC Live on Tour
AQL1-3826

Send in the Clowns
mw Stephen Sondheim, 1973
From the musical A Little Night Music.
29–31 Jul 1980 (Live) - PC Live on Tour
AQL1-3826
PC Spring in San Francisco - 10 May 1981

Jason
mw Debbie Hupp and Bob Morrison, 1979
Dec 1981–82 - So It Goes AFL1-4272

The Second Time
m Francis Lai, 1977, w Tim Rice, 1981
The theme from the film Bilitis.
Dec 1981–82 - So It Goes AFL1-4272

So It Goes
mw Barry Mason, Alec Gould
and Michael Heath Johnson, 1983
Dec 1981–82 - So It Goes AFL1-4272

What's One More Time
mw Richard Leigh, 1979
Dec 1981–82 - So It Goes AFL1-4272

The Best of Times
mw Jerry Herman, 1983
From the musical La Cage aux Folles.
17–18 Oct 1983 - PB-13690

Song on the Sand (La Da Da Da)
mw Jerry Herman, 1983
From the musical La Cage aux Folles.
17–18 Oct 1983 - PB-13690

Bless the Beasts and the Children
mw Barry DeVorzon
and Perry Botkin Jr., 1971
2–3 Feb 1987 - PC Today 6368-1-R

Making Love to You
m Nick Perito, w Sammy Cahn, 1987
2–3 Feb 1987 - PC Today 6368-1-R

My Heart Stood Still ■* ★
m Richard Rodgers, w Lorenz Hart, 1927
From the musical A Connecticut Yankee.
2–3 Feb 1987 - PC Today 6368-1-R

Sing Along with Me
m Nick Perito, w Dick Williams, 1987
2–3 Feb 1987 - PC Today 6368-1-R

That's What Friends Are For
m Burt Bacharach,
w Carole Bayer Sager, 1985
2–3 Feb 1987 - PC Today 6368-1-R

The Wind Beneath My Wings ★
mw Larry Henley and Jeff Silbar, 1982
2–3 Feb 1987 - PC Today 6368-1-R
PC Irish Christmas - Dec 1994

You're Nearer ■*
m Richard Rodgers, w Lorenz Hart, 1940
From the film Too Many Girls.
2–3 Feb 1987 - PC Today 6368-1-R

8

When You Come to the End of the Day

On 7 January 1990, Perry Como was one of seven inductees into the *Academy of Television Arts & Sciences Hall of Fame* at 20th Century-Fox studios in Los Angeles, California. Perry's biography in brief was narrated by Milton Berle, along with archival footage. Presenting Perry with his award was Frank Sinatra. As Frank approaches the microphone, suffering with a throat ailment, he says, 'If I sound very strange it's because I swallowed a shot glass!' In a heartfelt manner, Frank continues, 'The Television Academy and the Hall of Fame welcomes Perry Como, as I do – I adore him, and I know you do.'[1] From his guest table, Perry makes his way to the stage to a standing ovation. As he approaches Frank, Perry places his hands either side of Frank's face in a warm Italian greeting, and the pair embrace.

As the applause descends, and Frank exits the stage, Perry quips, 'I saw him swallow the glass!' It was a moment of great humour and deeply touching. In his acceptance speech Perry said, 'I never dreamed 40 or 50 years ago while I was cutting hair in Canonsburg that I'd be standing here tonight. You're looking at a very proud man right now, very proud. I'm sure that some of the ladies are thinking, "Well, where's Mrs. Como?" Well, she is kind of a white-knuckle flyer – she won't fly! So, I got to go do these things by myself, which is OK. But I'm sure that she's watching the show now and I can just hear her say, "You done good, Pops, you done good". For 57 years, she's been, if you'll pardon the expression, "the wind beneath my wings."'[2] It was a beautiful moment.

That March, Perry began an association with the *Sammy Davis Jr Variety Club Telethon* in St. Louis, Missouri. Producer Bob Wynn had asked Perry to appear, but Perry was initially negative about the idea. Perry had been most unhappy when Sammy withdrew from a live broadcast of the *Kraft Music Hall* at the last moment but was seen elsewhere on television enjoying himself. However, when he heard that Sammy had become seriously ill, Perry immediately offered to host. He did so for three consecutive years and didn't claim anything in expenses.[3]

After a three-year hiatus from Christmas specials, 1990 also saw a resurgence in Perry's Christmas activities. Rather than on television, though, Perry was now taking a show on the road across the United States – always concluding in Florida ahead of Christmas with his family. The concerts usually followed the pattern of around a third to half the duration of Perry's normal repertoire, followed by the remainder dedicated to Christmas music, and closing with 'Ave Maria'.

The concerts were very well received, often with capacity audiences. It was a period in which Perry and his audience were able to relive the glorious memories of his Christmas television specials. Speaking of a concert at Shea's Buffalo Theatre on 9 December 1990, Jim Santella of *The Buffalo News* said:

> From the moment he stepped out on the Shea's stage before a full orchestra, an intense love affair clearly was going on with the audience.... His smooth voice has lost little over the years. If there's one overriding quality to his music, it's a sincere delivery that transcends vocal quality and makes each song a brief and intimate shared moment with his audience.[4]

During a show at Westbury Music Fair in New York (a regular stop on Perry's concert tours), he recalled a visit to St. Francis' Hospital on Long Island (a charity he visited and supported for many years) where he encountered someone who looked troubled.

> This one little woman, she wasn't one of the sisters, but she was a nice little lady – and she was just lookin' at me and staring. You know when somebody starts to stare at you, how ya feel you wanna go and hide. And I picked her out, I said, 'Come here' and she looked kinda sad, then she looked happy.

And I finally said to her 'You got a problem?' She said 'No, no'. I said 'Well, what's your problem? What's wrong?' She says, 'Oh my god, I thought you were dead!'[5]

Perry had been visiting St. Francis' Hospital since 1950 to offer his help and was a major attraction of their Celebrity Golf Classic. 'Perry is the spirit of the tournament', remarked Dr Robert F. Vizza (president and chief executive of the hospital). 'You mention the St. Francis golf tournament and people say, "Oh, that's the one with Perry Como".[6] 'You do what you are able to do', said Perry of his long-lasting association with the cause. 'People say, "Why don't you just give them money and stay home?" That's not me. I want them to remember me, not the money'.[7]

Sister Jean, a Roman Catholic nun who had worked at St. Francis' Hospital since the early 1940s recalled how she and the other nuns attracted Perry's attention to their cause. 'We sent him a big photo of all the sisters lined up holding a sign that said "Perry, we need you." He's been helping us ever since.'[8] 'Who could turn down pleading nuns?' said Perry. Golf tournaments and dinners were Perry's closest interactions with the workings of the hospital, though. 'They asked me to view an operation once.' After the first incision I said, "I'll see you later."'[9]

Outside of his annual Christmas tour, the Como calendar continued to include numerous benefit performances and charity golf tournaments, including the Duke Children's Classic, which Perry had helped to establish in 1974. Perry worked tirelessly and elegantly at these events to raise smiles as well as money for the Duke University Pediatric Hospital in Durham, North Carolina – playing in the annual golf tournament and contributing to the celebrity shows. Another important part of Perry's involvement was his ability to invite famous friends along to the events, including Frank Sinatra, Bob Hope, Dinah Shore, Arnold Palmer and President Gerald Ford. Their first celebrity-amateur golf tournament was the idea of a group of Duke physicians led by Drs Jay Arena, John Griffith and Sam Katz. Perry was there from the start as both an enthusiastic supporter and chairman of the event.[10]

In June 1991, Perry was among many entertainers appearing at a benefit dinner at the Bel Age Hotel's Rooftop Atrium in Bel Air, West Hollywood,

California. The charity fundraiser was in support of singer John Gary, who was suffering from inoperable cancer. Among the stars in attendance were Esther Williams, Liza Minnelli, and Red Buttons. Johnny Mathis and Henry Mancini were among those performing at the charity concert that evening. Perry's songs included 'Where or When' and 'Look to Your Heart'. Press reports at the time indicated that Perry, Milton Berle, Mel Tormé and Jerry Vale had got stuck in an elevator. If walls could only talk!

While at the event, the television program *Hard Copy* took the opportunity to interview Perry and aired his profile in brief in a feature segment on 14 June. At one point, the 28-year-old reporter asked Perry how long he'd been married. Before offering an answer, he asked her how old she was. When she revealed her age, Perry paused with a comically vacant glance and said, 'As Bob Hope says, "I have a chicken that old!"'

Eddie Fisher was another attendee of the John Gary fundraiser. While there, he shared his thoughts with *Hard Copy* about one of his musical heroes. 'Any time, any moment that anyone can spend with Perry, has got to be a wonderful moment. He just exudes such charm and warmth'.

Concluding in a reflective mood, the interviewer asks Perry what he would consider the favourite part of his entire life. 'I couldn't really say one specific', said Perry. 'I really couldn't', but later quoted what he considered a great line from his friend Jackie Gleason. When an interviewer asked Jackie how he'd like to be remembered, he said, 'I just wanna be remembered'. The humble sentiment of the quote clearly struck a chord with Perry.[11]

1992 brought with it another milestone for Perry, his eightieth birthday year. It did not go unnoticed by the BBC, who broadcast a special two-hour radio programme, featuring an extensive interview with Chris Stuart, recorded two months earlier in Perry's hotel room in St. Louis, Missouri where Perry was again appearing at the *Sammy Davis Jr. Memorial Variety Club Telethon*.

Chris asked Perry if he had to work at his voice or whether it was a natural God-given instrument. Perry said that he owed everything to the man upstairs. He didn't have vocal lessons, nor did he do scales. If he felt good when he woke up, he could sing well.[12] Hearing the opening theme at the beginning of a show was enough to get him into the zone, and his opening number would be his warm-up. This isn't something that developed overnight though. Years of experience had resulted in this level of ease. Getting good sleep and eating well were his biggest keys, along with an occasional tea and honey.

'When I'm home, I eat a little more than I should, like all Italians,' said Perry in 1975. 'We Italians love salami and sausage and I tend to blow up a little. I used to be able to take off ten pounds "like that" – now, it doesn't come as easy. But, when I know I have to work, I go in training like a fighter would – I lay off all the pastas and lay off the drinking. I drink a little wine, but when I'm home I like a couple of shots of gin or scotch or whatever – so I kind of work up to a date.'[13]

'How can you get out of bed and put your tuxedo on and start to sing?' Nick Perito would ask Perry in bemusement. Mitchell Ayres shared Nick's puzzlement. They were both of the impression that he rehearsed at home, which Perry insisted he did not do. Even Perry's daughter Terri could verify this, saying that for a man who made a living singing, she never heard her dad practice. Ray Charles, however, got to the root of the matter. One day, Ray said to Perry, 'I have a theory that you think that you only have so many notes in your throat, and you aren't going to waste any of them'. Perry replied, 'That's possible'.[14] 'Why waste it?' was Perry's theory.

Soon after his birthday, Perry appeared at the *National Memorial Day Concert* in Washington, DC. The concert was broadcast live on PBS TV on the very wet evening of 24 May 1992. Perry opens his segment by singing a stunning version of his 1953 number one hit 'No Other Love'. The song was a fitting choice for the occasion. The melody was originally composed by Richard Rodgers for the NBC television series *Victory at Sea* which chronicled naval combat during the Second World War. Lyrics were later added by Oscar Hammerstein II and the song was included in the duo's musical *Me and Juliet*. Perry then moves into a performance of 'For Me and My Gal' (a major hit from the First World War) in which he invites the audience to sing along, then closes aptly with 'We'll Meet Again' bringing many rays of sunshine to the rainy spring weather.

In the spring of 1993, Perry made what would be his final tour of Japan. The tour was dubbed as a 'farewell tour', which amused Perry because he had never indicated it would be his final visit, although that did turn out to be the case. The three-concert tour included a performance at NHK Hall on 8 March, which was recorded for Japanese television. The concert is a wonderful example of professionalism, warmth and charisma – captured in widescreen and stereo. Nick Perito conducted the Japanese orchestra, and a group of female singers (including Cassie Miller) provided vocal support.

In his eighty-first year, Perry demonstrated with certainty that he had still got 'it'. Vocally, he is on excellent form – singing many of the staples of his concert repertoire. His interaction with the audience is, as always, sincere and heartfelt. Perry sings superb versions of 'I'm Sitting on Top of the World' in a medley with 'Hello, Young Lovers' followed by 'Where or When', 'And I Love You So', then later 'The Wind Beneath My Wings', 'That's What Friends Are For' and many more. During an encore, Perry sings 'It's Impossible' and closes the show with 'Always'. It was a fitting salute for the Como career, now in its sixtieth year.

During a backstage interview, Perry reflected on his age. 'I haven't changed too much. Oh, I lost some hair – getting a little shiny; but then, who cares? I don't sing with my hair!' adding later that a question he's been asked many times is 'You're 80 years old. How can you still sing?' to which Perry gestured upward and said, 'The man upstairs will tell me. The good Lord is gonna say to me one day – "You're finished! You can't sing anymore". Until he tells me that, I'll keep singing.'

Back home from Japan, the remainder of Perry's performance commitments for the year were charitable events. One such engagement was an appearance at the Roy Clark Golf Tournament in Palm Beach, Florida. Those in attendance included singer Don Cornell and his wife. At the end of his set, Perry and the audience sing 'Happy Birthday' to Roy, who was a few days away from his sixtieth birthday. Beaming from the gesture, Roy comes on to the stage and says, 'You wait till I tell my mother that Perry Como sang "Happy Birthday" to me!'[15]

In the autumn, RCA/BMG released a 3-CD boxed set titled *Yesterday & Today: A Celebration in Song* – a career-spanning box set of seventy-one songs, with an accompanying booklet – produced to commemorate what would have been Perry's fiftieth anniversary with the label. An attempt had been made to encourage Perry back to the recording studio, but it was generally agreed from both sides that Perry's most important recordings now lay in his back catalogue.

Perry's final major public appearance came the following January, when he travelled to Dublin, Ireland to record a Christmas concert special for PBS. Perry arrived in Dublin on 12 January, greeted by the Artane Boys Band playing 'Hey, Look Me Over'. It was a difficult concert for Perry, as he had developed a cold during the time since his arrival. Perry lived in Florida and to transport from there to Ireland in the depth of winter must have been quite a shock.

On 15 January, midway during his visit, he appeared as a guest on the television talk show *Kenny Live*, hosted by Pat Kenny. It was a poignant appearance. Perry spoke of the lovely reception he had on Grafton Street, his visit to a barbershop named Como (of no relation, as it turned out!) and sang a couple of impromptu songs with Nick Perito at the piano. Feeling conscious of his cold, Perry apologized to the audience but managed to deliver deeply moving renditions of 'How to Handle a Woman' and 'It Could Happen to You'.

The following Friday, 21 January 1994, *Perry Como's Irish Christmas* was presented at the Point Theatre in Dublin. The show got off to a fine start with Perry welcomed through the crowd to the sounds of 'Perito's March' inspired by 'MacNamara's Band' segueing into 'Consider Yourself'. As Perry arrives on stage he is in awe of the cheers and whistles from the 4000-strong audience. He then moves into a resplendent version of 'If I Could Almost Read Your Mind' accompanied with aplomb by the piano embellishments of Nick Perito. Following a rapturous applause, Perry welcomes his audience. In his opening remarks he says,

> Ireland is more than just a country, it's kind of a spirit of wit, humour, and heart. We've done many Christmas shows all over the world, and I've enjoyed a lot of 'em. In many countries they were wonderful, but I've never seen anything like I saw tonight – I could've gotten killed out there! But I would've died happily, believe me![16]

Despite a few lyric hiccups, the show started well, but then Perry began to experience some vocal difficulties, owing to his cold. Shortly after, Perry felt the need to stop, and in an emotional moment that followed, members of the audience could be heard singing 'And I Love You So' filling the auditorium in the absence of Perry's voice.

A 15-minute break was called while Perry composed himself, but so upset with his performance, he didn't want to go back on stage. After an hour, Perry had not returned, prompting one of Perry's guest stars, Irish singer Adele 'Twink' King, to beg for the audience's patience. She then headed backstage to assure

Perry shakes hands with some of his adoring fans at the Point Theatre in Dublin, Ireland. Photo courtesy of Liam Logan.

Perry that he was doing fine, which encouraged him to return to the stage. Before he did, though, he said a prayer saying, 'If you'll let me go out there and you'll let me finish, I'll never record anything again'. Perry went back on stage and not only got through the concert but turned it into a triumph. Perry sang 'And I Love You So' magnificently. The crowds cheered as he hit the high notes in each chorus! It's a wonderful, tear-jerking moment to see and hear. Perry proved against the odds that he could still do it! He never made another major personal appearance.

Christopher Logan was at the concert with his mother Molly, father Liam and sister Jennifer. He described the occasion as a treasured and momentous day – especially for his father, who had been a devoted fan of Perry's since he was a young man.

'There had been a number of opportunities that Dad could have seen Perry live in concert, over the years', said Christopher.

'Dad had given up his job to be a full-time carer for our mum Molly, who had become completely paralyzed with Motor Neuron disease, and to raise my sister Jennifer and I'. So, like Perry, he always put his family first. Perry was the soundtrack to our lives growing up and Dad found tremendous solace from his music. So, when the opportunity to see his hero live in Dublin arose, off we all went to the Point.'

> Because of Mum's severe disability we needed to get in there early with the wheelchair. Perry was doing some last-minute rehearsal in the theatre and saw us. He came down off the stage and with that radiant smile and those gentle dulcet tones could not have been more welcoming and kind. I'd never seen my dad starstruck before or since. There was his hero! 'I've been a fan all my life', Perry. Ever since 'Idle Gossip', said Dad. 'That's going back a bit!' Perry laughed. He embraced us all like old friends and held Mum's hand. He was worried that she might not be warm enough in the draughty auditorium. Jennifer was only 7 and I was 14. 'What great kids you have, Liam. Maybe I'll take them back with me!' Perry joked. He graciously posed for pictures with us all and then said he hoped we would enjoy the evening and off he went to get ready.

'We treasured the entire evening', continued Christopher. 'The waves of love for Perry were palpable from every corner of the huge auditorium, the moment he appeared. I still get goosebumps thinking of when he returned to the stage after speaking to Roselle on the phone – worried that he wasn't 100% and disappointing people – and then royally SOARED when he came to the chorus of "And I Love You So" and hit those sweet notes that only Mr. C. can hit!'

> We sent him a thank you letter enclosing a copy of the picture, sometime after the concert. We got the most wonderful letter back saying he was delighted to have met us and to have seen our faces popping up in close-up on the film of the concert – especially wee Jennifer during 'Toyland'. Enclosed with Perry's letter was a treasured signed photo personally inscribed to each of us, that was of course promptly framed and has had pride of place on the wall ever since.[17]

Sadly, Christopher and Jennifer's parents have now both died, but Christopher says that Perry's music continues to comfort and uplift both him and his sister.

Aside from fulfilling the promotional obligations of his *Irish Christmas* special, Perry began to wind down his professional activities. His last known

Liam Logan and his son Christopher with Perry inside the auditorium at the Point Theatre before Perry's Irish Christmas concert. Photo courtesy of Liam Logan.

public appearance was at the Duke Children's Classic in May 1995. With his trusted friend and colleague Nick Perito conducting, Perry (who had just celebrated his 83rd birthday) gave a final performance of four songs, pausing between numbers to engage in some dialogue with Nick. Preceding his performance were members of the cast of the revue *Forever Plaid* who tell and sing their 'Tribute to Mr. C'. and present Perry with a yellow sweater.

Perry opens in Como custom with a powerful performance of 'Where or When'. After finishing his opening number, with his new golden garment in hand, he kids, 'Anybody wanna buy a sweater?' As Nick noodles on the piano, hinting at 'And I Love You So' Perry passes the sweater to him and, to the delight of the audience, sings the opening line directly to Nick, then proceeds into a deeply touching performance of the song.

Perry then takes some time to speak with the audience, 'I wanna just tell ya, I'm happy to be here. I've been here for 22 years. I don't know if I'll make 22 more, but I'll get close!' he says.[18] After the applause settles, Perry says 'I think I see my girl here', referring to Roselle who is in the audience. Once he finds her in the low-lit auditorium, he tells the audience 'That's my baby', and Roselle receives a round of applause, during which she stands up to give a wave. 'Boy, I gonna catch hell for that!' jokes Perry.

Nick asks Perry how long he and Roselle have been married. Perry pauses for a sip of water and then responds, 'I can't count that high!' adding 'No, we've been together for a long time. I think – 60 years, honey, 50 years?' he asks Roselle. 'I forgot!' says Perry, then adds 'Oh will I get hell for that!'. 'Now you're in trouble!' calls Nick. The audience loves the whole interaction. What follows is a beautiful version of 'The Wind Beneath My Wings' which Perry dedicates to Roselle and delivers as always with great emotion and sensitivity.

Closing out with his swinging version of 'Almost Like Being in Love', Perry concluded a concert in miniature which demonstrated class and heart in equal measure. Nick's superb leading of the orchestra and loving interactions with Perry combine for what was a touching final collaboration between two dear friends. Perry's distinctive warmth and sincerity were abundantly clear throughout. It was the perfect swansong.

Perry was unable to attend the Duke Children's Classic in 1996, so Pat Boone acted as host; but in their absence, Perry and Roselle sent a gift of $100,000 to the charity. Over the following two years, Perry gradually settled into retirement. His time was spent golfing with buddies and fishing. Perry officially retired in 1998. During the process of closing his office in New York, he ensured that his staff could financially afford to retire – this included his secretary Vera Hamilton and his manager Mickey Glass. It was Perry's wish that they should be able to retire with him and be free from any future working obligation with respect to his career and legacy. It was a noble, final gesture from someone who had brought so much joy and happiness to so many people.

Perry and Roselle celebrated their sixty-fifth wedding anniversary that same year. It was a quiet celebration with close family. The *Pittsburgh Post-Gazette* reported on the occasion. 'He's still as handsome as ever', Roselle said, adding that there is no secret to their marriage (one of the longest in show business). 'It's simply a gift from God. When you make your wedding vows as a commitment to each other and to God, you will keep them'.[19] Just two weeks later, Roselle died at the age of eighty-six. Perry was heartbroken. Roselle had been the love and stay of his life from before he turned professional through his entire career. She'd been a part of all his major career moves and the one ever-constant presence in his life.

Before her death, Roselle had been instrumental in getting a tribute to Perry in his hometown of Canonsburg, Pennsylvania, and on 15 May 1999, a larger-than-life statue was unveiled. Perry was unable to attend, but many friends, family and colleagues were there to pay tribute. The statue, which is situated outside the Canonsburg Borough Building, is mounted on a marble plinth with the inscription 'To This Place God Has Brought Me'.[20] A sound system connected to the borough building pipes out Perry Como's music for the enjoyment of visitors and passers-by. Surrounding the statue are square and rectangular slabs sponsored by family, fans and colleagues, and a bench positioned opposite is adorned with a dedication by Perry's youngest son reading, 'Dad: Because you've always been "Just a man" you have my eternal respect and love. David'.

Perry winced at the idea of a statue of himself back in 1955. Recalling the occasion in 1962, Bernie Miller wrote:

Some years ago when Perry Como was about to inaugurate his full-hour network TV program, a meeting on how to announce and promote the new show was held high in one of Manhattan's Rockefeller Center towers. A bright-eyed and bushy-tailed young press agent came up with a suggestion that a 'National Perry Como Day' be declared. When word of this reached Perry, he said, 'Wait a minute. This is not George Washington; this is just Perry Como. Don't go putting up statues of Como in the parks.' 'Just Perry Como' is the modest self-appraisal of the man. But in another sense this quiet human being has erected statues of himself in every household in America and in countries around the world. For more years than he himself cares to remember, he has been rated as one of the great singing personalities of all time.[21]

On 12 May 2001, Perry Como died in his sleep, just days before his 89th birthday. In tribute to Perry, a *Billboard* Magazine memorial read, 'Perry Como – 50 years of music and a life well lived. An example to all'.

The Perry Como statue in Canonsburg, Pennsylvania. Author's photo.

In the years since his death, Perry's music has enjoyed several resurgences. His songs have been featured widely in television advertising, including campaigns for McDonalds and Nike. In the UK, several hits compilations have reached the charts along with a re-issue of the single 'It's Beginning to Look Like Christmas', which, courtesy of an advert for British high street chain Argos, brought awareness of the Como catalogue to a new generation. In the United States, Perry hit the top of the ringtone charts in 2006 with his 1946 recording of 'Jingle Bells'. He also simultaneously reached the No. 2 spot with his recording of 'Here We Come A-Carolling / We Wish You a Merry Christmas' from 1959.

The Perry Como legacy is a vast one, worthy of appreciation and representation in every music collection. His career, which spanned seven decades, exuded style, class and variety. His work on radio and television was pioneering and prolific; and in the recording studio he brought a wealth of beauty and musicianship together to create some of the finest recordings of the twentieth century. He was able to bring deep emotion and joy to a song without exaggerated affectation, and as a British fan once observed, 'he knows exactly how to handle a song, when to let it go, when to hold it down – he's just a complete professional'.[22]

Ray Charles considered Perry to be the most underrated artist of his generation. Perry would have been quite happy for it to be that way. He purposely declined to indulge in any kind of intentional self-flattery. 'Give yourself a chance to listen to a wonderful singer . . . and a nice man', said Ray. Humble as he was, Perry insisted that apart from his singing, he was 'a perfectly ordinary fellow', which Benny Green likened to saying 'apart from his career Napoleon Bonaparte was a perfectly ordinary Frenchman'. Green added that Perry's modesty was 'utterly genuine' and he was 'not one of those bores who wait to be cajoled into backing modestly into the limelight'.[23]

Many times, people would ask Nick Perito what Perry was really like, and Nick referred to a phrase coined by Flip Wilson 'What you see is what you get'.

'The audiences loved him', said Nick 'because he was the guy next door – he was Perry! He wasn't trying to impress you with anything. When he sang, he wasn't trying to impress you either – he sang from his heart – and that's what made him so special', later adding, 'He was a joy. A guy's guy, a gal's guy, an honest human being, a great talent. What else could you ask for?'[24]

A paperweight souvenir from the Perry Como statue dedication. Author's photo.

Perry's desire for simplicity and a lack of drama saw him at times ridiculed for not conforming to the so-called expectations of a superstar, but this was precisely Perry's USP (Unique Selling Point). He achieved worldwide fame on his own terms and by being himself in an industry where many would sell their souls for a taste of his success. His calm demeanour was the result of being well prepared and adjusted, personally and professionally. Yet, this at times was assumed to equate to a matter of blandness.

'This bland thing', Como reflected in 1961, 'Call it serenity. Possibly I was born with it ... my mother and father ... were very, very sound people. I could never be the man my father was. He made 35 bucks a week and he had 13 kids. He couldn't pay his bills but everybody went along with him on that 35 ... What people don't seem to see sometimes, is everything turned out right for me. I pushed through high school because I had work to do. I had my own barbershop in Canonsburg, Pa., before I was out of my teens ... and I was older than my years. At 21 I was married and had two families to take care of. I gave up band singing and I was going to stick with the shop. But I got talked into coming to New York and that turned out right. First radio and then the 15-minute show on TV and finally the hour show. I was scared to death every time, but they all turned out right. There's Roselle, my wife . . . she's a wonderful stabilizer – that's a very good word, maybe too big of a word for me – and that's turned out right. And the kids. I've had a very, very easy life,' Como said. 'It's not been a dramatic thing, but I've had a lot of fun. I'm no traveler at heart. We've all stayed together. I'm not antisocial, but we don't see a lot of people. All I want is to get home, put on a pair of old pants – the same pair all the time and when I take 'em off I don't have to hang 'em up, they stand up – throw a piece of meat on the fire, play with the kids, watch that box for a while and go to bed. I've had things so good, I've just never really had to worry. It's a hell of a feeling. If that's bland, then I'm bland. And pretty damned glad of it, at that'.[25]

Perry Como has touched the lives of millions around the world, and his music deserves to be remembered and held in the highest regard for the enjoyment of future generations. The world of music is all the richer for Perry's contributions to it. He brought joy to millions and continues to do so – the perfect antidote to an ever-hurried world. May his legacy live on for as long as there are people who appreciate wonderful music, beautifully sung – hopefully, till the end of time.

Quintessential Como
Recommended Christmas listening 1946–82

Winter Wonderland ★
m Felix Bernard, w Dick Smith, 1934
1 Aug 1946 - PC Sings
Merry Christmas Music LPM-1243

I'll Be Home for Christmas
mw Kim Gannon, Walter Kent
and Buck Ram, 1943
6 Aug 1946 - PC Sings
Merry Christmas Music LPM-1243

That Christmas Feeling
mw Bennie Benjamin
and George Weiss, 1946
6 Aug 1946 - PC Sings
Merry Christmas Music LPM-1243

Silent Night ★
m Franz Xaver Gruber, 1818,
w Joseph Mohr, 1816
20 Aug 1946 - PC Sings
Merry Christmas Music LPM-1243
PC Christmas in Austria - 13 Dec 1976
[in German]

O, Come All Ye Faithful (Adeste fideles) ★
mw Traditional (Lat.), 1751,
w Frederick Oakeley (Eng. transl.), 1841
20 Aug 1946 - PC Sings
Merry Christmas Music LPM-1243

O, Little Town of Bethlehem ★
m Lewis Redner, w Phillips Brooks, 1868
20 Aug 1946 - PC Sings
Merry Christmas Music P-161 (78)

Jingle Bells ★
mw James Lord Pierpont, 1857
22 Aug 1946 - PC Sings
Merry Christmas Music LPM-1243

Bless This House ★
mw May Brahe (under pseud.
May H. Morgan) and Helen Taylor, 1927
26–29 Jun 1950 - I Believe LPM-1172
PC Christmas in the Holy Land - 13 Dec 1980

There Is No Christmas Like a Home Christmas ★
m Mickey J. Addy, w Carl Sigman, 1950
15 Aug 1950 - 47-3933

The Christmas Symphony
mw Phil Perry, Joe Candullo
and Charles Faso Reade, 1950
15 Aug 1950 - 47-3933

It's Beginning to Look Like Christmas ★
with The Fontane Sisters
mw Meredith Willson, 1951
18 Sep 1951 - 47-4314

C-H-R-I-S-T-M-A-S
m Eddy Arnold, w Jenny Lou Carson, 1949
5 May 1953 - PC Sings
Merry Christmas Music LPM-1243

Frosty the Snowman
mw Steve Nelson and Jack Rollins, 1950
21 May 1953 - PC Sings
Merry Christmas Music LPM-1243

I Saw Mommy Kissing Santa Claus
mw Tommie Connor, 1952
21 May 1953 - PC Sings
Christmas Music for Kiddies WBY-42

Rudolph the Red-Nosed Reindeer
mw Johnny Marks, 1949
21 May 1953 - PC Sings
Merry Christmas Music LPM-1243

The Twelve Days of Christmas
mw Traditional, c. 1780,
w Frederic Austin (adapt.), 1909
26 May 1953 - PC Sings
Merry Christmas Music LPM-1243
PC Early American Christmas - 13 Dec 1978

Joy to the World ★
m George Frideric Handel (att.), 1742,
m Lowell Mason (arr.), 1848,
w Isaac Watts, 1719
26 May 1953 - PC Sings
Merry Christmas Music LPM-1243
PC NBC - 21 Dec 1957
[with The McGuire Sisters]

'Twas the Night Before Christmas
m Ray Charles, 1953,
w Clement Clarke Moore, 1823
22 Jun 1953 - PC Sings
Merry Christmas Music LPM-1243

Here We Come A-Carolling /
We Wish You a Merry Christmas ★
mw Traditional, c. pre-1850 /
mw Traditional, c. 16th Century
13 Jul 1959 - Season's Greetings from PC
LSP-2066

The Story of the First Christmas ★
m Mitchell Ayres (arr.),
w John A. Richards (adapt.), 1950
13 Jul 1959 - Season's Greetings from PC
LSP-2066

Santa Claus Is Comin' to Town ★
mw Haven Gillespie and J. Fred Coots, 1934
14 Jul 1959 - Season's Greetings from PC
LSP-2066

God Rest Ye Merry, Gentlemen ★
m Samuel Wesley, 1855,
w Anonymous, c. 1650s
14 Jul 1959 - Season's Greetings from PC
LSP-2066

(There's No Place Like)
Home for the Holidays ★
m Robert Allen, w Al Stillman, 1954
15 Jul 1959 - Season's Greetings from PC
LSP-2066

White Christmas ★
mw Irving Berlin, 1942
From the film Holiday Inn.
15 Jul 1959 - Season's Greetings from PC LSP-2066 / PC French Canadian Christmas - 12 Dec 1981 [with André Gagnon, piano]

**The Christmas Song
(Merry Christmas to You)** ★
m Mel Tormé, w Robert Wells, 1946
15 Jul 1959 - Season's Greetings from PC LSP-2066

The Lord's Prayer ★
m Albert Hay Malotte, 1935,
w Traditional, c. AD 150
26 Oct 1959 - The Lord's Prayer CAS-2299 (e)

Love Is a Christmas Rose
mw Earl Shuman and Leon Carr, 1967
24 Aug 1967 - 47-9367

Christmas Bells
mw Ray Stevens, 1967
24 Aug 1967 - 47-9367

Have Yourself a Merry Little Christmas
mw Hugh Martin and Ralph Blane, 1944
From the film Meet Me in St. Louis.
1 Aug 1968 - The PC Christmas Album LSP-4016 / PC Christmas in New York - 17 Dec 1983

Silver Bells
mw Jay Livingston and Ray Evans, 1951
From the film The Lemon Drop Kid.
1 Aug 1968 - The PC Christmas Album LSP-4016 / The Hollywood Palace - 20 Dec 1969 [with Diahann Carroll]

Ave Maria ★
m Franz Schubert, 1825, w Traditional,
c. AD 80–90, w Pope Pius V (add.), 1568
1 Aug 1968 - The PC Christmas Album LSP-4016

The First Noel
mw Traditional, c. 16th Century
1 Aug 1968 - The PC Christmas Album LSP-4016

Hark! The Herald Angels Sing
m Felix Mendelssohn, 1840,
w Charles Wesley, 1739,
w George Whitefield (adapt.), 1758
1 Aug 1968 - The PC Christmas Album LSP-4016

The Little Drummer Boy
mw Katherine Davis, Henry Onerati and Harry Simeone, 1958
3 Aug 1968 - The PC Christmas Album LSP-4016

Do You Hear What I Hear?
mw Noël Regney and Gloria Shayne, 1962
3 Aug 1968 - The PC Christmas Album LSP-4016

O Holy Night ★
m Adolphe Adam, 1847, w Placide
Cappeau (Fr.), 1843, w John Sullivan
Dwight (Eng. adapt.), 1855
3 Aug 1968 - The PC Christmas Album
LSP-4016

Christmas Eve
m Gerard Andre Biesel,
w Ray Charles, 1968
6 Aug 1968 - The PC Christmas Album
LSP-4016

Toyland
m Victor Herbert, w Glen MacDonough, 1903
From the musical Babes in Toyland.
6 Aug 1968 - The PC Christmas Album
LSP-4016

Christ Is Born ★
mw Domenico Bartolucci (Lat.), 1964,
w Ray Charles (Eng.), 1968
6 Aug 1968 - The PC Christmas Album
LSP-4016

Christmas Dream
m Andrew Lloyd Webber, w Tim Rice
(Eng.) and André Heller (Ger.), 1974
From the film The Odessa File.
7 Aug 1974 - I Wish It Could Be
Christmas Forever AYL1-4526

I Wish It Could Be Christmas Forever
m Nick Perito, w Richard Matheson, 1981
From the television special
Perry Como's French Canadian Christmas.
Oct 1981 - I Wish It Could
Be Christmas Forever AYL1-4526
PC French Canadian Christmas -
12 Dec 1981

Appendix

The Songs He Loved and More

Perry Como recordings and performances from the Great American Songbook and beyond

A

Abide with Me •
m William Henry Monk, 1861,
w Henry Francis Lyte, 1847
29 Sep 1953 - I Believe LPM-1172

Act of Contrition •
m Joseph J. Leahy, 1953,
w Traditional, 1888
29 Sep 1953 - I Believe LPM-1172

An Affair to Remember (Our Love Affair)
m Harry Warren, w Harold Adamson and Leo McCarey, 1957
From the film An Affair to Remember.
PC NBC - 28 Feb 1959

Ah! Sweet Mystery of Life
m Victor Herbert,
w Rida Johnson Young, 1910
From the musical Naughty Marietta.
CSC - 1 Feb 1946

Ain't Misbehavin' •* ★
m Fats Waller and Harry Brooks,
w Andy Razaf, 1929
From the revue Hot Chocolates.
20 Jan 1955 - So Smooth XQAM-1078

Ain't We Got Fun?
m Richard A. Whiting, w Gus Kahn and Raymond B. Egan, 1921
PC NBC - 6 Oct 1956 [with Kathryn Grayson]

Alexander's Ragtime Band ★
mw Irving Berlin, 1911
PC KMH - 17 Feb 1960

All I Do Is Dream of You •
*m Nacio Herb Brown, w Arthur
Freed, 1934
From the film Sadie McKee.
17 May 1961 - Sing to Me, Mr. C.
LSP-2390*

All I Have to Do Is Dream
*mw Boudleaux Bryant, 1958
PC NBC - 31 May 1958 [with Patti Page]*

All of Me
*mw Seymour Simons
and Gerald Marks, 1931
PC KMH - 6 Apr 1960*

All of My Life
*mw Irving Berlin, 1944
CSC - 24 May 1945*

All or Nothing at All ★
*mw Jack Lawrence and Arthur
Altman, 1940
CPPC - 1943 / PC NBC - 4 May 1957*

All the Things You Are
*m Jerome Kern,
w Oscar Hammerstein II, 1939
From the musical Very Warm for May.
PC NBC - 25 May 1957*

All the Way
*m Jimmy Van Heusen, w Sammy
Cahn, 1957
From the film The Joker Is Wild.
PC NBC - 7 Dec 1957 [blooper]*

All Through the Night •
*m Traditional, 1784,
w John Ceiriog Hughes (Wel.), 1873,
w Harold Boulton (Eng.), 1884
18 Jun 1958 - When You Come
to the End of the Day LSP-1885*

All-American Girl
*mw Al Lewis, 1932
PC NBC - 7 Dec 1957*

Allegheny Moon
*mw Al Hoffman and Dick Manning, 1956
PC NBC - 22 Sep 1956*

Aloha Oe (Farewell to Thee)
*mw HM Queen Lili'uokalani, 1878
PC KMH - 14 Mar 1962*

Alone Together
*m Arthur Schwartz, w Howard Dietz, 1932
From the musical Flying Colours.
PC KMH - 18 Jan 1961 & 23 Jan 1963*

Along the Navajo Trail
*mw Dick Charles, Eddie DeLange
and Larry Markes, 1942
PC KMH - 28 Mar 1962*

Always ★
*mw Irving Berlin, 1925
PC NBC - 31 Jan 1959*

America the Beautiful
m Samuel Augustus Ward, 1892,
w Katharine Lee Bates, 1910
PC Summer of '74 - 12 Sep 1974

And Roses and Roses ●
mw Dorival Caymmi (Port.), 1964,
w Ray Gilbert (Eng.), 1965
25 Feb 1966 - Lightly Latin LSP-3552

Anema e core ●
m Salve d'Esposito, w Tito
Manlio (Nea.), 1950, w Mann Curtis
and Harry Akst (Eng.), 1954
17 May 1966 - PC in Italy LSP-3608

Angel
m Harry Warren, w Arthur Freed, 1945
From the film Yolanda and the Thief.
CSC - 5 Dec 1945

Angry ● ★
m Henry Brunies, Jules Cassard
and Merritt Brunies, w Dudley Mecum, 1925
12 Feb 1957 - We Get Letters LPM-1463
PC KMH - 6 Jan 1960

Another Op'nin', Another Show
mw Cole Porter, 1949
From the musical Kiss Me Kate.
PC NBC - 10 Nov 1956

Any Old Time (I'm Feeling Blue)
m Fud Livingston and Irving Melsher,
w Jack Wolf, 1945
CSC - 27 Apr 1945

Anything You Can Do
mw Irving Berlin, 1946
From the musical Annie Get Your Gun.
PC NBC - 8 Jun 1957 [with Ethel Merman]

April in Paris ★
m Vernon Duke, w E. Y. Harburg, 1932
From the musical Walk a Little Faster.
PC NBC - 12 Apr 1958

April Love
m Sammy Fain,
w Paul Francis Webster, 1957
From the film April Love.
PC NBC - 9 Nov 1957

Are These Really Mine?
mw Sunny Skylar, David Saxon
and Robert Cook, 1945
CSC - 4 Jan 1946

Aren't You Glad You're You?
m Jimmy Van Heusen, w Johnny
Burke, 1945
From the film The Bells of St. Mary's.
CSC - 2 Jan 1946

Around the World
m Victor Young, w Harold
Adamson, 1956
The theme from the film
Around the World in 80 Days.
PC NBC - 14 Sep 1957

**Arrivederci Roma
(Goodbye to Rome)** •
m Renato Rascel, w Pietro Garinei
and Sandro Giovannini (It.), 1954,
w Carl Sigman (Eng.), 1955
18 May 1966 - PC in Italy LSP-3608
PC NBC - 4 Oct 1958

As Time Goes By •
mw Herman Hupfeld, 1931
From the musical Everybody's Welcome.
20 Jan 1955 - So Smooth LPM-1085

At Last
m Harry Warren, w Mack Gordon, 1942
From the film Orchestra Wives.
PC CBS - 2 May 1952

At the Balalaika
m George Posford, w Eric Maschwitz,
1936, w Robert Wright and George
Forrest (under pseud. Chet Forrest) (new
lyric), 1939
From the film Balalaika.
BB - 28 Jan 1940

Aubrey •
mw David Gates, 1972
27 Mar 1973 - And I Love You So
APL1-0100

Auld Lang Syne ★
m Traditional, 1799, w Robert
Burns, 1788
PC KMH - 30 Dec 1959

Autumn in New York ★
mw Vernon Duke, 1934
From the revue Thumbs Up!
PC NBC - 5 Oct 1957 / PC KMH - 5
Oct 1960

Autumn Leaves ★
m Joseph Kosma, w Jacques Prévert
(Fr.), 1946, w Johnny Mercer (Eng.), 1950
PC NBC - 28 Sep 1957 / PC KMH - 1
Nov 1961

B

Back in Your Own Back Yard •* ★
mw Dave Dreyer, Al Jolson
and Billy Rose, 1928
17 May 1961
PC NBC - 21 Mar 1959 [blooper]

Baia •
mw Ary Barroso (Port.), 1939,
w Ray Gilbert (Eng.), 1944
From the animated film
The Three Caballeros.
25 Feb 1966 - Lightly Latin LSP-3552

Ballerina
mw Bob Russell and Carl Sigman, 1947
CSC - 17 Dec 1947

Bally Mena
m Traditional, mw Robert De Cormier
and Irving Burgie, 1961
PC Bahamas Holiday - 21 May 1980
[with Toni Tennille]

The Banana Boat Song
mw Traditional, c. 1900s, mw Alan Arkin,
Bob Carey and Erik Darling, 1957
PC NBC - 26 Jan 1957

Barney Google
mw Billy Rose and Con Conrad, 1923
PC NBC - 21 Mar 1959

Basin Street Blues
mw Spencer Williams, 1928
PC KMH - 15 Nov 1961
PC Spring in New Orleans - 7 Apr 1976

Be a Clown
mw Cole Porter, 1948
From the film The Pirate.
PC KMH - 4 May 1960 [with guests]

Be My Love
m Nicholas Brodszky, w Sammy
Cahn, 1950
From the film The Toast of New Orleans.
PC KMH - 10 Feb 1960

Be the Good Lord Willing (I'll See You in the Morning)
mw Jack Fulton, 1949
CSC TV - 27 Nov 1949

Beady Eyed Buzzard •
mw Eddie Snyder and Richard
Ahlert, 1965
23 Jun 1965 - Seattle LSP-4183

Beats There a Heart So True •
mw Noel Sherman and Jack Keller, 1958
5 Jun 1958 - Love Makes the World
Go 'Round CAS-805 (e)

Beautiful Dreamer
mw Stephen Foster, posth. 1864
PC KMH - 25 Oct 1961

Beautiful Hawaii
mw Randy Farden, 1967
PC Hawaiian Holiday - 22 Feb 1976
[with Petula Clark]

Beautiful Noise •
mw Neil Diamond, 1976
29–31 Jul 1980 (Live) - PC Live on
Tour AQL1-3826

Before the Parade Passes By
mw Jerry Herman, 1964
From the musical Hello, Dolly!
The PC Sunshine Show - 10 Apr 1974
[with guests]

Behind Closed Doors •
mw Kenny O'Dell, 1973
1 May 1974 - Perry CPL1-0585

Bella Bella Sue ●*
mw Barry Parker, Anthony Roberto
and Fran Smith (aka Franco Riccio), 1958
17 Dec 1958 - Juke Box Baby BFX 15306

The Bells of St. Mary's ●*
m A. Emmett Adams, w Douglas
Furber, 1917
14 Jun 1962 - A PC Christmas
0786368041-2

Beloved
m Joe Sanders, w Gus Kahn, 1928
CSC - 27 Jun 1945

**The Best Thing for You
(Would Be Me)** ●
mw Irving Berlin, 1950
From the musical Call Me Madam.
31 Aug 1950 - 47-3922

The Best Things in Life Are Free
m Ray Henderson, w B. G. DeSylva
and Lew Brown, 1927
From the musical Good News.
CSC - 19 Jan 1948

Better Luck Next Time ●
mw Irving Berlin, 1948
From the film Easter Parade.
16 Oct 1947 - 20-2888

Between the Devil and the Deep Blue Sea ●
m Harold Arlen, w Ted Koehler, 1931
From the revue Rhyth-mania.
5 Mar 1958 - Saturday Night with Mr. C.
LSP-1971

Beyond the Sea
mw Charles Trenet (Fr.), 1945,
w Jack Lawrence (Eng.), 1947
PC KMH - 10 Feb 1960

**Beyond Tomorrow
(Love Theme from *Serpico*)** ●
mw Mikis Theodorakis and Larry Kusik, 1973
The theme from the film Serpico.
4 Jan 1974 - Perry CPL1-0585

The Birth of the Blues ● ★
m Ray Henderson, w B. G. DeSylva
and Lew Brown, 1926
From the revue George White's
Scandals of 1926.
11 Mar 1958 - Saturday Night with Mr. C.
LSP-1971

Black Moonlight ● ★
mw Arthur Johnston and Sam Coslow, 1933
From the film Too Much Harmony.
5 Dec 1950 - TV Favourites LPM-3013 (10")

Blame It on the Bossa Nova
mw Cynthia Weil and Barry Mann, 1962
PC KMH - 6 Feb 1963

Blue Hawaii
m Ralph Rainger, w Leo Robin, 1937
From the film Waikiki Wedding.
PC KMH - 2 Jan 1963

The Blue Tail Fly (Jimmy Crack Corn)
mw Traditional, c. 1840s
PC KMH - 10 Feb 1960
[with Raymond Massey]

Blueberry Hill
mw Al Lewis, Larry Stock
and Vincent Rose, 1940
BB - 11 Aug 1940

Brazil
mw Ary Barroso (Port.), 1939,
w Bob Russell (Eng.), 1942
PC NBC - 9 Nov 1957

Breezin' Along with the Breeze ● ★
mw Haven Gillespie, Seymour Simons
and Richard A. Whiting, 1926
25 Jan 1955 - So Smooth LPM-1085

Bridge Over Troubled Water ●
mw Paul Simon, 1970
30 Apr 1971 - I Think of You LSP-4539

Brother, Can You Spare a Dime?
m Jay Gorney, w E. Y. Harburg, 1932
From the revue Americana.
PC NBC - 25 Apr 1959

Bummin' Around ●*
mw Pete Graves, 1953
22 Jun 1965 - Yesterday & Today - A
Celebration in Song 0786366098-2

Buongiorno Teresa ●
mw Dick Manning and Jimmy Lytell, 1968
7 Oct 1968 - Seattle LSP-4183

But Beautiful ● ★
m Jimmy Van Heusen, w Johnny Burke, 1947
From the film Road to Rio.
29-31 Jul 1980 (Live) - PC Live on Tour
AQL1-3826 / PC KMH - 5 Oct 1960

Button Up Your Overcoat
m Ray Henderson, w B. G. DeSylva
and Lew Brown, 1929
From the musical Follow Thru.
PC NBC - 13 Dec 1958

Buttons and Bows
mw Jay Livingston and Ray Evans, 1948
From the film Paleface.
CSC - 27 Dec 1948
[with The Fontane Sisters]

By the Light of the Silvery Moon ★
m Gus Edwards, w Edward Madden, 1909
The American Veterans Committee
Salutes Al Jolson - 1 Oct 1946
PC NBC - 7 Jun 1958 [with Eydie Gormé]

C

Call Me Irresponsible
m Jimmy Van Heusen, w Sammy
Cahn, 1963
From the film Papa's Delicate Condition.
PC KMH - 21 May 1964

The Call of the Canyon
mw Billy Hill, 1940
BB - 20 Oct 1940

**Can You Look Me in the Eyes
(and Say We're Thru)**
m Judd McMichael, w Paul Herrick, 1947
CSC - 17 Sep 1947

Canadian Sunset
m Eddie Heywood, w Norman Gimbel, 1956
PC KMH - 22 May 1967
[with Monique Leyrac
and Oscar Peterson, piano]

Can't We Talk It Over?
m Victor Young, w Ned Washington, 1931
PC KMH - 2 Nov 1960

Carolina Moon •
m Joe Burke, w Benny Davis, 1928
10 Jul 1947 - A Sentimental Date with PC
LPM-1177

Carry On, Brother, Carry On
mw Bob Carroll and Howard
Phillips, 1945
CSC - 24 Jan 1945

C'est magnifique
mw Cole Porter, 1953
From the musical Can-Can.
PC KMH - 30 Mar 1960
PC French Canadian Christmas -
12 Dec 1981 [with Diane Tell]

C'est si bon
m Henri Betti, w André Hornez
(Fr.), 1948, w Jerry Seelen (Eng.), 1950
PC NBC - 16 Mar 1960 [with Genevieve]
PC French Canadian Christmas -
12 Dec 1981 [with Diane Tell]

Chances Are
m Robert Allen, w Al Stillman, 1957
PC NBC - 30 Nov 1957

Changing Partners
m Larry Coleman, w Joe Darion, 1953
PC CBS - 18 Jan 1954

Chanson d'amour (Song of Love)
mw Wayne Shanklin, 1958
PC NBC - 26 Apr 1958

Chantez, Chantez
m Irving Fields, w Albert Gamse, 1957
PC NBC - 23 Feb 1957

Chattanooga Choo Choo
m Harry Warren, w Mack Gordon, 1941
From the film Sun Valley Serenade.
PC NBC - 26 Jan 1957

Cheek to Cheek
mw Irving Berlin, 1935
From the film Top Hat.
PC KMH - 11 May 1960

Cherry Pink and Apple Blossom White
m Louis Guglielmi (Louiguy),
w Jacques Larue (Fr.), 1950,
w Mack David (Eng.), 1951
PC KMH - 29 Mar 1961 [with
Dorothy Collins]

Chicago
mw Fred Fisher, 1922
PC NBC - 14 Dec 1957

Chlo-e (Song of the Swamp)
m Charles N. Daniels (under
pseud. Neil Morét), w Gus Kahn, 1927
CSC - 24 Jan 1945

Christmas Is a Birthday
mw Dick Manning
and Gregory Paul Deutsch, 1964
PC KMH - 20 Dec 1965 [with
Roberta Peters]

Christmas Is My Time of Year
mw Traditional (Ger.), c. 1820,
w Ray Charles (adapt. and Eng.), 1976
From the television special
Perry Como's Christmas in Austria.
PC Christmas in Austria - 13 Dec 1976

Cielito lindo (I yi yi yi amigo)
mw Quirino Mendoza y Cortés
(Sp.), 1882, mw John Redmond
and James Cavanaugh (Eng.), 1941
PC NBC - 7 Feb 1959
[with The Mills Brothers]

The Cinderella Waltz
m Al Mack, w Johnny Mercer, 1961
PC NBC - 28 Mar 1959

Cindy, Oh Cindy
mw Traditional, 1942,
mw Bob Barron and Burt Long, 1956
PC NBC - 17 Nov 1956

The City of Tradition
mw Ray Charles, 1980
From the television special
Perry Como's Christmas in the Holy Land.
PC Christmas in the Holy Land - 13 Dec 1980 [with Ilanit]

Climb Ev'ry Mountain
m Richard Rodgers,
w Oscar Hammerstein II, 1959
From the musical The Sound of Music.
PC KMH - 11 Oct 1961

Close as Pages in a Book
m Sigmund Romberg, w Dorothy
Fields, 1945
From the musical Up in Central Park.
CSC - 16 Apr 1945

Close to You
mw Al Hoffman, Jerry Livingston
and Carl Lampl, 1943
CPPC - Jul 1943

Come Closer to Me (Acércate más)
m Osvaldo Farres (Sp.), 1940,
w Al Stewart (Eng.), 1945
From the film Easy to Wed.
CSC - 11 Feb 1946

Come to Me, Bend to Me
m Frederick Loewe, w Alan Jay
Lerner, 1947
From the musical Brigadoon.
PC KMH - 9 Mar 1960

Comin' In on a Wing and a Prayer
m Jimmy McHugh, w Harold
Adamson, 1943
CPPC - 29 Apr 1943

Cominciamo ad amarci ●
m Gino Mescoli, w Vito Pallavicini, 1965
19 May 1966 - PC in Italy LSP-3608

Coo Coo Roo Coo Coo Paloma ●
mw Tomás Méndez (Sp.), 1954,
w Pat Valando and
Ronnie Carson (Eng.), 1959
29 Dec 1965 - Lightly Latin LSP-3552

Country Is
mw Tom T. Hall, 1974
Como Country: Perry and His Nashville
Friends - 17 Feb 1975 [with guests]

Country Style
m Jimmy Van Heusen, w Johnny Burke, 1947
From the film Welcome Stranger.
PC NBC - 4 Jan 1958 [with Jimmy Dean]

Crying in the Chapel
mw Artie Glenn, 1953
PC CBS - 9 Sep 1953

Cuddle Up a Little Closer
m Karl Hoschna, w Otto Harbach, 1908
From the musical The Three Twins.
PC KMH - 6 Feb 1963

Cynthia's in Love
m Earl Gish and Billy White,
w Jack Owens, 1946
CSC - 6 Mar 1946

D

Dance Only with Me •
m Jule Styne, w Betty Comden
and Adolph Green, 1958
From the musical Say, Darling.
4 Mar 1958 - Love Makes the World
Go 'Round CAS-805 (e)

Dancing in the Dark
m Arthur Schwartz, w Howard
Dietz, 1931
From the musical The Band Wagon.
PC NBC - 5 Oct 1957

Dancing on the Ceiling
m Richard Rodgers, w Lorenz Hart, 1930
From the musical Ever Green.
PC KMH - 11 Oct 1961

Danny Boy
mw Frederic Edward Weatherly, 1913
Adapted from the traditional
'Londonderry Air'.
PC KMH - 27 Mar 1963
[with Tex Beneke, tenor sax]

Dardanella
m Felix Bernard and Johnny S. Black,
w Fred Fisher, 1919
PC KMH - 10 Oct 1962

Darling, je vous aime beaucoup
mw Anna Sosenko, 1935
PC CBS - 28 Mar 1955

Dear Heart
m Henry Mancini, w Jay Livingston
and Ray Evans, 1964
From the film Dear Heart.
PC KMH - 7 Jan 1965

Dearie
mw Bob Hilliard and David Mann, 1950
From the revue The Copacabana Show
of 1950.
PC NBC - 23 Nov 1957 [with Pearl Bailey]

Devil May Care
m Harry Warren, w Johnny Burke, 1940
BB - 16 Jun 1940

The Dickey-Bird Song
m Sammy Fain, w Howard Dietz, 1948
From the film Three Daring Daughters.
CSC - 13 May 1948

Did You Ever See a Dream Walking?
m Harry Revel, w Mack Gordon, 1933
From the film Sitting Pretty.
PC NBC - 20 Apr 1957

Did Your Mother Come from Ireland? ★
mw Jimmy Kennedy and Michael
Carr, 1936
PC NBC - 14 Mar 1959

Didn't We? •
mw Jimmy Webb, 1967
25–27 Jun 1970 (Live) - PC in Person at the
International Hotel, Las Vegas LSPX-1001
The Doris Mary Anne Kappelhoff Special -
14 Mar 1971

Dindi •
m Antônio Carlos Jobim,
w Aloysio de Oliveira (Port.), 1959,
w Ray Gilbert (Eng.), 1965
28 Feb 1966 - Lightly Latin LSP-3552

Do I Know What I'm Doing?
m Joanne Costello, w Joanne Costello
and Freddie Stewart, 1943
CPPC - Jul 1943

**Do You Know What It Means
to Miss New Orleans?**
m Louis Alter, w Eddie DeLange, 1946
From the film New Orleans.
PC Spring in New Orleans - 7 Apr 1976

The Donkey Serenade •
m Rudolf Friml, 1920, m Herbert
Stothart, w Robert Wright and George
Forrest (under pseud. Chet Forrest), 1937
From the film The Firefly.
16 Apr 1959 - Como Swings LSP-2010

Don't Be Ashamed of Your Age
mw Cindy Walker and Bob Wills, 1947
PC NBC - 3 May 1958
[with Tennessee Ernie Ford]

Don't Blame Me ★
m Jimmy McHugh, w Dorothy
Fields, 1933
CSC - 27 Mar 1946 / PC NBC - 25
Oct 1958

**Don't Cry, Joe
(Let Her Go, Let Her Go, Let Her Go)**
mw Joe Marsala, 1949
CSC - 1 Dec 1949

Don't Fence Me In
mw Cole Porter, 1944
From the film Hollywood Canteen.
CSC - 1 Feb 1945

Don't Get Around Much Anymore
m Duke Ellington, w Bob Russell, 1942
CPPC - 1943

Don't Go to Strangers
m Arthur Kent and David Mann,
w Redd Evans, 1954
PC KMH - 4 Jan 1961

Don't Take Your Love from Me
mw Henry Nemo, 1941
PC NBC - 23 May 1959

Don't Worry 'Bout Me
m Rube Bloom, w Ted Koehler, 1939
From the revue Cotton Club Parade
(World's Fair Edition).
PC CBS - 31 May 1954

Door of Dreams •
m Robert Allen, w Al Stillman, 1953
22 Feb 1955 - PC Wednesday Night
Music Hall CAL-511

Do-Re-Mi
m Richard Rodgers,
w Oscar Hammerstein II, 1959
From the musical The Sound of Music.
PC KMH - 21 Dec 1960 [with Ginny Tiu]
PC Christmas in Austria - 13 Dec 1976
[with Senta Berger]

Down by the Station
mw Paul Mills (under
pseud. Lee Ricks) and Slim Gaillard, 1948,
w Anonymous, 1931
CSC - 31 Jan 1949 [with
The Fontane Sisters and Mitchell Ayres]

Dream ★
mw Johnny Mercer, 1944
PC KMH - 9 Dec 1959

Dream Along with Me
(I'm on My Way to a Star) ● ★
mw Carl Sigman, 1956
The theme song of Perry Como.
7 Jun 1956 - Dream Along with Me
CAL-403
12 Mar 1958 (Theme) - Saturday Night
with Mr. C. LSP-1971

Dream Baby (How Long Must I
Dream) ●
mw Cindy Walker, 1962
29 Apr 1971 - I Think of You LSP-4539

Dreamer with a Penny
mw Allan Roberts and Lester Lee, 1949
From the musical All for Love.
CSC - 14 Mar 1949

E

E lei (To You) ●
mw Ugo Calise (It.),
w Ray Charles (Eng.), 1965
19 May 1966 - PC in Italy LSP-3608

Easter Parade ● ★
mw Irving Berlin, 1933
23 Jan 1947 - Make Someone Happy
CAL-694

Easter Sunday with You
mw Don Reid and Henry Tobias, 1944
PC NBC - 5 Apr 1958

Easy Street
mw Alan Rankin Jones, 1941
PC NBC - 17 May 1958

Easy to Love
mw Cole Porter, 1936
From the film Born to Dance.
PC NBC - 6 Apr 1957

Ebb Tide
m Robert Maxwell, w Carl Sigman, 1953
PC CBS - 18 Jan 1954

Edelweiss
m Richard Rodgers,
w Oscar Hammerstein II, 1959
From the musical The Sound of Music.
PC Christmas in Austria - 13 Dec 1976
[with Senta Berger]

Eli, Eli ●
m Jacob Koppel Sandler,
w Boris Thomashefsky, c. 1896
17 Nov 1953 - I Believe LPM-1172

Embraceable You
m George Gershwin, w Ira
Gershwin, 1930
From the musical Girl Crazy.
PC NBC - 4 Oct 1958

Empty Saddles
m Billy Hill, w J. Keirn Brennan, 1936
From the film Rhythm on the Range.
CSC - 8 Feb 1945

The End (At the End of the Rainbow)
m Jimmy Krondes, w Sid Jacobson, 1958
PC NBC - 25 Oct 1958

Eternally
m Charles Chaplin, 1952,
w Geoffrey Parsons, 1953
The theme from the film Limelight.
PC KMH - 3 Feb 1960

Everybody Is Looking for an Answer ●
mw Evangeline Seward, 1970
24 Nov 1970 - It's Impossible LSP-4473

Everybody Knew but Me
mw Irving Berlin, 1945
CSC - 8 Feb 1946

Everybody Loves a Lover
m Robert Allen, w Richard Adler, 1958
PC NBC - 11 Oct 1958
[self-duet via split screen]

Everybody Loves Somebody
m Ken Lane, w Irving Taylor, 1948
PC KMH - 29 Oct 1964

Everybody's Talkin' ●
mw Fred Neil, 1967
From the film Midnight Cowboy.
25–27 Jun 1970 (Live) - PC in Person at the
International Hotel, Las Vegas LSPX-1001
The Many Moods of PC - 22 Feb 1970

Everything Happens to Me
m Matt Dennis, w Tom Adair, 1941
PC NBC - 28 Mar 1959 [with
Dorothy Collins]

Everything I Have Is Yours
m Burton Lane, w Harold Adamson, 1933
From the film Dancing Lady.
PC NBC - 26 Jan 1957

Everything Is Peaches Down in Georgia
m Milton Ager and George W. Meyer, w Grant Clarke, 1918
CSC - 2 Nov 1945

Everything Is Rosy Now for Rosie
m Irving Berlin, w Irving Berlin and Grant Clarke, 1919
PC KMH - 25 Oct 1961

Ev'ry Time (Ev'ry Time I Fall in Love)
mw Gordon Jenkins, 1944
CSC - 24 May 1945
[with The Fontane Sisters]

Ev'rything I Love
mw Cole Porter, 1941
From the musical Let's Face It.
PC KMH - 7 Oct 1959

F

Faithful Forever
m Ralph Rainger, w Leo Robin, 1939
From the animated film Gulliver's Travels.
BB - 18 Feb 1940

Far Above Cayuga's Waters
m Henry S. Thompson, 1857, w Archibald Croswell Weeks and Wilmot Moses Smith, c. 1870
CSC TV - 20 Nov 1949 [with cast]

Fascination
m Fermo Dante Marchetti, 1904, w Dick Manning, 1957
The theme from the film Love in the Afternoon.
PC NBC - 26 Oct 1957

Feelin' Groovy (The 59th Street Bridge Song)
mw Paul Simon, 1967
The PC Holiday Special - 30 Nov 1967

The Ferryboat Serenade
m Eldo Di Lazzaro, w Mario Panzeri (It.), w Harold Adamson (Eng.), 1940
PC NBC - 1 Feb 1958

Fiddle Dee Dee
m Jule Styne, w Sammy Cahn, 1949
From the film It's a Great Feeling.
CSC TV - 16 Oct 1949

Fine and Dandy
m Kay Swift, w Paul James, 1930
From the musical Fine and Dandy.
PC NBC - 30 Nov 1957

Five Foot Two, Eyes of Blue (Has Anybody Seen My Girl?)
m Ray Henderson, w Sam M. Lewis and Joe Young, 1925
PC KMH - 8 Nov 1961

Fly Me to the Moon (In Other Words) •
mw Bart Howard, 1954
18–26 Mar 1963 - *The Songs I Love*
LSP-2708

A Foggy Day
m George Gershwin,
w Ira Gershwin, 1937
From the film *A Damsel in Distress*.
PC KMH - 25 Jan 1961

Fools Rush In
m Rube Bloom, w Johnny Mercer, 1940
BB - 14 Jul 1940

For a Little While
m Vic Mizzy, w Irving Taylor, 1943
The theme song from the radio series Columbia Presents Perry Como.
CPPC - 1943

For All We Know •
m Fred Karlin, w Arthur James
and Robb Wilson, 1970
From the film *Lovers and Other Strangers*.
27 Apr 1971 - *I Think of You* LSP-4539

Forget-Me-Nots in Your Eyes
m Harry Warren, w Edgar Leslie, 1944
Radio broadcast - c. 1944 - V-Disc 269

Forgive Me
m Milton Ager, w Jack Yellen, 1927
PC NBC - 16 Feb 1957

A Friend of Yours
m Jimmy Van Heusen,
w Johnny Burke, 1945
CSC - 19 Oct 1945 / PC NBC - 23 Feb 1957

Full Moon and Empty Arms
mw Buddy Kaye and
Ted Mossman, 1946
Adapted from the second movement of Sergei Rachmaninov's 'Piano Concerto No. 2 in C Minor', Op. 18.
CSC - 14 May 1946

Fun and Fancy Free
mw Bennie Benjamin
and George Weiss, 1947
From the animated film *Fun and Fancy Free*.
CSC - Sep–Oct 1947

Funny How Time Slips Away
mw Willie Nelson, 1961
9 Feb 1965 - *The Scene Changes* LSP-3396

G

A Garden in the Rain •
m Carroll Gibbons,
w James Dyrenforth, 1929
14 Mar 1946 - *The Lord's Prayer* CAS-2299 (e)

Georgia on My Mind
m Hoagy Carmichael,
w Stuart Gorrell, 1930
PC KMH - 30 Nov 1960

Get Out Those Old Records
mw Carmen Lombardo
and John Jacob Loeb, 1951
PC NBC - 25 Jan 1958
[with Pat Boone, Peggy Lee
and John Bubbles]

Getting to Know You
m Richard Rodgers,
w Oscar Hammerstein II, 1951
From the musical The King and I.
PC NBC - 28 Sep 1957
[with Irene Dunne and Kukla & Ollie]

Gigi ● ★
m Frederick Loewe, w Alan Jay
Lerner, 1958
From the film Gigi.
17 May 1961 - Sing to Me, Mr. C.
LSP-2390
PC NBC - 12 Apr 1958

The Girl Next Door
mw Hugh Martin and Ralph Blane, 1944
From the film Meet Me in St. Louis.
PC NBC - 29 Nov 1958

Girl of My Dreams ● ★
mw Sunny Clapp, 1927
21 Mar 1946 - Dream Along with Me
CAL-403

The Girl That I Marry
mw Irving Berlin, 1946
From the musical Annie Get Your Gun.
CSC - Jan–Feb 1947

Girls
mw Cole Porter, 1944
From the musical Mexican Hayride.
PC KMH - 3 Feb 1960 [with guests]

Give Me an Old-Fashioned Christmas Card
m Nick Perito, 1977, w Ogden Nash, 1945
From the television special
Perry Como's Olde Englishe Christmas
PC Olde Englishe Christmas - 14 Dec 1977

Give Myself a Party ●
mw Don Gibson, 1958
9 Feb 1965 - The Scene Changes LSP-3396

The Glory of Love ★
mw Billy Hill, 1936
PC NBC - 8 Feb 1958

Gonna Build a Mountain
mw Leslie Bricusse
and Anthony Newley, 1962
From the musical Stop the World –
I Want to Get Off.
PC KMH - 23 Jan 1963 [with cast]

Goodnight, Sweet Jesus ● ★
mw Reverend James Curry, 1913
29 Sep 1953 - I Believe LPM-1172

Great Day
m Vincent Youmans, w Billy Rose
and Edward Eliscu, 1929
From the musical Great Day!
Guest Star (477) - 13 May 1956

The Greatest Love of All
m Michael Masser, w Linda Creed, 1977
From the film The Greatest.
PC Christmas in New York - 17 Dec
1983 [excerpt]

Green Fields
mw Terry Gilkyson, Richard Dehr
and Frank Miller, 1960
PC KMH - 18 May 1960

Green, Green Grass of Home
mw Curly Putman, 1966
Como Country: Perry and
His Nashville Friends - 17 Feb 1975

Gringo's Guitar ●
mw Cindy Walker, 1965
9 Feb 1965 - The Scene Changes LSP-3396

Guilty
m Richard A. Whiting and Harry Akst,
w Gus Kahn, 1931
PC NBC - 19 Jan 1957

The Gypsy in My Soul •
m Clay Boland, w Moe Jaffe, 1938
From the revue Fifty-Fifty.
19 Feb 1958 - Saturday Night
with Mr. C. LSP-1971

H

Hallelujah!
m Vincent Youmans, w Leo Robin
and Clifford Grey, 1927
From the musical Hit the Deck.
PC NBC - 14 Sep 1957

Happy Easter
mw Irving Berlin, 1948
From the film Easter Parade.
PC KMH - 20 Mar 1967 [excerpt]

Happy Holiday ★
mw Irving Berlin, 1942
From the film Holiday Inn.
PC KMH - 23 Dec 1959
PC Irish Christmas - Dec 1994

Happy Man (If I Ever Find the Time) •
mw Bob McDill, 1966
24 Aug 1967 - 47-9533

The Happy Wanderer
(Val-De-Ri, Val-De-Ra)
m Wilhelm Möller, w Florenz Sigismund
and Edith Möller (Ger.),
w Antonia Ridge (Eng.), 1954
PC Christmas in Austria - 13 Dec 1976

Harmony •*
mw Artie Kaplan and Norman Simon, 1972
7 Jan 1974
The PC Winter Show - 10 Dec 1973

Harrigan
mw George M. Cohan, 1908
From the musical Fifty Miles from Boston.
PC KMH - 14 Mar 1962

Have You Ever Been Lonely?
(Have You Ever Been Blue?)
m Peter De Rose, w Billy Hill
(under pseud. George Brown), 1933
PC NBC - 23 May 1959
[with Gisele MacKenzie, violin]

The Hawaiian Wedding Song
(Ke Kali Nei Au) •
mw Charles E. King (Haw.), 1926,
w Al Hoffman and
Dick Manning (Eng.), 1959
25 Mar 1963 - The Songs I Love LSP-2708

Heartaches
m Al Hoffman, w John Klenner, 1931
PC KMH - 22 May 1963

Hearts Will Be Hearts •
mw Cindy Walker, 1964
24 Aug 1967 - Seattle LSP-4183

Hello, Dolly!
mw Jerry Herman, 1964
From the musical Hello, Dolly!
PC KMH - 13 Feb 1964 [special lyrics]

Here
mw Dorcas Cochran and Harold Grant, 1954
Based on the aria 'Caro nome' from Giuseppe Verdi's opera Rigoletto.
PC CBS - 2 Jun 1954

He's Got the Whole World in His Hands •
mw Geoff Love, 1958
23 Jun 1958 - When You Come to the End of the Day LSP-1885

Hey There
mw Richard Adler and Jerry Ross, 1954
From the musical The Pajama Game.
PC NBC - 15 Nov 1958

Hey! Jealous Lover
mw Sammy Cahn, Kay Twomey and Bee Walker, 1956
PC NBC - 8 Dec 1956

Hey, Good Lookin'
mw Hank Williams, 1951
PC CBS - 28 Dec 1951
[with The Fontane Sisters]

Hi, Neighbor!
mw Jack Owens, 1941
From the film San Antonio Rose.
PC KMH - 2 Mar 1960 [with guests]

Hi-Lili, Hi-Lo
m Bronislau Kaper, w Helen Deutsch, 1952
From the film Lili.
PC CBS - 16 Oct 1953
[with The Fontane Sisters]

The Holy City
m Michael Maybrick,
w Frederic Edward Weatherly, 1892
PC Christmas in the Holy Land - 13 Dec 1980

Holy God, We Praise Thy Name •
m Traditional, c. 1774,
w Ignaz Franz (Ger.), 1771,
w Clarence Augustus Walworth (transl.), 1858
26–29 Jun 1950 - The Lord's Prayer CAS-2299 (e)

Home (When Shadows Fall)
mw Peter Van Steeden, Harry Clarkson and Geoff Clarkson, 1931
PC KMH - 22 Nov 1961

Home on the Range ★
m Daniel E. Kelley, c. 1872,
w Brewster M. Higley, c. 1871-3
27 Jan 1941 - Decca Mx. 68628
[with Ted Weems with PC
and Garry Moore] PC NBC - 24 Nov 1956

Homesick – That's All
mw Gordon Jenkins, 1945
CSC - 18 Oct 1945

Honeycomb
mw Bob Merrill, 1957
PC NBC - 23 Nov 1957

Honolulu
m Harry Warren, w Gus Kahn, 1939
From the film Honolulu.
PC NBC - 17 May 1958 [with guests]

Hooray for Hollywood
m Richard A. Whiting,
w Johnny Mercer, 1938
From the film Hollywood Hotel.
PC NBC - 26 Oct 1957 [special lyrics]

Hooray for Love
m Harold Arlen, w Leo Robin, 1948
From the film Casbah.
PC KMH - 10 Feb 1960 [with
Dorothy Collins]

A House Is Not a Home ●
m Burt Bacharach, w Hal David, 1964
From the film A House Is Not a Home.
24 Nov 1970 - It's Impossible LSP-4473

How About Me?
mw Irving Berlin, 1928
PC NBC - 7 Jan 1965

How About You?
m Burton Lane, w Ralph Freed, 1941
From the film Babes on Broadway.
PC KMH - 18 May 1960
[with Edie Adams]

How Are Things in Glocca Morra?
m Burton Lane, w E. Y. Harburg, 1947
From the musical Finian's Rainbow.
PC KMH - 14 Mar 1962

How Deep Is the Ocean? ● ★
mw Irving Berlin, 1932
17 May 1961 - Sing to Me, Mr. C. LSP-2390

How Insensitive (Insensatez) ●
m Antonio Carlos Jobim,
w Vinícius de Moraes (Port.), 1961,
w Norman Gimbel (Eng.), 1963
29 Dec 1965 - Lightly Latin LSP-3552

How Little We Know
m Hoagy Carmichael,
w Johnny Mercer, 1944
From the film To Have and Have Not.
PC Summer of '74 - 12 Sep 1974
[with Michele Lee]

How Soon (Will I Be Seeing You?)
mw Carroll Lucas and Jack Owens, 1947
CSC - 20 Nov 1945

How to Handle a Woman •
m Frederick Loewe, w Alan Jay
Lerner, 1960
From the musical Camelot.
7 Jun 1968 - Look to Your Heart
LSP-4052

I

I Believe in Music •
mw Mac Davis, 1972
27 Mar 1973 - And I Love You So
APL1-0100

I Can't Begin to Tell You
m James V. Monaco,
w Mack Gordon, 1945
From the film The Dolly Sisters.
CSC - 28 Nov 1945

I Didn't Know About You
m Duke Ellington, w Bob Russell, 1944
CSC - 8 Feb 1945

I Do, Do You? (Do You Believe in Love?)
mw Lew Quadling, 1940
BB - 29 Dec 1940

I Don't Believe in Rumors
m Jimmy Lambert, w Harry Glick, 1943
CPPC - 3 May 1943

I Don't Know Enough About You
mw Peggy Lee and Dave Barbour, 1946
CSC - 28 May 1946

I Don't Want to Walk Without You
m Jule Styne, w Frank Loesser, 1942
From the film Sweater Girl.
PC NBC - 6 Oct 1956

I Fall in Love with You Ev'ry Day
mw Sam H. Stept, 1946
CSC - 20 Feb 1946

I Found a Million Dollar Baby (in a Five and Ten Cent Store) •
m Harry Warren, w Billy Rose
and Mort Dixon, 1931
From the revue Billy Rose's Crazy Quilt.
1 Feb 1951 - Door of Dreams CAS-2482 (e)

I Give You My Word
mw Al Kavelin and Merril Lyn, 1940
BB - 8 Dec 1940

I Gotta Right to Sing the Blues • ★
m Harold Arlen, w Ted Koehler, 1932
From the revue Earl Carroll's
Vanities of 1932.
25 Jan 1955 - So Smooth LPM-1085

I Guess I'll Get the Papers (and Go Home)
mw Hughie Prince and Hal Kanner, 1946
CSC - 20 Dec 1946

I Guess I'll Have to Change My Plan
m Arthur Schwartz,
w Howard Dietz, 1929
From the revue The Little Show.
PC NBC - 16 May 1959

I Had the Craziest Dream •
m Harry Warren, w Mack Gordon, 1942
From the film Springtime in the Rockies.
12 Feb 1957 - We Get Letters LPM-1463

I Have Faith (So Have You)
mw Lew Brown and Sam H. Stept, 1943
CPPC - Aug 1943

I Haven't Time to Be a Millionaire
m James V. Monaco,
w Johnny Burke, 1940
BB - 7 Jul 1940

I Hear Music
m Burton Lane, w Frank Loesser, 1940
From the film Dancing on a Dime.
PC KMH - 2 Dec 1959

I Heard You Cried Last Night (and So Did I)
m Ted Grouya, w Jerrie Kruger, 1943
From the film Cinderella Swings It.
CPPC - 1943

I Just Called to Say I Love You
mw Stevie Wonder, 1984
From the film The Woman in Red.
PC Christmas in Hawaii - 14 Dec 1985
[with Marie Osmond]

I Lost My Sugar in Salt Lake City
mw Leon René and Johnny Lange, 1942
From the film Stormy Weather.
CPPC - 1943

I Love
mw Tom T. Hall, 1974
PC Lake Tahoe Holiday - 28 Oct 1975

I Love Paris
mw Cole Porter, 1953
From the musical Can-Can.
PC CBS - 16 Oct 1953
Cole Porter in Paris - 17 Jan 1973

I Love to Dance Like They Used to Dance
m Billy Goldenberg, w Alan Bergman
and Marilyn Bergman, 1975
From the film Queen
of the Stardust Ballroom.
PC Springtime Special - 9 Apr 1979

(I Love You) For Sentimental Reasons
m William Best, w Deek Watson, 1946
CSC - c. Nov-Dec 1946

I Love You So (The Merry Widow Waltz)
m Franz Lehár, w Adrian Ross, 1907
From the operetta The Merry Widow.
PC KMH - 30 Jan 1963

I Love You So Much It Hurts
mw Floyd Tillman, 1948
CSC - 6 Dec 1948

I Love You Truly •
mw Carrie Jacobs Bond, 1906
27 Mar 1945 - Make Someone Happy
CAL-694

**I May Be Wrong
(but, I Think You're Wonderful!)** •
m Henry Sullivan, w Harry Ruskin, 1929
From the revue Murray Anderson's Almanac.
5 Mar 1958 - Saturday Night with Mr. C.
LSP-1971

I Never Knew (That Roses Grew)
m Ted Fio Rito, w Gus Kahn, 1925
PC NBC - 7 Dec 1957

I Really Don't Want to Know •
m Don Robertson,
w Howard Barnes, 1954
9 Feb 1965 - The Scene Changes LSP-3396

I Should Care
mw Sammy Cahn, Axel Stordahl
and Paul Weston, 1945
From the film Thrill of a Romance.
CSC - 2 Mar 1945

I Surrender, Dear
m Harry Barris, w Gordon Clifford, 1931
PC NBC - 4 Jan 1958

I Think I Love You •
mw Tony Romeo, 1970
25 Nov 1970 - It's Impossible LSP-4473

I Thought About You
m Jimmy Van Heusen, w Johnny Burke, 1939
PC NBC - 13 Sep 1958

I Tipped My Hat (and Slowly Rode Away)
mw Larry Markes and Dick Charles, 1947
CSC - 20 Dec 1946

I Walk with Music
m Hoagy Carmichael,
w Johnny Mercer, 1940
From the musical Walk with Music.
BB - 24 Mar 1940

I Walked In (with My Eyes Wide Open)
m Jimmy McHugh,
w Harold Adamson, 1945
From the film Nob Hill.
CSC - 10 Jan 1945

I Wanna Be Around •
mw Johnny Mercer
and Sadie Vimmerstedt, 1963
19–25 March 1963 - The Songs I Love
LSP-2708

**I Want a Girl (Just Like the Girl
That Married Dear Old Dad)** ★
m Harry Von Tilzer,
w William Dillon, 1911
PC KMH - 8 May 1963

I Was Young and Foolish •
mw Dick Manning, 1960
2 Nov 1960 - For the Young at Heart
LSP-2343

I Wish We Didn't Have to Say Goodnight ● ■
m Jimmy McHugh,
w Harold Adamson, 1944
From the film Something for the Boys.
8 Dec 1944 - 20-1630
Something for the Boys - 1944

I Wish You Love
mw Charles Trenet (Fr.),
w Albert Beach (Eng.), 1955
PC KMH - 28 Nov 1962

I Wonder as I Wander
mw John Jacob Niles, 1934
PC Christmas in the Holy Land - 13 Dec 1980

I Wonder What's Become of Sally ★
m Milton Ager, w Jack Yellen, 1924
CPPC - 1943

I Write the Songs
mw Bruce Johnston, 1976
PC – Las Vegas Style - 11 Sep 1976

I'd Love to Live in Loveland
mw Will Rossiter (under pseud. W. R. Williams), 1910
CSC - 31 Jan 1945

If Ever I Would Leave You
m Frederick Loewe, w Alan Jay Lerner, 1960
From the musical Camelot.
PC KMH - 2 Jan 1963

If I Could Be with You (One Hour Tonight) ●* ★
m James P. Johnson,
w Henry Creamer, 1930
18 Jun 1956 - Door of Dreams CAS-2482 (e)

If I Had a Hammer ●
mw Lee Hays and Pete Seeger, 1958
25–27 Jun 1970 (Live) - PC in Person at the International Hotel, Las Vegas LSPX-1001
PC KMH - 7 Jan 1965

If I Had My Life to Live Over
mw Henry Tobias,
Larry Vincent and Moe Jaffe, 1947
The Doris Mary Anne Kappelhoff Special - 14 Mar 1971 [with Doris Day]

If I Ruled the World
m Cyril Ornadel, w Leslie Bricusse, 1965
From the musical Pickwick.
PC Spring in New Orleans - 7 Apr 1976

If I'm Lucky ● ■
m Josef Myrow, w Eddie DeLange, 1946
From the film If I'm Lucky.
15 Jul 1946 - 20-1945
If I'm Lucky - 1946

If There Is Someone Lovelier Than You ● ★
m Arthur Schwartz, w Howard Dietz, 1934
From the musical Revenge with Music.
11 Mar 1952 - TV Favourites LPM-3013 (10")

If We Can't Be the Same Old Sweethearts, We'll Just Be the Same Old Friends •
m James V. Monaco,
w Joseph McCarthy, 1915
25 Sep 1947 - A Sentimental Date with
PC LPM-1177

If You Are But a Dream
mw Moe Jaffe, Jack Fulton
and Nat Bonx, 1942
Based on Anton Rubinstein's
'Romance, No. 1 in E-Flat Major'.
PC NBC - 12 Jan 1957

If You Love Me (Really Love Me)
m Marguerite Monnot, w Edith Piaf
(Fr.), 1950, w Geoffrey Parsons (Eng.), 1953
PC KMH - 26 Apr 1961

If You Were the Only Girl in the World • ★
m Nat D. Ayer, w Clifford Grey, 1916
21 Mar 1946 - 20-1857
PC NBC - 15 Nov 1958 [with The Buffalo Bills]

I'll Be with You in Apple Blossom Time
m Albert Von Tilzer, w Neville Fleason, 1920
PC KMH - 29 Mar 1961 [with Dorothy Collins]

I'll Never Smile Again
mw Ruth Lowe, 1940
PC NBC - 18 Apr 1959

I'll String Along with You
m Harry Warren, w Al Dubin, 1934
From the film Twenty Million Sweethearts.
PC NBC - 22 Nov 1958

I'll Walk Alone
m Jule Styne, w Sammy Cahn, 1944
From the film Follow the Boys.
CSC - 14 Dec 1944

I'm a Fool to Want You
mw Jack Wolf, Joel Herron
and Frank Sinatra, 1951
PC KMH - 11 Nov 1959

I'm an Old Cowhand (from the Rio Grande) ★
mw Johnny Mercer, 1936
From the film Rhythm on the Range.
PC CBS - 31 Mar 1954
[with The Fontane Sisters]

I'm Beginning to See the Light
mw Duke Ellington, Don George,
Johnny Hodges and Harry James, 1944
CSC - 25 May 1945

I'm Gonna Sit Right Down and Write Myself a Letter •
m Fred E. Ahlert, w Joe Young, 1936
17 May 1961 - Sing to Me, Mr. C.
LSP-2390
PC NBC - 21 Sep 1957

I'm in Love with Vienna
m Johann Strauss II, 1874,
m Dimitri Tiomkin (adapt.), 1938,
w Oscar Hammerstein II, 1938
From the film The Great Waltz.
PC Christmas in Austria - 13 Dec 1976

I'm in the Mood for Love
m Jimmy McHugh, w Dorothy
Fields, 1935
From the film Every Night at Eight.
CSC - 16 Feb 1950 [with Mae West]
PC NBC - 23 May 1959 [excerpt]

I'm Nobody's Baby
mw Benny Davis, Milton Ager
and Lester Santly, 1921
PC NBC - 1 Mar 1958

I'm Sitting on Top of the World ★
m Ray Henderson, w Sam M. Lewis
and Joe Young, 1925
PC NBC - 8 Nov 1958 / Concert at
NHK Hall, Tokyo, Japan - 8 Mar 1993

I'm Sorry I Didn't Say I'm Sorry
mw Allan Roberts and Lester Lee, 1947
From the film When a Girl's Beautiful.
CSC - 17 Dec 1947

I'm Stepping Out with a Memory Tonight
m Allie Wrubel, w Herb Magidson, 1940
BB - 21 Jul 1940

I'm Thinking Tonight of My Blue Eyes
mw A. P. Carter, 1930
CPPC - 1943

Imagination
m Jimmy Van Heusen,
w Johnny Burke, 1940
PC CBS - 2 Sep 1953

In a Little Spanish Town
('Twas on a Night Like This)
m Mabel Wayne, w Sam M. Lewis
and Joe Young, 1926
PC NBC - 7 Apr 1956

In Acapulco
m Harry Warren, w Mack Gordon, 1945
From the film Billy Rose's
Diamond Horseshoe.
PC NBC - 12 Apr 1958

In My Dream of Tomorrow
m Vic Mizzy and Irving Taylor,
w Nat Burton, 1943
CPPC - 3 May 1943

In the Cool, Cool, Cool of the
Evening ● ★
m Hoagy Carmichael,
w Johnny Mercer, 1951
From the film Here Comes the Groom.
PC NBC - 1 Jun 1957 [with Patrice Munsel]

In the Garden •
mw C. Austin Miles, 1912
18 Jun 1958 - When You Come to the End of the Day LSP-1885

In the Wee Small Hours of the Morning
m David Mann, w Bob Hilliard, 1955
PC KMH - 14 Feb 1962

Indian Summer
m Victor Herbert, 1919, w Al Dubin, 1939
BB - 25 Feb 1940

Isn't It Romantic?
m Richard Rodgers, w Lorenz Hart, 1932
From the film *Love Me Tonight*.
CSC - 21 May 1946

It All Depends on You •* ★
m Ray Henderson, w B. G. DeSylva and Lew Brown, 1926
From the musical *Big Boy*.
15 May 1961
PC KMH - 3 Feb 1960

It All Seems to Fall into Line •
m Ben Weisman, w Al Stillman, 1973
16 Jan 1973 - And I Love You So APL1-0100

It Came upon the Midnight Clear
m Richard Storrs Willis, w Edmund Sears, 1850
PC NBC - 21 Dec 1957
[with The McGuire Sisters]

It Can't Be Wrong
m Max Steiner, w Kim Gannon, 1943
The theme from the film *Now, Voyager*.
CPPC - 1943

It Could Happen to You • ★
m Jimmy Van Heusen, w Johnny Burke, 1944
From the film *And the Angels Sing*.
6 Mar 1958 - Saturday Night with Mr. C. LSP-1971
29–31 Jul 1980 (Live) - PC Live on Tour AQL1-3826 / PC Bahamas Holiday - 21 May 1980

It Couldn't Please Me More
m John Kander, w Fred Ebb, 1966
From the musical *Cabaret*.
PC Early American Christmas - 13 Dec 1978 [with Diana Canova]

It Happened in Monterey •
m Mabel Wayne, w Billy Rose, 1930
From the film *The King of Jazz*.
25 Jan 1955 - So Smooth LPM-1085

It Isn't Fair
m Richard Himber, Frank Warshauer and Sylvester Sprigato, w Richard Himber, 1933
CSC - 2 Mar 1950

It Might as Well Be Spring
m Richard Rodgers,
w Oscar Hammerstein II, 1945
From the film State Fair.
PC NBC - 11 Apr 1959 [excerpt]
PC – Las Vegas Style - 11 Sep 1976
[with Ann-Margret]

It Must Be True
mw Gus Arnheim, Harry Barris
and Gordon Clifford, 1930
PC NBC - 30 Mar 1957

It Only Happens When I Dance with You •
mw Irving Berlin, 1948
From the film Easter Parade.
21 Oct 1947 - 20-2888

It Was Such a Good Day •*
mw Joe Brooks, 1973
17 Jan 1973 - Just out of
Reach – Rarities from Nashville
Produced by Chet Atkins RGM-0191

It's a Big Wide Wonderful World ★
mw John Rox, 1940
From the musical All in Fun.
PC CBS - 24 Jun 1955

It's a Grand Night for Singing ★
m Richard Rodgers,
w Oscar Hammerstein II, 1945
From the film State Fair.
PC NBC - 27 Dec 1958

It's a Great Day for the Irish
mw Roger Edens, 1940
From the film Little Nellie Kelly.
PC NBC - 14 Mar 1959

It's a Lovely Day Tomorrow
mw Irving Berlin, 1940
From the musical Louisiana Purchase.
BB - 28 Jul 1940

It's a Miracle
mw Barry Manilow and Marty Panzer, 1975
PC Spring in San Francisco - 10 May 1981

It's a Most Unusual Day
m Jimmy McHugh, w Harold Adamson, 1948
From the film A Date with Judy.
PC CBS - 13 Apr 1955

It's All in the Game
m Charles Gates Dawes, 1912,
w Carl Sigman, 1951
PC NBC - 18 Oct 1958

It's Always You
m Jimmy Van Heusen,
w Johnny Burke, 1941
From the film Road to Zanzibar.
CPPC - 22 Apr 1943

It's Been a Long, Long Time •* ★
m Jule Styne, w Sammy Cahn, 1945
18 Jun 1956
CSC - 23 Oct 1945 / PC NBC - 24 Jan 1959
Concert at NHK Hall, Tokyo, Japan - 8 Mar 1993

It's Better in the Bahamas
mw Ray Charles, 1980
From the television special
Perry Como's Bahamas Holiday
PC Bahamas Holiday - 21 May 1980
[with Loretta Swit and Toni Tennille]

**It's Breaking My Heart
to Keep Away from You**
mw D. Anthony, 1943
CSC - 3 May 1945

It's Easter Time ● ★
mw Meredith Willson, 1951
4 Mar 1952 - 47-4631

It's Easy to Remember ● ★
m Richard Rodgers, w Lorenz Hart, 1935
From the film Mississippi.
19 Feb 1957 - We Get Letters LPM-1463

It's Just a Matter of Opinion
m Carl Lampl, w Moe Jaffe, 1946
CSC - 29 Mar 1946

It's Like Old Times
mw Dave Franklin, 1942
From the film One Exciting Night.
CPPC - 18 Jun 1943

It's Magic
m Jule Styne, w Sammy Cahn, 1948
From the film Romance on the High Seas.
CSC - 27 Dec 1948
PC NBC - 18 Oct 1958 [excerpt]

It's Not for Me to Say
m Robert Allen, w Al Stillman, 1957
From the film Lizzie.
PC NBC - 21 Sep 1957

It's Only a Paper Moon • ★
m Harold Arlen, w E. Y. Harburg
and Billy Rose, 1933
From the play The Great Magoo
and the film Take a Chance.
1 Feb 1951 - PC Sings Just for You
CAL-440

I've Got a Feeling I'm Falling •
m Fats Waller and Harry Link,
w Billy Rose, 1929
14 Oct 1947 - Dream Along with Me
CAL-403

I've Got My Love to Keep Me Warm
mw Irving Berlin, 1937
From the film On the Avenue.
PC NBC - 10 Jan 1959

I've Got the World on a String •
m Harold Arlen, w Ted Koehler, 1932
From the revue Cotton Club Parade.
20 Jan 1955 - So Smooth LPM-1085

I've Grown Accustomed to Her Face • ★
m Frederick Loewe, w Alan Jay Lerner, 1956
From the musical My Fair Lady.
15 May 1961 - Sing to Me, Mr. C.
LSP-2390

J

Jeannine, I Dream of Lilac Time
m Nathaniel Shilkret,
w L. Wolfe Gilbert, 1928
The theme song from the film Lilac Time.
PC KMH - 10 Oct 1962

Jeepers Creepers
m Harry Warren, w Johnny Mercer, 1938
From the film Going Places.
PC NBC - 9 May 1959

Jesus Was Born Today
mw Ray Bunch, 1982
PC Christmas in Hawaii - 14 Dec 1985
[with Marie Osmond]

A Journey to a Star
m Harry Warren, w Leo Robin, 1943
From the film The Gang's All Here.
CPPC - 1943

June in January
m Ralph Rainger, w Leo Robin, 1935
From the film Here Is My Heart.
PC KMH - 27 Jan 1960

June Is Bustin' Out All Over
m Richard Rodgers,
w Oscar Hammerstein II, 1945
From the musical Carousel.
PC NBC - 31 May 1958

June Night
m Abel Baer, w Cliff Friend, 1924
PC NBC - 1 Jun 1957

Just a Cottage Small (by a Waterfall)
m James F. Hanley, w B. G. DeSylva, 1925
PC KMH - 7 Oct 1959

Just a Little Fond Affection
mw Lewis Ilda, Elton Box
and Desmond Cox, 1946
CSC - 6 Dec 1945

Just A-Sittin' and A-Rockin'
m Billy Strayhorn and Duke Ellington,
w Lee Gaines, 1945
CSC - 17 Dec 1945

Just Friends
m John Klenner, w Sam M. Lewis, 1931
CPPC - 1943

Just in Time
m Jule Styne, w Betty Comden
and Adolph Green, 1956
From the musical The Bells Are Ringing.
PC NBC - 8 Mar 1958

Just One of Those Things
mw Cole Porter, 1935
From the musical Jubilee.
PC NBC - 3 May 1958

Just out of Reach ●
mw Pappy Stewart, 1953
27 May 1975 - Just out of Reach
APL1-0863

K

Kentucky Babe ● ★
m Adam Geibel,
w Richard Henry Buck, 1896
14 Mar 1946 - Make Someone Happy
CAL-694

Killing Me Softly with Her Song ●
m Charles Fox, w Norman Gimbel, 1972
27 Mar 1973 - And I Love You So
APL1-0100

Kissing Bridge ●
with The Fontane Sisters
m Robert Allen, w Al Stillman, 1953
1953 - 47-5524

Kol Nidrei ●
mw Traditional, c. 1400s
17-23 Nov 1953 - I Believe LPM-1172

L

La vie en rose
m Louis Guglielmi (Louiguy), w Edith Piaf
(Fr.), 1946, w Mack David (Eng.), 1950
PC CBS - 16 Oct 1953

The Lady's in Love with You
m Burton Lane, w Frank Loesser, 1939
From the film Some Like It Hot (aka
Rhythm Romance).
PC KMH - 22 Mar 1961

The Last Time I Saw Paris
m Jerome Kern,
w Oscar Hammerstein II, 1941
Featured in the film Lady Be Good.
PC NBC - 11 Apr 1959
[with Oscar Hammerstein II]

The Latin Quarter
m Harry Warren, w Al Dubin, 1938
From the film Gold Diggers in Paris.
PC NBC - 26 Apr 1958

Laughing on the Outside (Crying on the Inside)
m Bernie Wayne, w Ben Raleigh, 1946
CSC - 2 May 1946

Laughter in the Rain
mw Neil Sedaka and Phil Cody, 1975
PC Springtime Special - 27 Mar 1975
[with Olivia Newton-John]

Laura
m David Raksin, w Johnny Mercer, 1945
CSC - 31 May 1945

Lazybones
mw Johnny Mercer
and Hoagy Carmichael, 1933
CPPC - c. Jun–Jul 1943

Let a Smile Be Your Umbrella •
m Sammy Fain, w Irving Kahal
and Francis Wheeler, 1928
16 Apr 1959 - Como Swings LSP-2010

Let It Be Love •
mw Ben Peters, 1973
8 Jan 1975 - Just out of Reach APL1-0863

Let It Snow! Let It Snow! Let It Snow!
m Jule Styne, w Sammy Cahn, 1946
CSC - 21 Jan 1946
The PC Winter Show - 4 Dec 1972

Let Me Call You Sweetheart
mw Beth Slater Whitson
and Leo Friedman, 1910
The Doris Mary Anne Kappelhoff Special -
14 Mar 1971 [with Doris Day]

Let's All Sing Like the Birdies Sing
m Tolchard Evans and Henry B. Tilsley,
w Robert Hargreaves
and Stanley J. Damerell, 1932
PC KMH - 30 Mar 1960 [with guests]

Let's Call the Whole Thing Off
m George Gershwin, w Ira Gershwin, 1937
From the film Shall We Dance.
PC NBC - 17 May 1958
[with Sally Ann Howes]

Let's Do It (Let's Fall in Love)
mw Cole Porter, 1928
From the musical Paris.
Cole Porter in Paris - 17 Jan 1973 [with
Diahann Carroll and Connie Stevens]

Let's Face the Music and Dance
mw Irving Berlin, 1936
From the film Follow the Fleet.
PC KMH - 1 Mar 1961

Let's Take a Walk Around the Block
m Harold Arlen, w Ira Gershwin and
E. Y. Harburg, 1934
From the musical Life Begins at 8:40.
PC Springtime Special - 27 Mar 1975

Let's Take the Long Way Home
m Harold Arlen, w Johnny Mercer, 1944
From the film Here Come the Waves.
CSC - c. Jan–Mar 1945

Lida Rose / Will I Ever Tell You?
mw Meredith Willson, 1957
From the musical The Music Man.
PC KMH - 4 Feb 1965 [with Shirley Jones]

Lies •
m Harry Barris, w George E. Springer, 1930
4 Nov 1952 - A Sentimental Date with PC LPM-1177

Life Is Just a Bowl of Cherries
m Ray Henderson, w B. G. DeSylva and Lew Brown, 1931
From the revue George White's Scandals of 1931.
PC KMH - 21 Oct 1959
[with Rosemary Clooney and Nat King Cole]

Like Someone in Love •
m Jimmy Van Heusen, w Johnny Burke, 1944
From the film Belle of the Yukon.
6 Mar 1958 - Saturday Night with Mr. C. LSP-1971
CSC - c. Jan–Feb 1945 - V-Disc 444

Linda •
mw Jack Lawrence, 1947
21 May 1959 - Como Swings LSP-2010

Listen to My Heart
mw Ted Weems, Harry Budka and Mildred Livesay, 1941
BB - 5 Jan 1941

A Little Bit of Heaven
m Ernest R. Ball, w J. Keirn Brennan, 1914
From the musical The Heart of Paddy Whack.
PC Irish Christmas - Dec 1994 [excerpt]

The Little Gray House
m Kurt Weill, w Maxwell Anderson, 1949
From the musical Lost in the Stars.
CSC - 16 Feb 1950

Little Green Apples
mw Bobby Russell, 1968
The PC Holiday Special - 1 Dec 1968

The Little Old Mill (Went Round and Round)
mw Don Pelosi, Lewis Ilda and Leo Towers, 1947
CSC - 18 Feb 1948

A Little on the Lonely Side
mw Dick Robertson, Frank Weldon and James Cavanaugh, 1944
CSC - 16 Apr 1945

A Little Street Where Old Friends Meet
m Harry Woods, w Gus Kahn, 1932
PC KMH - 25 Nov 1959
[with The Lennon Sisters]
& 7 Dec 1960 [excerpt]

The Little White Duck
m Bernard Zaritzky, w Walt Barrows, 1950
PC KMH - 18 Jan 1961 [with George Gobel]

Lollipops and Roses ●
mw Tony Velona, 1962
8 Jun 1962 - By Request LSP-2567

Lonely Love
m Ray Sinatra, w Everett Carter, 1945
CSC - 25 May 1945

The Lonesome Road
m Nathaniel Shilkret, w Gene Austin, 1928
PC KMH - 14 Oct 1959

Look to Your Heart ●
m Jimmy Van Heusen, w Sammy
Cahn, 1955
From the television series
Producers' Showcase ('Our Town').
12 Jun 1968 - Look to Your Heart
LSP-4052

Louise
m Richard A. Whiting, w Leo Robin, 1929
From the film Innocents of Paris.
PC NBC - 19 Apr 1958

Love and Marriage
m Jimmy Van Heusen, w Sammy
Cahn, 1955
From the television series
Producers' Showcase ('Our Town').
PC KMH - 22 Feb 1961

Love Don't Care (Where It Grows) ●
mw Tupper Saussy, 1973
9 Aug 1973 - APB0-0096

Love in a Home ●
m Gene De Paul, w Johnny Mercer, 1956
From the musical L'il Abner.
19 Jun 1968 - Look to Your Heart LSP-4052
The Hollywood Palace - 20 Dec 1969

Love Is a Many-Splendoured Thing
m Sammy Fain,
w Paul Francis Webster, 1955
From the film Love Is a
Many-Splendoured Thing.
PC KMH - 30 Dec 1959

Love Is a Simple Thing
m Arthur Siegel, w June Carroll, 1952
From the revue New Faces of 1952.
PC NBC - 22 Nov 1958 [with
Dorothy Collins]

Love Is Here to Stay
m George Gershwin, w Ira Gershwin, 1938
From the film The Goldwyn Follies.
PC NBC - 9 May 1959

Love Is Just Around the Corner ★
m Lewis E. Gensler, w Leo Robin, 1935
From the film Here Is My Heart.
PC KMH - 6 Jan 1960

Love Is Spreading over the World •
m Neil Sedaka, w Howard Greenfield, 1970
25–27 Jun 1970 (Live) - PC in Person at the
International Hotel, Las Vegas LSPX-1001

Love Is Sweeping the Country
m George Gershwin, w Ira
Gershwin, 1932
From the musical Of Thee I Sing.
PC NBC - 28 Sep 1957

Love Is the Reason
m Arthur Schwartz, w Dorothy
Fields, 1951
From the musical A Tree Grows
in Brooklyn.
PC KMH - 10 Feb 1960 [with
Dorothy Collins]

Love Is the Sweetest Thing
mw Ray Noble, 1933
From the film Say It with Music.
CSC - c. Feb 1945 - V-Disc 444

Love Letters in the Sand
m J. Fred Coots, w Nick Kenny
and Charles Kenny, 1931
PC KMH - 8 May 1963

Love Me Again
mw Eddie Snyder, 1958
PC NBC - 8 Mar 1958

Love Me Tender
m George R. Poulton, w W. W. Fosdick,
1861, w Elvis Presley and Ken Darby
(under pseud. Vera Matson), 1956
From the film Love Me Tender.
PC NBC - 24 Nov 1956

Love of My Life •
mw Cole Porter, 1948
From the film The Pirate.
21 Oct 1947 - PC Wednesday Night
Music Hall CAL-511

**Love Theme from *La Strada*
(Travelling down a Lonely Road)** •
m Nino Rota, w Angelo Faccenna
and Michele Galdieri (It.), 1954,
w Don Raye (Eng.), 1956
The theme from the film La Strada.
11 May 1966 - PC in Italy LSP-3608

Love Walked In
m George Gershwin, w Ira Gershwin, 1938
From the film The Goldwyn Follies.
PC NBC - 1 Jun 1957

A Lovely Way to Spend an Evening
m Jimmy McHugh,
w Harold Adamson, 1944
From the film Higher and Higher.
PC NBC - 25 Oct 1958 [excerpt]
PC KMH - 21 Nov 1966
[excerpt with Angela Lansbury]

Lover, Come Back to Me
m Sigmund Romberg,
w Oscar Hammerstein II, 1928
From the operetta The New Moon.
PC NBC - 10 Mar 1956

**Loving Her Was Easier
(Than Anything I'll Ever Do Again)** •
mw Kris Kristofferson, 1971
8 Jan 1975 - Just out of Reach APL1-0863

Lucky Day
m Ray Henderson, w B. G. DeSylva
and Lew Brown, 1926
From the revue George White's
Scandals of 1926.
PC NBC - 2 Nov 1957

Lullaby of Broadway
m Harry Warren, w Al Dubin, 1935
From the film Gold Diggers of 1935.
PC NBC - 4 May 1957

M

Ma Blushin' Rosie
m John Stromberg, w Edgar Smith, 1900
From the musical Fiddle Dee Dee.
PC KMH - 25 Oct 1961

MacNamara's Band
m Shamus O'Connor, w John J.
Stamford, 1917
PC NBC - 14 Mar 1959

Make Love with a Guitar
mw Maria Grever (Sp.),
w Raymond Leveen (Eng.), 1940
BB - 17 Mar 1940

Make Your Own Kind of Music
mw Barry Mann and Cynthia Weil, 1969
The PC Winter Show - 4 Dec 1972

Manhattan
m Richard Rodgers, w Lorenz Hart, 1925
From the revue Garrick Gaieties.
PC CBS - 14 Mar 1955

Marcheta •
mw Victor Schertzinger, 1913
4 Dec 1947 - PC Sings Just for You
CAL-440

Maria •
m Leonard Bernstein,
w Stephen Sondheim, 1957
From the musical West Side Story.
8 Jun 1962 - By Request LSP-2567

Married
m John Kander, w Fred Ebb, 1966
From the musical Cabaret.
PC French Canadian Christmas - 12 Dec
1981 [with Debby Boone]

Marrying for Love
mw Irving Berlin, 1950
From the musical Call Me Madam.
31 Aug 1950 - PC Sings Hits
from Broadway Shows LPM-1191

May the Good Lord Bless and Keep You •
mw Meredith Willson, 1950
19 Jun 1958 - When You Come
to the End of the Day LSP-1885

Me and My Shadow •
m Al Jolson and Dave Dreyer,
w Billy Rose, 1927
1 Feb 1951 - Dream Along with Me
CAL-403

Me and You and a Dog Named Boo •
mw Kent Lavoie, 1971
29 Apr 1971 - I Think of You LSP-4539

Meditation (Meditação) •
m Antonio Carlos Jobim,
w Newton Mendonça (Port.), 1959,
w Norman Gimbel (Eng.), 1963
25 Feb 1966 - Lightly Latin LSP-3552

Mele Kalikimaka
mw R. Alex Anderson, 1949
PC Christmas in Hawaii - 14 Dec 1985
[with Marie Osmond]

Melodie d'amour (Melody of Love)
m Henri Salvador and Leona Gabriel,
w Leona Gabriel and Marc Lanjean
(Fr.), 1931, w Leo Johns (Eng.), 1957
PC NBC - 26 Oct 1957

Miami
mw Con Conrad, B. G. DeSylva
and Al Jolson, 1925
From the musical Big Boy.
PC NBC - 1 Mar 1958

Mighty lak' a Rose
m Ethelbert Nevin,
w Frank Lebby Stanton, 1901
CSC - 3 Apr 1945
[with The Golden Gate Quartet]

A Million Miles Away
m Nat Simon, w Charles Tobias, 1949
CSC - 20 Apr 1949

Mister Meadowlark
m Walter Donaldson,
w Johnny Mercer, 1940
BB - 23 Jun 1940

**Mister Moon, Kindly Come
Out and Shine**
mw Leham Smith and
Harry Bowman, 1903
PC NBC - 1 Nov 1958
[with Kukla & Ollie]

Mister Sandman
mw Pat Ballard, 1954
PC CBS - Jan 1955

Misty
m Erroll Garner, w Johnny Burke, 1954
PC KMH - 30 Jan 1963
[with Phyllis McGuire and Erroll Garner]

Molly Malone (Cockles and Mussels)
mw James Yorkston,
m Edmund Forman (arr.), 1884
PC KMH - 2 Mar 1960
[with Theodore Bikel]

The Moment I Met You
mw Buck Ram and Gail Meredith, 1945
CSC - 18 Feb 1946

Moments in the Moonlight
mw Richard Himber, Irving Gordon
and Al Kaufman, 1940
BB - 14 Apr 1940

Mona Lisa
mw Jay Livingston and Ray Evans, 1950
From the film Captain Carey, U.S.A.
PC Christmas in Paris - 18 Dec 1982

The Mood I'm In
mw Paul Francis Webster
and Pete King, 1964
The Many Moods of PC - 22 Feb 1970

Mood Indigo •
m Duke Ellington, Barney Bigard
and Irving Mills, w Mitchell Parish, 1931
21 May 1959 - Como Swings LSP-2010

Moon River •
m Henry Mancini, w Johnny Mercer, 1961
From the film Breakfast at Tiffany's.
21 Jun 1962 - By Request LSP-2567

The Moon Won't Talk
m Helen Bliss, w Charles Hathaway, 1940
BB - 9 Feb 1941

Moonlight Becomes You
m Jimmy Van Heusen,
w Johnny Burke, 1942
From the film Road to Morocco.
PC NBC - 13 Sep 1958

The More I See You
m Harry Warren, w Mack Gordon, 1945
From the film Billy Rose's
Diamond Horseshoe.
CSC - 2 Mar 1945

More than Ever
m Jesse Greer, w Chick Adams, 1943
CPPC - 1943

More than Likely •
m Jimmy Van Heusen,
w Sammy Cahn, 1962
26 Jun 1962 - By Request LSP-2567

M-O-T-H-E-R
(A Word That Means the World to Me)
m Theodore Morse, w Howard Johnson, 1915
PC NBC - 10 May 1958
[with Rusty Hamer and Sherry Jackson]

Mother Dear, O Pray for Me ●
mw I. B. Woodbury, 1850
26–29 Jun 1950 - The Lord's Prayer
CAS-2299 (e)

Mountain Greenery ■ ★
m Richard Rodgers, w Lorenz Hart, 1926
From the revue Garrick Gaieties
and featured in the film Words and Music.
25 May 1948 - MGM Mx. 27490 / Sc. 2415
[with Allyn Ann McLerie]
(Words and Music - 1948)

Muskrat Ramble
m Kid Ory, 1926, w Ray Gilbert, 1950
PC KMH - 9 Jan 1963 [excerpt]

My Baby Just Cares for Me
m Walter Donaldson, w Gus Kahn, 1930
From the film Whoopee.
PC KMH - 31 Jan 1962

My Blue Heaven ●* ★
m Walter Donaldson,
w George Whiting, 1927
19 Mar 1946 - PC Book-of-the-Month Club
11-7775

My Buddy
m Walter Donaldson, w Gus Kahn, 1922
PC KMH - 8 Nov 1961

My Colouring Book ●
m John Kander, w Fred Ebb, 1962
26 Mar 1963 - The Songs I Love LSP-2708

My Darling, My Darling
mw Frank Loesser, 1948
From the musical Where's Charley?
CSC - 5 Nov 1948

My Days of Loving You ●
m Eddie Snyder, w Richard Ahlert, 1971
26 Apr 1971 - I Think of You LSP-4539

My Dreams Are Getting Better All the Time
m Vic Mizzy, w Mann Curtis, 1945
From the film In Society.
CSC - c. Jan 1945 V-Disc 410

My Favourite Things ● ★
m Richard Rodgers,
w Oscar Hammerstein II, 1959
From the musical The Sound of Music.
14 Jun 1962 - By Request LSP-2567

My Funny Valentine ●
m Richard Rodgers, w Lorenz Hart, 1937
From the musical Babes in Arms.
20 Jan 1955 - So Smooth LPM-1085

My Happiness
m Borney Bergantine, w Betty Peterson, 1948
PC NBC - 17 Jan 1959 [with Rosemary June]

My Ideal
m Richard A. Whiting and Newell Chase,
w Leo Robin, 1930
From the film Playboy of Paris.
CPPC - 1943 / PC KMH - 19 Apr 1961

My Kind of Girl ●
mw Leslie Bricusse, 1961
6–10 Jun 1977 - The Best of British
PL 12373 (UK)

My Kind of Town (Chicago Is)
m Jimmy Van Heusen,
w Sammy Cahn, 1964
From the film Robin and the Seven Hoods.
PC KMH - 27 May 1965

My Mammy
m Walter Donaldson, w Sam M. Lewis and Joe Young, 1918
CSC - 23 May 1945

My Melancholy Baby ● ★
m Ernie Burnett, w George A. Norton, 1912
4 Nov 1947 - Dream Along with Me
CAL-403

My Mother's Eyes
m Abel Baer, w L. Wolfe Gilbert, 1929
From the film Lucky Boy.
PC KMH - 8 May 1963

My One and Only Highland Fling
m Harry Warren, w Ira Gershwin, 1949
From the film The Barkleys of Broadway.
CSC - 18 May 1949

My Own Peculiar Way •
mw Willie Nelson, 1964
9 Feb 1965 - The Scene Changes LSP-3396

N

Nearer, My God to Thee •
m Lowell Mason, 1856,
w Sarah Flower Adams, 1841
29 Sep 1953 - I Believe LPM-1172

Never a Day Goes By
mw Walter Donaldson, Peter De Rose
and Mitchell Parish, 1943
CPPC - Jul 1943

Never Too Late to Pray
m Fud Livingston, w Willard
Robison, 1945
CSC - 20 Nov 1945

Next Door to Paradise
mw Gordon Jenkins, 1968
PC Hawaiian Holiday - 22 Feb 1976

Nice 'n' Easy
m Lew Spence, w Alan Bergman
and Marilyn Bergman, 1960
PC KMH - 7 Dec 1960

Nice Work If You Can Get It
m George Gershwin, w Ira
Gershwin, 1937
From the film A Damsel in Distress.
CSC - 29 Oct 1947 / PC NBC - 25
May 1957

Night and Day ★
mw Cole Porter, 1932
From the musical Gay Divorce.
PC NBC - 8 Jun 1957
Cole Porter in Paris - 17 Jan 1973

The Night Is Young and You're So Beautiful ★
m Dana Suesse, w Billy Rose
and Irving Kahal, 1936
From the revue Billy Rose's Casa Mañana.
PC KMH - 11 Nov 1959

A Nightingale Sang in Berkeley Square •
m Manning Sherwin,
w Eric Maschwitz, 1940
From the revue New Faces of 1940.
6–10 Jun 1977 - The Best of British
PL 12373 (UK)
BB - 15 Dec 1940

No Love, No Nothin'
m Harry Warren, w Leo Robin, 1943
From the film The Gang's All Here.
CPPC - 1943

No, No, No
mw Tommy Tucker and Lige McKelvy, 1943
CPPC - 20 May 1943

Nobody • ★
m Bert Williams, w Alex Rogers, 1905
From the musical Abyssinia.
8 Feb 1955 - 47-6059

Nobody but You ●
mw Tom Springfield
(under pseud. Dion O'Brien), 1966
24 Aug 1967 - Seattle LSP-4183

Non dimenticar (Don't Forget)
m Gino Redi (under pseud. P. G. Redi),
w Michele Galdieri (It.), 1951,
w Shelley Dobbins (Eng.), 1954
From the film Anna.
PC NBC - 1 Nov 1958

Not One Minute More
mw Don Robertson, Lou Dinning
and Hal Blair, 1959
PC KMH - 14 Oct 1959

Nothing in Common
m Jimmy Van Heusen,
w Sammy Cahn, 1957
From the film Paris Holiday.
PC NBC - 12 Apr 1958 [with Bob Hope]

Now
m Jack Shaindlin, w Marcel Vavin, 1943
From the newsreel series
The March of Time ('Upbeat in Music').

Now Is the Hour (Maori Farewell Song)
mw Maewa Kaihan, Clement Scott
and Dorothy Stewart, 1948
CSC - 3 Mar 1948

Now the Day Is Over ★
m Joseph Barnby, 1868,
w Sabine Baring-Gould, 1865
PC NBC - 13 Sep 1958

O

**O bambino
(One Cold and Blessed Winter)**
mw Alphonsus Maria de Liguori, 1732,
m Tony Velona and Remo Capra
(adapt.), 1964
PC KMH - 19 Dec 1966
[with Anna Moffo]

O, Christmas Tree (O Tannenbaum)
m Melchior Franck, 16th century,
w Ernst Anschütz, 1824
PC KMH - 19 Dec 1966 [with Anna Moffo]
PC Christmas in Austria - 13 Dec 1976
[with The Vienna Boys' Choir]

The Object of My Affection
mw Pinky Tomlin, Coy Poe
and Jimmie Grier, 1934
PC KMH - 14 Nov 1962 [with
Bill Hinnant]

Oh, How I Miss You Tonight ● ★
mw Benny Davis, Joe Burke
and Mark Fisher, 1925
20 Nov 1947 - Dream Along with Me
CAL-403

Oh, Lady, Be Good!
m George Gershwin, w Ira
Gershwin, 1924
From the musical Lady, Be Good!
PC KMH - 1 Nov 1961

Oklahoma
m Richard Rodgers,
w Oscar Hammerstein II, 1943
From the musical Oklahoma!
PC NBC - 10 May 1958

Old Cape Cod
mw Claire Rothrock, Milt Yakus
and Allan Jeffrey, 1957
PC KMH - 4 Mar 1965
[with Lena Horne]

Old Devil Moon ★
m Burton Lane, w E. Y. Harburg, 1947
From the musical Finian's Rainbow.
PC NBC - 19 Oct 1957

Old Folks at Home (Swanee River)
mw Stephen Foster, 1851
CSC - 16 Nov 1945

The Old Lamp-Lighter
m Nat Simon, w Charles Tobias, 1946
PC KMH - 18 May 1960

On a Clear Day (You Can See Forever)
m Burton Lane, w Alan Jay Lerner, 1965
From the musical On a Clear Day You
Can See Forever.
PC KMH - 22 Nov 1965

On a Slow Boat to China
mw Frank Loesser, 1948
CSC - 31 Dec 1948

On the Isle of May
m André Kostelanetz, w Mack
David, 1940
Based on the second movement
of Pyotr Ilych Tchaikovsky's String
Quartette No. 1 ('Andante cantabile').
BB - 31 Mar 1940

On the Street Where You Live
m Frederick Loewe, w Alan Jay
Lerner, 1956
From the musical My Fair Lady.
PC KMH - 31 Jan 1962

On the Sunny Side of the Street
m Jimmy McHugh, w Dorothy
Fields, 1930
From the revue Lew Leslie's
International Revue.
CSC - 2 Jan 1945

Once I Loved (O amor em paz) •
m Antonio Carlos Jobim,
w Vinícius de Moraes (Port.), 1960,
w Ray Gilbert (Eng.), 1965
1 Mar 1966 - Lightly Latin LSP-3552

Once in a While
m Michael Edwards, w Bud Green, 1937
CPPC - 1 Jul 1943 / PC NBC - 7 Apr 1956

Once upon a Time •
m Charles Strouse, w Lee Adams, 1962
From the musical All American.
14 Jun 1962 - By Request LSP-2567

**One for My Baby
(and One More for the Road)** •
m Harold Arlen, w Johnny Mercer, 1943
From the film The Sky's the Limit.
17 Feb 1955 - So Smooth LPM-1085

**The One I Love
(Belongs to Somebody Else)**
m Isham Jones, w Gus Kahn, 1924
PC KMH - 18 Oct 1961

One More Mountain •
mw Paul Vance and Eddie Snyder, 1963
1 May 1963 - Love Makes the World
Go 'Round CAS-805 (e)

Only One •
m Andy Ackers, w Sunny Skylar,
mw Tom Glazer (changed), 1957
30 Apr 1958 - When You Come
to the End of the Day LSP-1885

Onward, Christian Soldiers •
m Arthur Sullivan, 1871,
w Sabine Baring-Gould, 1865
24 Sep 1953 - I Believe LPM-1172

Only Forever
m James V. Monaco, w Johnny Burke, 1940
From the film Rhythm on the River.
PC CBS - 3 Mar 1952 / PC KMH - 2 Dec
1959; 22 May 1963 & 9 Apr 1964

Our Love Affair
m Roger Edens, w Arthur Freed, 1940
From the film Strike Up the Band.
BB - 29 Sep 1940

Out California Way
mw Foster Carling and Jack Meakin, 1946
From the film Out California Way.
CSC - 21 May 1946

Out of the Night
m Harry Sosnik, w Walter Hirsch, 1936
The theme song of Ted Weems.
PC KMH - 22 May 1963 [excerpt]

Over the Rainbow ● ★
with Sally Sweetland
m Harold Arlen, w E. Y. Harburg, 1939
From the film The Wizard of Oz.
4 Mar 1952 - TV Favourites LPM-3013 (10")

P

Padre
m Alain C. Romans, w Marcel Algeron
and Jacques Larue (Fr.),
w Paul Francis Webster (Eng.), 1958
PC NBC - 7 Jun 1958

Paper Doll
mw Johnny S. Black, 1915
CPPC - 1943

Passé
mw Joseph Meyer, Carl Sigman
and Eddie DeLange, 1946
CSC - 22 Nov 1946

Peace of Mind
mw Grace LeBoy Kahn, 1944
Max Liebman Presents: Variety - 30 Jan 1955

Pearly Shells
mw Webley Edwards and Leon Pober, 1964
PC Hawaiian Holiday - 22 Feb 1976
[with Petula Clark]

Peg o' My Heart
m Fred Fisher, w Alfred Bryan, 1913
From the revue Ziegfeld Follies of 1913.
PC NBC - 14 Mar 1959

Pennies from Heaven ●
m Arthur Johnston, w Johnny Burke, 1936
From the film Pennies from Heaven.
29-31 Jul 1980 (Live) - PC Live on Tour
AQL1-3826 / PC KMH - 28 Oct 1959

People
m Jule Styne, w Bob Merrill, 1964
From the musical Funny Girl.
PC KMH - 29 Oct 1964

Peter Cottontail
mw Jack Rollins and Steve Nelson, 1950
PC NBC - 20 Apr 1957

Picture a World
mw Joe Raposo, 1970
From the television series Sesame Street.
Julie on Sesame Street - 23 Nov 1973
[with Julie Andrews and The Muppets]

Play a Simple Melody
mw Irving Berlin, 1914
From the musical Watch Your Step.
PC KMH - 20 Mar 1967
[with Woody Allen, vibraphone]

Please Be Kind
m Saul Chaplin, w Sammy Cahn, 1938
PC CBS - 16 Sep 1953

Poor Butterfly
m Raymond Hubbell, w John Golden, 1916
From the revue The Big Show.
PC KMH - 6 Mar 1963
[with Gene Sheldon, banjo]

Portrait of My Love •
m Cyril Ornadel, w David West, 1961
17 May 1961 - Sing to Me, Mr. C.
LSP-2390

Prayer of Thanksgiving •
m Eduard Kremser, 1877,
mw Adrianus Valerius (Dut.), 1626,
w Theodore Baker (Eng.), 1894
26–29 Jun 1950 - The Lord's Prayer
CAS-2299 (e)

Put Your Arms Around Me, Honey
m Albert Von Tilzer, w Junie McCree, 1910
CPPC - 1943 / PC KMH - 30 Sep 1959

Put Your Hand in the Hand •
mw Gene Maclellan, 1971
30 Apr 1971 - I Think of You LSP-4539
The Barber Comes To Town - 14 Dec 1975

Q
No titles

R

Rags to Riches
mw Richard Adler and Jerry Ross, 1953
PC CBS - 20 Jan 1954

Red Roses for a Blue Lady
mw Sid Tepper and Roy C. Bennett
(under pseud. Roy Brodsky), 1949
PC KMH - 20 Mar 1967

Remember
mw Irving Berlin, 1925
Treasury Star Parade (177) -
The Music of Irving Berlin - 4 Apr 1943

Remember When
m Mickey Addy, w Buck Ram, 1945
CSC - 17 Apr 1945

Return to Me (Ritorna a me)
mw Carmen Lombardo and Danny DiMinno, 1958
PC NBC - 19 Apr 1958

The Right Kind of Love
m Mabel Wayne, w Kermit Goell, 1943
CPPC - 1943

Rock of Ages •
m Thomas Hastings, 1830,
w Augustus Toplady, 1776
26–29 Jun 1950 - The Lord's Prayer
CAS-2299 (e)

Rock-a-Bye Your Baby with a Dixie Melody
m Jean Schwartz, w Sam M. Lewis and Joe Young, 1918
PC KMH - 2 Nov 1960
[with Rosemary Clooney]

A Romantic Guy I
mw Del Sharbutt, Richard Uhl and Frank Stanton, 1941
PC NBC - 3 May 1958

The Rosary • ★
m Ethelbert Nevin,
w Robert Cameron Rogers, 1898
26–29 Jun 1950 - I Believe LPM-1172

Roses of Picardy •
m Haydn Wood,
w Frederic Edward Weatherly, 1916
4 Nov 1947 - PC Wednesday Night Music Hall CAL-511

(Get Your Kicks on) Route 66 •
mw Bobby Troup, 1946
23 Apr 1959 - Como Swings LSP-2010

Row, Row, Row
m James V. Monaco, w William Jerome, 1912
From the revue Ziegfeld Follies of 1912.
PC KMH - 14 Oct 1959 [with Phil Harris]

Rum and Coca-Cola
m Massie Patterson and Lionel Belasco, 1906,
mw Morey Amsterdam, Paul Baron and Jeri Sullivan, 1945
PC NBC - 23 Feb 1957
[with The Andrews Sisters]

S

'S Wonderful
m George Gershwin,
w Ira Gershwin, 1927
From the musical Funny Face.
PC NBC - 1 Jun 1957

Sail Along, Silv'ry Moon
m Percy Wenrich, w Harry Tobias, 1937
PC NBC - 8 Feb 1958 [with Julius La Rosa]

Sakura
mw Traditional c. 1600s–1800s
Concert at Sun Plaza Hall, Tokyo, Japan - 22 Apr 1979

San Francisco
m Bronislaw Kaper and Walter Jurmann,
w Gus Kahn, 1936
From the film San Francisco.
PC Spring in San Francisco - 10 May 1981

Santa Lucia •
mw Achille Longo (Nea.) (att.),
w Teodoro Cottrau (It. transl.), 1849,
m Nick Perito, w Ray Charles (It. and Eng. adapt.), 1966
11 May 1966 - PC in Italy LSP-3608

Save Me the Dance •
mw Luciano Angeleri, 1979,
w Ervin Drake, 1980
8–17 Apr 1980 - Perry Como AFL1-3629

Say It Over Again (Para que sufras)
mw Osvaldo Farres (Sp.),
w Sunny Skylar (Eng.), 1944
CSC - 26 Oct 1945

Say One for Me
m Jimmy Van Heusen, w Sammy
Cahn, 1959
From the film Say One for Me.
PC NBC - 6 Jun 1959

Secret Love
m Sammy Fain,
w Paul Francis Webster, 1953
From the film Calamity Jane.
PC NBC - 14 Feb 1959

Secretly •*
m Al Kaufman, w Marty Symes, 1943
20 Jun 1943
CPPC - 1943

September Song
m Kurt Weill, w Maxwell Anderson, 1938
From the musical Knickerbocker Holiday.
PC CBS - 9 Sep 1953

Seven Little Girls Sitting in the Back Seat
m Lee Pockriss, w Bob Hilliard, 1959
PC KMH - 9 Dec 1959

Shenandoah
mw Traditional, c. early 1800s
PC KMH - 21 Feb 1962

A Shine on Your Shoes
m Arthur Schwartz, w Howard Dietz, 1932
From the musical Flying Colours.
PC NBC - 16 May 1959

Shine On, Harvest Moon
m Nora Bayes and Jack Norworth,
w Jack Norworth, 1908
From the revue Ziegfeld Follies of 1908.
PC NBC - 1 Nov 1958 [with Kukla & Ollie]

Shoo-Fly Pie and Apple Pan Dowdy
m Guy Wood, w Sammy Gallop, 1946
CSC - 11 Mar 1946

Side by Side
mw Harry Woods, 1927
The All Star Revue - 14 Feb 1953
[with Patti Page]

Sierra Sue
mw Joseph Buell Carey, 1916
BB - 30 Jun 1940

Silver and Gold
m Del Sharbutt and Bob Crosby,
w Henry Prichard, 1952
PC CBS - 27 Feb 1952
[with The Fontane Sisters]

Sing •
mw Joe Raposo, 1971
26 Mar 1973 - And I Love You So APL1-0100

Sing, Sing, Sing
mw Louis Prima, 1936
PC KMH - 18 Nov 1959

Singin' in the Bathtub
mw Herb Magidson, Ned Washington
and Michael H. Cleary, 1929
From the film The Show of Shows.
PC KMH - 16 May 1962

Singin' in the Rain
m Nacio Herb Brown, w Arthur
Freed, 1929
From the film The Hollywood Revue of 1929.
PC KMH - 29 Mar 1961 [with
Dorothy Collins]

Sleep Well, Little Children
mw Alan Bergman and Leon
Klatzkin, 1956
PC Christmas Show - 17 Dec 1974
[with Karen Carpenter]

Sleepy Time Gal •
m Ange Lorenzo and Richard A. Whiting,
w Joseph R. Alden
and Raymond B. Egan, 1925
19 Feb 1957 - We Get Letters LPM-1463

Sleigh Ride
m Leroy Anderson, w Mitchell
Parish, 1949
PC Christmas in Hawaii - 14 Dec 1985
[with Marie Osmond]

Sloop John B
mw Traditional, 1964,
mw Brian Wilson (adapt.), 1966
PC Bahamas Holiday - 21 May 1980

Smile • ★
m Charles Chaplin, 1935,
w John Turner and Geoffrey Parsons, 1954
The theme from the silent film
Modern Times.
17 May 1961 - Sing to Me, Mr. C. LSP-2390

Smoke Gets in Your Eyes
m Jerome Kern, w Otto Harbach, 1933
From the musical Roberta.
PC NBC - 24 Jan 1959

Snowbird •
mw Gene Maclellan, 1970
23 Nov 1970 - It's Impossible LSP-4473

So Far •
m Richard Rodgers,
w Oscar Hammerstein II, 1947
From the musical Allegro.
28 Jul 1947 - PC Wednesday Night
Music Hall CAL-511

So in Love • ★
mw Cole Porter, 1949
From the musical Kiss Me, Kate.
15 May 1961 - Sing to Me, Mr. C.
LSP-2390

So Rare
m Jerry Herst, w Jack Sharpe, 1937
PC NBC - 25 May 1957

Softly and Tenderly Jesus Is Calling
mw Will Thompson, 1880
PC NBC - 1 Nov 1958

Solamente una vez
(You Belong to My Heart)
mw Agustín Lara (Sp.), 1942,
w Ray Gilbert (Eng.), 1944
From the animated film
The Three Caballeros.
PC Christmas in Mexico - 15 Dec 1975
[with Vikki Carr]

Some Children See Him ●*
m Wihla Hutson, w Alfred Burt, 1954
6 Aug 1968 - Greatest Christmas Songs
0786367790-2

Somebody Cares ●
m Ernest G. Schweikert and Johnny
Robba, w Frank Reardon, 1962
26 Jun 1962 - By Request LSP-2567

Somebody Somewhere
mw Frank Loesser, 1956
From the musical The Most Happy Fella.
PC KMH - 4 Feb 1965

Somebody up There Likes Me ●
m Bronislau Kaper, w Sammy Cahn, 1956
From the film Somebody up There Likes Me.
7 Jun 1956 - 47-6590

Someone Is Waiting ●
mw Richard Ahlert and Ettore Stratta, 1980
8–17 Apr 1980 - Perry Como AFL1-3629

Someone to Watch over Me ★
m George Gershwin, w Ira
Gershwin, 1926
From the musical Oh, Kay!
PC CBS - 13 Oct 1954

Someone Who Cares ●
mw Alex Harvey, 1970
The theme from the film Fools.
29 Apr 1971 - I Think of You LSP-4539

Something to Remember You By
m Arthur Schwartz, w Howard Dietz, 1930
From the musical Three's a Crowd.
PC NBC - 16 May 1959 [with Kay Starr]

Something's Gotta Give
mw Johnny Mercer, 1955
From the film Daddy Long Legs.
PC KMH - 21 Feb 1962

The Song Is You
m Jerome Kern,
w Oscar Hammerstein II, 1932
From the musical Music in the Air.
PC NBC - 11 Apr 1959 [excerpt]

Song Sung Blue
mw Neil Diamond, 1972
The PC Winter Show - 4 Dec 1972
[with Joey Heatherton]

The Songs I Love ●
m Jimmy Van Heusen, w Sammy Cahn, 1963
26 Mar 1963 - The Songs I Love LSP-2708

The Sound of Music ★
m Richard Rodgers,
w Oscar Hammerstein II, 1959
From the musical The Sound of Music.
PC KMH - 6 Jan 1960
PC Christmas in Austria - 13 Dec 1976

South Bound Track
mw Irene Higginbotham, Milton Leeds
and Mary Schaeffer, 1943
CPPC - c. Apr-May 1943

South of the Border (down Mexico Way) ● ★
mw Jimmy Kennedy and Michael Carr, 1939
12 Feb 1957 - We Get Letters LPM-1463

Speak Low
m Kurt Weill, w Ogden Nash, 1943
From the musical One Touch of Venus.
PC KMH - 2 Jan 1963

Speak to Me of Love
mw Jean Lenoir (Fr.), 1930,
w Bruce Siever (Eng.), 1932
PC NBC - 8 Mar 1958

S'posin' ● ★
m Paul Denniker, w Andy Razaf, 1929
18 Jun 1956 - We Get Letters LPM-1463
PC NBC - 8 Feb 1958

Spring Is Here
m Richard Rodgers, w Lorenz Hart, 1938
From the musical I Married an Angel.
PC NBC - 21 Mar 1959

Spring, Spring, Spring
m Gene De Paul, w Johnny Mercer, 1954
From the film Seven Brides for
Seven Brothers.
PC KMH - 28 Mar 1966

St. Louis Blues ● ★
mw W. C. Handy, 1914
9 Apr 1959 - Como Swings LSP-2010

Stairway to the Stars
m Matty Malneck and Frank Signorelli,
w Mitchell Parish, 1939
PC NBC - 7 Apr 1956

Star Dust
m Hoagy Carmichael,
w Mitchell Parish, 1927
CSC - 22 Mar 1946 / PC NBC - 25 Apr 1959

Stay as Sweet as You Are
m Harry Revel, w Mack Gordon, 1934
From the film College Rhythm.
PC NBC - 25 May 1957

Stay with Me ●
m Nick Perito, w Ray Charles, 1965
1 Mar 1966 - Lightly Latin LSP-3552

A Still Small Voice ●
m Ben Weisman, w Al Stillman, 1958
23 Jun 1958 - When You Come to
the End of the Day LSP-1885

Stranger in Paradise
mw Robert Wright and George
Forrest, 1953
Based on the first theme of the
'Polovetsian Dances' from
Alexander Borodin's opera Prince Igor.
From the musical Kismet.
PC CBS - 27 Jan 1954

Street of Dreams
m Victor Young, w Sam M. Lewis, 1933
PC CBS - 28 Oct 1953

The Streets of Laredo
m Jay Livingston, w Ray Evans, 1948
CSC - 27 Apr 1949

Strike Up the Band
m George Gershwin, w Ira
Gershwin, 1930
From the musical Strike Up the Band.
PC NBC - 22 Feb 1958

Sugar Moon
mw Danny Wolfe, 1958
PC NBC - 7 Jun 1958 [with Eydie Gormé]

Sugartime
mw Charlie Phillips and Odis
Echols, 1958
PC NBC - 15 Mar 1958
[with The McGuire Sisters]

Summer Wind ●
m Heinz Meier (under pseud. Henry Mayer),
w Hans Bradtke (Ger.),
w Johnny Mercer (Eng.), 1965
23 Jun 1965 - 47-8636

Summertime ● ★
with Sally Sweetland
m George Gershwin,
w DuBose Heyward, 1935
From the musical Porgy and Bess.
11 Mar 1952 - TV Favourites
LPM-3013 (10")

Sunday, Monday or Always
m Jimmy Van Heusen, w Johnny
Burke, 1943
From the film Dixie.
CPPC - 30 Sep 1943 / PC NBC -
2 May 1959

Sunshine Cake
m Jimmy Van Heusen, w Johnny
Burke, 1950
From the film Riding High.
PC NBC - 10 Jan 1959
[with Jane Wyman and Rosemary Clooney]

Sway
m Luis Demetrio and Pablo Beltrán Ruiz,
w Pablo Beltrán Ruiz (Sp.), 1953,
w Norman Gimbel (Eng.), 1954
PC CBS - 13 Oct 1954

Sweet Adorable You ●
mw Baker Knight, 1964
12 Feb 1965 - The Scene
Changes LSP-3396

Sweet Lorraine
m Cliff Burwell, w Mitchell Parish, 1928
CSC - 14 Dec 1945

The Sweetheart of Sigma Chi ★
m F. Dudleigh Vernor, w Byron D.
Stokes, 1912
CSC TV - 20 Nov 1949

Swingin' down the Lane ●
m Isham Jones, w Gus Kahn, 1923
12 Feb 1957 - We Get Letters LPM-1463

Symphony
m Alex Alstone, 1942, w André Tabet
and Roger Bernstein (Fr.),
w Jack Lawrence (Eng.), 1945
CSC - 1 Nov 1945

T

Take a Look at Me ●*
mw Ronal McCown, 1972
16 Jan 1973 - Just out of Reach –
Rarities from Nashville
Produced by Chet Atkins RGM-0191

Take Care (When You Say 'Te quiero')
mw Henry Prichard, 1946
CSC - 27 Mar 1946

Take It Easy
mw Xavier Cugat (under pseud.
Albert DeBrue), Irving Taylor and Vic
Mizzy, 1943
From the film Two Girls and a Sailor.
PC KMH - 27 Feb 1963

Take It from There
m Ralph Rainger, w Leo Robin, 1942
From the film Coney Island.
CPPC - 1943

Take Me Home ●*
m Johnny Mandel, w Alan Bergman
and Marilyn Bergman, 1973
From the film Molly and Lawless John.
17 Jan 1973 - Just out of Reach –
Rarities from Nashville
Produced by Chet Atkins RGM-0191

Take Me Home, Country Roads
mw Bill Danoff, John Denver
and Taffy Nivert, 1971
Como Country: Perry and His
Nashville Friends - 17 Feb 1975

Take Me in Your Arms
m Fred Markush, w Fritz Rotter
and Fred Markush (Gr.), 1931,
w Mitchell Parish (Eng.), 1932
CPPC - 26 Apr 1943

Take Me Out to the Ball Game ★
m Albert Von Tilzer, w Jack Norworth, 1908
PC NBC - 18 Apr 1959

Appendix

Talk to the Animals
mw Leslie Bricusse, 1967
From the film Doctor Dolittle.
The PC Holiday Special - 30 Nov 1967
[with Bobbie Gentry]
PC Christmas in New York - 17 Dec 1983
[with Sarah Litzsinger]

Tammy
mw Jay Livingston and Ray Evans, 1957
From the film Tammy and the Bachelor.
PC NBC - 19 Oct 1957

Tangerine
m Victor Schertzinger,
w Johnny Mercer, 1942
From the film The Fleet's In.
PC NBC - 15 Sep 1956

A Taste of Honey
m Bobby Scott, w Ric Marlow, 1962
From the play A Taste of Honey.
PC KMH - 22 Nov 1965

Tea for Two
m Vincent Youmans, w Irving
Caesar, 1925
From the musical No, No, Nanette.
PC KMH - 24 Jan 1966 [with
Lena Horne]

Tell Me a Story
m Larry Stock, w Maurice Sigler, 1948
Guest Star (54) - 4 Apr 1948

Tell Me Why
m Marty Gold, w Al Alberts, 1952
PC CBS - 27 Feb 1952

Tenderly
m Walter Gross, w Jack Lawrence, 1946
PC CBS - 27 Jan 1954

The Test of Time
m Pyotr Ilyich Tchaikovsky, 1877,
w Bernie Wayne and Miriam Lewis, 1959
Adapted from Pyotr Ilyich Tchaikovsky's
ballet Swan Lake (Act 1, Sc. 1 'Scène').
PC NBC - 23 May 1959

Thank Heaven for Little Girls ●
m Frederick Loewe, w Alan Jay Lerner, 1958
From the musical Gigi.
17 May 1961 - Sing to Me, Mr. C. LSP-2390

Thank Your Lucky Stars
m Arthur Schwartz, w Frank Loesser, 1943
From the film Thank Your Lucky Stars.
CPPC - c. Jun–Jul 1943

That Ain't All ●
mw John D. Loudermilk, 1965
11 Feb 1965 - The Scene Changes
LSP-3396

That Moon's in My Heart
mw Albert Von Tilzer
and Harry McPherson, 1944
CSC - 3 Jan 1945 - V-Disc 410

That Old Black Magic ★
m Harold Arlen, w Johnny Mercer, 1942
From the film Star Spangled Rhythm.
PC NBC - 1 Nov 1958

That Old Feeling
m Sammy Fain, w Lew Brown, 1937
From the film Walter Wanger's
Vogues of 1938.
PC KMH - 18 Nov 1959

That's Entertainment
m Arthur Schwartz, w Howard
Dietz, 1953
From the film The Band Wagon.
PC NBC - 4 Jan 1958 [special lyrics]

That's My Desire
m Helmy Kresa, w Carroll Loveday, 1931
CSC - 3 Oct 1947

That's You (Eres tú) •
m Mojmir Sepe, w Elza Budau (Sl.),
1966, mw Juan Carlos Calderón (Sp.),
1973, w Jay Livingston and Ray Evans
(Eng.), 1974
29 Apr 1974 - Perry CPL1-0585

Them There Eyes
mw Maceo Pinkard, William Tracey
and Doris Tauber, 1930
PC NBC - 7 Mar 1959

There Goes My Heart
m Abner Silver, w Benny Davis, 1934
PC NBC - 8 Nov 1958

There Goes That Song Again
m Jule Styne, w Sammy Cahn, 1944
From the film Carolina Blues.
CSC - 9 Feb 1945

There! I've Said It Again
mw Redd Evans and David Mann, 1945
CSC - 12 Jan 1945

**There'll Be a Hot Time
in the Old Town Tonight**
m Theodore H. Metz, w Joe Hayden, 1896
PC NBC - 12 Jan 1957

There'll Be Some Changes Made
m W. Benton Overstreet,
w Billy Higgins, 1924
CSC - 24 Nov 1947

There'll Soon Be a Rainbow •
mw Henry Nemo and David Saxon, 1943
20 Jun 1943 - 20-1538
CPPC - c. May 1943

**There's a Kind of Hush
(All over the World) •**
mw Les Reed and Geoff Stevens, 1966
6–10 Jun 1977 - The Best of British
PL 12373 (UK)

There's No Two Ways About Love
m James P. Johnson and Irving Mills,
w Ted Koehler, 1943
From the film Stormy Weather.
CPPC - 23 Jul 1943

They Didn't Believe Me
m Jerome Kern, w Herbert Reynolds, 1914
From the musical *The Girl from Utah*.
PC KMH - 22 Nov 1965

Thinking of You
m Harry Ruby, w Bert Kalmar, 1927
From the musical *The Five O'Clock Girl*.
PC NBC - 13 Dec 1958

This Heart of Mine
m Harry Warren, w Arthur Freed, 1943
From the film *Ziegfeld Follies*.
CSC - 1 Jan 1945

This Nearly Was Mine ●
m Richard Rodgers,
w Oscar Hammerstein II, 1949
From the musical *South Pacific*.
17 May 1961 - Sing to Me, Mr. C.
LSP-2390

Three Little Words
m Harry Ruby, w Bert Kalmar, 1930
From the film *Check and Double Check*.
PC NBC - 13 Dec 1958

Till There Was You
mw Meredith Willson, 1957
From the musical *The Music Man*.
PC KMH - 7 Oct 1959

Time on My Hands
m Vincent Youmans,
w Harold Adamson and
Mack Gordon, 1930
From the musical *Smiles*.
CSC - 21 Mar 1945

A Time to Be Jolly
mw Les Brown, Sonny Burke
and Lee Hale, 1971
The PC Winter Show - 10 Dec 1973

Tiny Bubbles
mw Leon Pober, 1966
PC Hawaiian Holiday - 22 Feb 1976
[with Don Ho]

Tip Toe Through the Tulips with Me
m Joe Burke, w Al Dubin, 1929
From the film *Gold Diggers of Broadway*.
PC NBC - 28 Mar 1959

'Tis Autumn
mw Henry Nemo, 1941
PC KMH - 17 Oct 1962 [with
Sandy Stewart]

Together Wherever We Go
m Jule Styne, w Stephen Sondheim, 1959
From the musical *Gypsy*.
PC Springtime Special - 9 Apr 1979
[with Bernadette Peters]

Tonight I Celebrate My Love for You ●
m Michael Masser, w Gerry Goffin, 1983
2–3 Feb 1987 - PC Today 6368-1-R

Too Marvelous for Words ★
m Richard A. Whiting,
w Johnny Mercer, 1937
From the film *Ready, Willing and Able*.
PC KMH - 5 Dec 1962

Too Young ●
m Sidney Lippman, w Sylvia Dee, 1951
26 Oct 1960 - For the Young at Heart
LSP-2343

Too Young to Go Steady ●
m Jimmy McHugh, w Harold
Adamson, 1955
2 Nov 1960 - For the Young at Heart
LSP-2343

Toot, Toot, Tootsie, Goodbye
mw Ted Fio Rito, Robert King,
Gus Kahn and Ernie Erdman, 1922
PC NBC - 25 May 1957

Toselli's Serenade (Dreams and Memories) ●
m Enrico Toselli, 1900,
w Carl Sigman (Eng. and adapt.), 1966
19 May 1966 - PC in Italy LSP-3608

Trees ●* ★
m Otto Rasbach, w Joyce Kilmer, 1922
17 Feb 1955 - So Smooth XQAM-1078

The Trolley Song
mw Hugh Martin and Ralph Blane, 1944
From the film Meet Me in St. Louis.
PC NBC - 24 May 1958

True Love ★
mw Cole Porter, 1956
From the film High Society.
PC NBC - 7 Jun 1958

Trust in Me
m Milton Ager and Jean Schwartz,
w Ned Wever, 1937
PC NBC - 16 Feb 1957

Try a Little Tenderness ●* ★
mw Harry Woods, Jimmy Campbell
and Reg Connelly, 1933
13 Jun 1956 - Yesterday & Today – A
Celebration in Song 0786366098-2
PC KMH - 6 Jan 1960

Tulsa
m Allie Wrubel, w Mort Greene, 1949
CSC - 20 Apr 1949

Tumbling Tumbleweeds ● ★
with The Sons of the Pioneers
mw Bob Nolan, 1934
18 Dec 1950 - Dreamer's Holiday CAL-582

Twilight on the Trail ● ★
m Louis Alter, w Sidney D. Mitchell, 1936
From the film Trail of the Lonesome Pine.
6 Mar 1958 - Saturday Night with Mr. C.
LSP-1971

Two Lost Souls ●
with Jaye P. Morgan
mw Richard Adler and Jerry Ross, 1955
From the musical Damn Yankees.
28 Apr 1955 - 47-6137

Two Loves Have I ●
m Vincent Scotto, w Géo Koger
and Henri Varna (Fr.), 1930,
w Jack Murray
and Barry Trivers (Eng.), 1931
7 Oct 1947 - 20-2545

U

**Un giorno dopo l'altro
(One Day Is Like Another)** ●
*mw Luigi Tenco (It.), w Earl Shuman
(Eng.), 1966
11–16 May 1966 - PC in Italy LSP-3608*

Unchained Melody ●* ★
*m Alex North, w Hy Zaret, 1955
The theme from the film Unchained.
13 Jun 1956 - Yesterday & Today –
A Celebration in Song 0786366098-2*

Until It's Time for You to Go
*mw Buffy Sainte-Marie, 1967
PC Christmas in New Mexico - 14 Dec
1979 [with Buffy Sainte-Marie]*

V

**Vaya con Dios
(May God Be with You)** ●
*mw Larry Russell, Inez James
and Buddy Pepper, 1953
13 Feb 1958 - Saturday Night with
Mr. C. LSP-1971*

A Very Precious Love
*m Sammy Fain,
w Paul Francis Webster, 1958
From the film Marjorie Morningstar.
PC NBC - 4 Apr 1959*

The Village of St. Bernadette
*mw Eula Parker, 1960
PC KMH - 20 Jan 1960*

Violets for Your Furs
*m Matt Dennis, w Tom Adair, 1941
PC KMH - 7 Dec 1960*

Volare (Nel blu, dipinto di blu)
*m Domenico Modugno, w Franco Migliacci
and Domenico Modugno (It.),
w Mitchell Parish (Eng.), 1958
PC NBC - 13 Sep 1958*

W

Waitin' for the Train to Come In
*mw Sunny Skylar and Martin Block, 1945
CSC - 5 Dec 1945*

Watch What Happens
*m Michel Legrand, w Jacques Demy
(Fr.), 1964, w Norman Gimbel (Eng.), 1965
From the film The Umbrellas of Cherbourg.
PC Summer of '74 - 12 Sep 1974
[with Michele Lee]*

Watermelon Weather ●
*with Eddie Fisher
m Hoagy Carmichael,
w Paul Francis Webster, 1952
13 May 1952 - 47-4744*

Way Back Home
*mw Al Lewis and Tom Waring, 1935
PC NBC - 7 Mar 1959 [with Eve Arden]*

Way Down Yonder in New Orleans
*m Turner Layton, w Henry Creamer, 1922
From the revue Spice of 1922.
PC CBS - 27 Jan 1954*

We Need a Little Christmas
mw Jerry Herman, 1966
From the musical Mame.
PC Irish Christmas - Dec 1994

Welcome to My Dream
m Jimmy Van Heusen, w Johnny
Burke, 1945
From the film Road to Utopia.
CSC - 16 May 1946

We'll Be Together Again
m Carl Fischer, w Frankie Laine, 1945
CSC - 1 Mar 1946

We'll Meet Again •
m Ross Parker, w Hugh Charles, 1941
6–10 Jun 1977 - The Best of British
PL 12373 (UK)

We've Only Just Begun •
mw Paul Williams and Roger Nichols, 1970
25 Nov 1970 - It's Impossible LSP-4473

What Are You Doing New Year's Eve?
mw Frank Loesser, 1947
CSC - 29 Oct 1947

What Is This Thing Called Love?
mw Cole Porter, 1930
From the revue Wake Up and Dream.
PC NBC - 9 Nov 1957

What Love Is Made Of •
mw Paul Vance, Jack Segal
and Eddie Snyder, 1967
1 Jun 1967 - A PC Christmas 0786368041-2

What the World Needs Now Is Love
m Burt Bacharach, w Hal David, 1965
PC KMH - 24 Jan 1966

**Whatever Will Be,
Will Be (Que será, será)**
mw Jay Livingston and Ray Evans, 1956
From the film The Man
Who Knew Too Much.
PC NBC - 15 Sep 1956

What'll I Do? •
mw Irving Berlin, 1924
25 Sep 1947 - A Sentimental Date with PC
LPM-1177

When •
mw George Fischoff, 1980
8–17 Apr 1980 - Perry Como AFL1-3629

When Day Is Done •
m Robert Katscher, w B. G. DeSylva, 1926
30 Sep 1947 - A Sentimental Date with PC
LPM-1177

When I Fall in Love • ★
m Victor Young, w Edward Heyman, 1952
From the film One Minute to Zero.
20 Feb 1958 - Saturday Night with Mr. C.
LSP-1971
PC Bahamas Holiday - 21 May 1980

When I Grow Too Old to Dream
m Sigmund Romberg,
w Oscar Hammerstein II, 1935
From the film The Night Is Young.
PC KMH - 18 Jan 1961

When I Need You •
m Albert Hammond,
w Carole Bayer Sager, 1977
5 Oct 1977 - Where You're Concerned
AFL1-2641

When Irish Eyes Are Smiling
m Ernest R. Ball, w Chauncey Olcott
and George Graff Jr., 1912
From the musical The Isle o' Dreams.
PC NBC - 14 Mar 1959
PC Irish Christmas - Dec 1994
[with Adele King (Twink)]

When It's Sleepy Time Down South
mw Leon René, Otis René
and Clarence Muse, 1931
PC Spring in New Orleans - 7 Apr 1976
[with Louis Cottrell's Heritage Hall
Jazz Band]

When It's Springtime in the Rockies
m Robert Sauer, w Mary Hale Woolsey
and Milton Taggert, 1930
PC NBC - 28 Mar 1959 [with cast]

When My Dreamboat Comes Home
mw Cliff Friend and Dave Franklin, 1936
PC CBS - 14 Oct 1953

**When the Red, Red Robin
Comes Bob-Bob-Bobbin' Along** ★
mw Harry Woods, 1926
PC NBC - 7 Dec 1957 [with
Ethel Merman]

**When the World Was Young
(Ah, the Apple Trees)**
m Philippe-Gérard, w Angela Vannier (Fr.),
w Johnny Mercer (Eng.), 1950
PC NBC - 15 Nov 1958

When Winter Comes
mw Irving Berlin, 1939
From the film Second Fiddle.
The PC Winter Show - 10 Dec 1973
[with Sally Struthers]

When You and I Were Young, Maggie •
m James Austin Butterfield, 1866,
w George Washington Johnson, 1864
15 Nov 1960 - For the Young at Heart
LSP-2343

When You Come to the End of the Day • ★
m Frank Westphal, w Gus Kahn, 1929
19 Jun 1958 - When You Come
to the End of the Day LSP-1885

When You Wish upon a Star
m Leigh Harline, w Ned
Washington, 1940
From the animated film Pinocchio.
PC NBC - 19 Jan 1957

**When Your Hair Has Turned to Silver
(I Will Love You Just the Same)** • ★
m Peter De Rose, w Charles Tobias, 1930
25 Sep 1947 - A Sentimental Date with PC
LPM-1177

When Your Lover Has Gone
mw Einar Aaron Swan, 1931
PC KMH - 14 Feb 1962

When You're Away ●* ★
m Victor Herbert, w Henry Blossom, 1914
From the musical The Only Girl.
8 Feb 1955 - So Smooth XQAM-1078

When You're in Love ●
m Gene De Paul, w Johnny Mercer, 1954
From the film Seven Brides
for Seven Brothers.
5 Jun 1968 - Look to Your Heart
LSP-4052

When You're Smiling
(the Whole World Smiles with You) ● ★
mw Mark Fisher, Joe Goodwin
and Larry Shay, 1928
25 Nov 1947 - PC Wednesday Night
Music Hall CAL-511

Where Does a Little Tear Come From? ●
mw Marge Barton and Fred Macrae, 1964
12 Feb 1965 - The Scene Changes
LSP-3396

Where Is Love? ●
mw Lionel Bart, 1963
From the musical Oliver!
6–10 Jun 1977 - The Best of British
PL 12373 (UK)

The Whiffenpoof Song ● ★
m Tod B. Galloway, w Meade Minnigerode
and George S. Pomeroy, 1909
Adapted from Rudyard Kipling's
poem 'Gentlemen-Rankers'.
12 Feb 1958 - Saturday Night with Mr. C.
LSP-1971

While the Angelus Was Ringing
(Les trois cloches)
mw Jean Villard (Gilles) (Fr.), 1945,
w Dick Manning (Eng.), 1948
CSC - 23 Mar 1949

While We're Young ● ★
m Alec Wilder and Morty Palitz,
w Bill Engvick, 1943
26 Oct 1960 - For the Young at Heart
LSP-2343

Whispering
mw Richard Coburn, Vincent Rose
and John Schonberger, 1920
PC KMH - 3 Apr 1963
[with Caterina Valente]

Whither Thou Goest ●
mw Guy Singer, 1954
30 Apr 1958 - When You Come
to the End of the Day LSP-1885

Who Can I Turn To?
mw Leslie Bricusse
and Anthony Newley, 1964
From the musical The Roar of the
Greasepaint – The Smell of the Crowd.
PC KMH - 7 Jan 1965

Who Put That Dream in Your Eyes
m Nacio Porter Brown, w Al Stewart, 1947
Guest Star (54) - 4 Apr 1948

Who Wants to Be a Millionaire?
mw Cole Porter, 1956
From the film High Society.
PC Christmas in England - 15 Dec 1984
[with Ann-Margret]

Who Will Buy?
mw Lionel Bart, 1963
From the musical Oliver!
PC Spring in New Orleans - 7 Apr 1976

Who?
m Jerome Kern, w Otto Harbach
and Oscar Hammerstein II, 1925
From the musical Sunny.
PC KMH - 6 Feb 1963

Who's Sorry Now?
m Ted Snyder, w Bert Kalmar
and Harry Ruby, 1923
PC NBC - 12 Apr 1958

Why Does It Have to Rain on Sunday?
mw Bob Merrill and Vi Ott, 1947
CSC - 17 Dec 1947

With a Little Bit of Luck
m Frederick Loewe, w Alan Jay Lerner, 1956
From the musical My Fair Lady.
PC NBC - 6 Oct 1956

With the Wind and the Rain in Your Hair
mw Jack Lawrence and Clara Edwards, 1940
BB - 7 Apr 1940

Without a Penny in Your Pocket
m Fud Livingston, w Jack Wolf, 1946
CSC - 14 May 1946

Without a Word of Warning
m Harry Revel, w Mack Gordon, 1935
From the film Two for Tonight.
PC KMH - 8 Mar 1961

Wonderful Baby ●
mw Don McLean, 1974
7 Jan 1975 - RCA 2541 (UK)

Wonderful, Wonderful Day
m Gene De Paul, w Johnny Mercer, 1954
From the film Seven Brides
for Seven Brothers.
PC Christmas in Mexico - 15 Dec 1975
[with Zavala Brothers and Sisters]

A World of Love (That I Found in Your Arms) (Le ciel, le soleil et la mer) •
mw François Deguelt (Fr.), 1965,
w Judy Spencer (Eng.), 1967
1 Jun 1967 - 47-9262

Would You Like to Take a Walk?
m Harry Warren, w Mort Dixon and Billy Rose, 1930
From the revue Sweet and Low.
PC CBS - 9 Sep 1953

Wouldn't It Be Loverly?
m Frederick Loewe, w Alan Jay Lerner, 1956
From the musical My Fair Lady.
PC KMH - 21 Nov 1966
[with Angela Lansbury]

Wouldn't It Be Nice?
m Jimmy McHugh, w Harold Adamson, 1944
From the film Something for the Boys.
CSC - Jan 1945 - V-Disc 410

Wrap Your Troubles in Dreams
m Harry Barris, w Ted Koehler and Billy Moll, 1931
PC CBS - 16 Jan 1953

X

No titles

Y

Yesterdays
m Jerome Kern, w Otto Harbach, 1933
From the musical Roberta.
PC KMH - 4 Jan 1961 & 10 Oct 1962

You
m Walter Donaldson,
w Harold Adamson, 1936
From the film The Great Ziegfeld.
PC NBC - 8 Mar 1958

You and the Night and the Music
m Arthur Schwartz, w Howard Dietz, 1934
From the musical Revenge with Music.
PC NBC - 16 May 1959

You Are My Sunshine
mw Jimmie Davis and Charles Mitchell, 1940
PC NBC - 4 Jan 1958 [with Jimmy Dean]

You Are Never Far Away •* ★
m Robert Allen, w Allan Roberts, 1952
The closing theme song of Perry Como.
17 July 1952 - Yesterday & Today –
A Celebration in Song 0786366098-2
12 Mar 1958 (Theme) -
Saturday Night with Mr. C. LSP-1971

You Are So Beautiful •
mw Billy Preston and Bruce Fischer, 1975
10–11 Dec 1978 - So It Goes AFL1-4272

You Are the Sunshine of My Life •
mw Stevie Wonder, 1973
29 Apr 1974 - Perry CPL1-0585

You Call It Madness (but I Call It Love)
mw Con Conrad, Gladys DuBois,
Russ Columbo and Paul Gregory, 1931
PC NBC - 18 Jan 1958

You Came a Long Way from St. Louis •
m John Benson Brooks, w Bob Russell, 1948
23 Apr 1959 - Como Swings LSP-2010

You Came Along (from out of Nowhere)
m John Green, w Edward Heyman, 1931
CSC - 15 Oct 1945

You Can Do No Wrong •
mw Cole Porter, 1948
From the film The Pirate.
16 Oct 1947 - 20-2784

You Don't Kno' What Lonesome Is ('Til You Get to Herdin' Cows •
with The Sons of the Pioneers
mw Foster Carling
and Country Washburn, 1947
18 Dec 1950 - 47-4081

You Gotta Be a Football Hero (to Get Along with the Beautiful Girls)
mw Al Lewis, Al Sherman
and Buddy Fields, 1933
PC NBC - 8 Dec 1956

You Light Up My Life •
mw Joe Brooks, 1977
From the film You Light Up My Life.
5 Oct 1977 - Where You're Concerned
AFL1-2641

You Made Me Love You (I Didn't Want to Do It) • ★
m James V. Monaco,
w Joseph McCarthy, 1913
6 Mar 1958 - Saturday Night with Mr. C.
LSP-1971

You Must Have Been a Beautiful Baby • ★
m Harry Warren, w Johnny Mercer, 1938
From the film Hard to Get.
21 Mar 1946 - 20-1916

You Needed Me •
mw Randy Goodrum, 1978
29–31 Jul 1980 (Live) - PC Live on Tour
AQL1-3826

(You Only Want Me) When There's Nobody Else Around
m Larry Stock, w Teddy Powell, 1949
CSC - 16 Apr 1945

You Turned the Tables on Me
m Louis Alter, w Sidney D. Mitchell, 1936
From the film Sing, Baby, Sing.
PC KMH - 25 May 1960

You Were Meant for Me • ★
m Nacio Herb Brown, w Arthur Freed, 1929
From the film The Broadway Melody.
17 May 1961 - Sing to Me, Mr. C. LSP-2390

You, You, You
m Lotar Olias, w Walter Rothenburg
(Ger.), 1952, w Robert Mellin (Eng.), 1953
PC CBS - 2 Sep 1953
[with The Fontane Sisters]

You'd Be So Nice to Come Home To
mw Cole Porter, 1943
From the film Something to Shout About.
Cole Porter in Paris - 17 Jan 1973

You'll Never Go Home
mw Leon Pober, 1967
PC Hawaiian Holiday - 22 Feb 1976 [with Petula Clark, George Carlin and Don Ho]

You'll Never Know ★
m Harry Warren, w Mack Gordon, 1943
From the film Hello, Frisco, Hello.
PC NBC - 19 Oct 1957

You're Breaking My Heart
mw Pat Genaro and Sunny Skylar, 1948
Based on Ruggero Leoncavallo's 'Mattinata'.
CSC - 8 Sep 1949

You're Gonna Get My Letter in the Morning
mw Bob Merrill and Vi Ott, 1947
CSC - 18 Feb 1948

You're Nobody 'Til Somebody Loves You
mw Russ Morgan, Larry Stock and James Cavanaugh, 1944
CSC - 9 Jan 1946

You're So Understanding
m Bernie Wayne, w Ben Raleigh, 1949
CSC - 27 Apr 1949
[with The Fontane Sisters]

You're the Top
mw Cole Porter, 1934
From the musical Anything Goes.
PC KMH - 5 Oct 1960 [with Ethel Merman]

You've Changed
m Carl Fischer, w Bill Carey, 1942
CSC - 4 Feb 1948

You've Got a Friend
mw Carole King, 1971
The PC Winter Show - 4 Dec 1972
PC Spring in New Orleans - 7 Apr 1976
[with Leslie Uggams]

Z

Zing a Little Zong
m Harry Warren, w Leo Robin, 1952
From the film Just for You.
The Bing Crosby Show - 29 Feb 1960
[with Bing Crosby]

Zing Zing – Zoom Zoom ●
m Sigmund Romberg, w Charles Tobias, 1951
5 Dec 1950 - 47-3997

Zip-a-Dee-Doo-Dah
m Allie Wrubel, w Ray Gilbert, 1946
From the film Song of the South.
PC NBC - 5 Oct 1957

Notes

Introduction

1 Perry Como, interview by Michael Parkinson, *Parkinson*, 26 November 1977.
2 Ray Charles, email correspondence with George Townsend.
3 Gene Lees, liner notes for the album *Look to Your Heart*, 1968.

Chapter 1

1 Anon., 'The Aluminum Dam', *The Bridgeville Area Historical Society*, 20 May 2021. https://bridgevillehistory.org/the-aluminum-dam/.
2 Perry Como, interview by Michael Parkinson, *Parkinson*, 26 November 1977.
3 Perry Como, interview by Chris Stuart, *Perry Como* (80th Birthday Tribute), 18 May 1992.
4 Perry Como, interview by Arlene Herson, *The Arlene Herson Show*, 1984.
5 Perry Como, 'Perry Como: I've been Married Three Times', by Claire Primus, *TV and Movie Screen*, July 1958.
6 Perry Como, booklet notes by Colin Escott for the Compilation *Yesterday and Today: A Celebration in Song*, 1993.
7 Ted Weems, *Reader's Digest Music Guide*, January 1962.
8 Perry Como, interview by Phil Donahue, *Donahue*, 10 September 1979.
9 Perry Como, interview by William B. Williams, *William B. & Company*, December 1976.
10 Perry Como, 'The Perry Como You Should Know', by Richard Heller, *TV Stage*, October 1955.

Chapter 2

1. Perry Como, booklet notes by Colin Escott for the Compilation *Yesterday and Today: A Celebration in Song*, 1993.
2. Perry Como, booklet notes by Colin Escott for the Compilation *Yesterday and Today: A Celebration in Song*, 1993.
3. Harriet Van Horne, *New York World-Telegram*, c. June 1943.
4. Abel Green, *Variety*, 16 June 1943.
5. Vic Damone, 'A&E Biography: The Singing Barber', Hal Lewis, dir., 22 December 2000.
6. Perry Como, interview by Chris Stuart, *Perry Como* (80th Birthday Tribute), 18 May 1992.
7. Perry Como, 'The Barber Comes to Town', 14 December 1975.
8. Margaret Whiting, interview by David Jacobs, 'Magic Moments – The Perry Como Story', 18 May 1997.
9. *Billboard*, 28 July 1945.
10. Anon., *Perry Como Album* (A Dell Magazine), 1950.
11. Perry Como, 'The Doris Mary Anne Kappelhoff Special', 14 March 1971.
12. Perry Como, 'Perry Como – In Person', 19 May 1971.
13. *Collier's*, 6 January 1956.
14. Dee Belline, 'Como: The Pied Piper of TV', by Martin Cohen, *TV Radio Mirror*, December 1957.

Chapter 3

1. *Time*, 27 December 1948.
2. http://www.boo-ga-loo.demon.co.uk
3. Perry Como, interview by Arlene Herson, *The Arlene Herson Show*, 1984.
4. Mel Tormé, interview by Lilyan Chauvin, *Hollywood Structured*, 1991. https://www.youtube.com/watch?v=-yJRpalARZo
5. Hank Snow, *This Is My Story*, 1966.
6. Perry Como, 'The Barber Comes to Town', 14 December 1975.

7 Perry Como, interview by William B. Williams, *William B. & Company*, December 1976.

8 Warren Covington, interview by David Jacobs, 'Magic Moments – The Perry Como Story', 18 May 1997.

9 Perry Como, interview by William B. Williams, *William B. & Company*, December 1976.

10 Perry Como, interview by Chris Stuart, *Perry Como* (80th Birthday Tribute), 18 May 1992.

11 Dick Stark, *The Perry Como Show*, 2 May 1952.

12 Irving Berlin, liner notes for the compilation *Como's Golden Records*, 1954.

13 Perry Como, 'Como: The Pied Piper of TV' by Martin Cohen, *TV Radio Mirror*, December 1957.

14 Rudyard Kipling, 'If', 1910.

15 Perry Como, interview by William B. Williams, *William B. & Company*, December 1976.

16 Perry Como, 'Guideposts Classics: Perry Como on Faith, Family and Prayer', *Guideposts*, December 1953. https://guideposts.org/faith-prayer-devotions/guideposts-classics-perry-como-on-faith-family-and-prayer/

17 Perry Como, interview by Phil Donahue, *Donahue*, 10 September 1979.

18 Perry Como, interview by Chris Stuart, *Perry Como* (80th Birthday Tribute), 18 May 1992.

19 *Variety*, 25 August 1954.

20 Richard Heller, 'The Perry Como You Should Know', *TV Stage*, October 1955.

Chapter 4

1 *Variety*, 21 September 1955.

2 Kirk Douglas, *The Perry Como Show*, 17 December 1955.

3 *Time*, 19 December 1955.

4 Ray Charles, email message to author.

5 Ray Charles, interview by David Jacobs, 'Magic Moments – The Perry Como Story', 18 May 1997.

6 Anon., 'Ye Olde Free-For-All', *TV Guide*, 11 February 1956.

7   Perry Como, 'A&E Biography: The Singing Barber', Hal Lewis, dir., 22 December 2000.
8   Anon., 'Ye Olde Free-For-All', *TV Guide*, 11 February 1956.
9   Perry Como, interview by William B. Williams, *William B. & Company*, December 1976.
10 Goodman Ace, 'Perry Como: The Millionaire Behind the Smile', by Ted Constable, *TV Best*, December 1957.
11 William B. Williams quoting Goodman Ace, *William B. & Company*, December 1976.
12 Perry Como, 'Perry Como: The Millionaire Behind the Smile', by Ted Constable, *TV Best*, December 1957.
13 Dinah Shore, 'Why I Love Perry – by Dinah Shore as told to Bill Tusher', *TV and Movie Screen*, February 1958.
14 Ervin Drake, email message to George Townsend, c. December 2001.
15 Ethel Gabriel, email message to George Townsend.
16 George Townsend, text message to Matthew Long.
17 Millicent Morton, 'Kid With the Beat', *TV Star Parade*, February 1957.
18 Jimmy Van Heusen, *The Perry Como Show*, 13 September 1958.
19 Perry Como, 'The Barber Comes to Town', 14 December 1975.
20 Perry Como, 'Christmas with Nationwide: Journey to Bethlehem', 21 December 1977.
21 Nick Perito, 'Christmas at the Hollywood Palace', December 2004.

Chapter 5

1   George Eells, 'Perry Como: How Much Is His $25,000,000 Worth?', *Look*, 12 May 1959.
2   George Eells, 'Perry Como: How Much Is His $25,000,000 Worth?', *Look*, 12 May 1959.
3   Michael Parkinson, *Parkinson*, 26 November 1977.
4   Andy Williams, interview by David Jacobs, 'Magic Moments – The Perry Como Story', 18 May 1997.
5   Val Doonican, interview by David Jacobs, 'Magic Moments – The Perry Como Story', 18 May 1997.
6   Perry Como, *Perry Como's Kraft Music Hall*, 16 March 1960.

7   *Variety*, 4 May 1960.
8   Yvonne Littlewood, interview by David Jacobs, 'Magic Moments – The Perry Como Story', 18 May 1997.
9   Myrna Oliver, 'Nick Vanoff, 61; Producer Won Tony, Five Emmys', *Los Angeles Times*, 22 March 1991. https://www.latimes.com/archives/la-xpm-1991-03-22-mn-649-story.html.
10 Felisa Vanoff, 'Christmas at the Hollywood Palace', December 2004.
11 Dwight Hemion, interview by Michael Rosen for the Television Academy Foundation, 9 July 2001. https://interviews.televisionacademy.com/interviews/dwight-hemion?clip=1#interview-clips.
12 Jimmy Durante, *Perry Como's Kraft Music Hall*, 22 February 1961.
13 Lena Horne, *The 6th Annual American Music Awards*, 12 January 1979.
14 Hugh Wilson, dir., *Blast from the Past*, 1999.
15 Perry Como and Ted Weems, *Perry Como's Kraft Music Hall*, 18 October 1961.
16 Anon., cover caption for the album *By Request*, 1962.
17 Perry Como, 'The Barber Comes to Town', 14 December 1975.
18 Anita Kerr, email message to author, 28 November 2009.
19 Nick Perito, 'The Barber Comes to Town', 14 December 1975.
20 Hank Wiswell, email message to George Townsend, 1999.
21 Nick Perito, interview by David Jacobs, 'Magic Moments - The Perry Como Story', 18 May 1997.
22 Anon., liner notes for the album *Lightly Latin*, 1966.
23 Vic Damone, interview by David Jacobs, 'Magic Moments – The Perry Como Story', 18 May 1997.
24 Gene Lees, liner notes for the album *Look to Your Heart*, 1968.

Chapter 6

1   Felisa Vanoff, 'Christmas at the Hollywood Palace', December 2004.
2   Felisa Vanoff, 'Christmas at the Hollywood Palace', December 2004.
3   Benny Green, 'The Barber Comes to Town', 14 December 1975.
4   George Townsend quoting Nick Perito, text message to author.

5   *The Gramophone*, 1971.
6   Val Doonican, interview by David Jacobs, 'Magic Moments – The Perry Como Story', 18 May 1997.
7   Perry Como, *Associated Press*, November 1972.
8   Perry Como, *Associated Press*, November 1972.
9   Perry Como, interview by William B. Williams, *William B. & Company*, December 1976.
10 Perry Como, Gala Midnight Charity Concert at the London Palladium, 9 May 1974.
11 Perry Como, interview by Michael Parkinson, *Parkinson*, 26 November 1977.
12 Brian Mulligan, *Music Week*, 18 May 1974.
13 James Green, *Evening News*, 10 May 1974.
14 Perry Como, *The Royal Variety Performance*, 23 November 1974.
15 Micmarsus, 'Perry Como and His Nashville Friends are a Hit at the Opry House', *Nashville Sound*, September 1975.
16 Perry Como, 'The Barber Comes to Town', 14 December 1975.
17 Perry Como, 'The Barber Comes to Town', 14 December 1975.
18 Perry Como, interview by Michael Parkinson, *Parkinson*, 26 November 1977.
19 Perry Como, 'The Barber Comes to Town', 14 December 1975.
20 Tommy Loftus, interview by Matthew Long, October 2011.
21 Benny Green, 'The Barber Comes to Town', 14 December 1975.
22 Perry Como, 'Val Doonican's Very Special Christmas', 24 December 1984.
23 Tommy Loftus, interview by Matthew Long, October 2011.
24 Yvonne Littlewood, 'Christmas with Nationwide: Journey to Bethlehem', 21 December 1977.
25 Perry Como, 'Christmas with Nationwide: Journey to Bethlehem', 21 December 1977.
26 Yvonne Littlewood, interview by David Jacobs, 'Magic Moments – The Perry Como Story', 18 May 1997.
27 Perry Como, interview by Chris Stuart, *Perry Como* (80th Birthday Tribute), 18 May 1992.
28 Anne Murray, interview by Matthew Long, 16 February 2024.

Chapter 7

1. Jay Leno, *Duke Children's Classic*, 20 May 1995.

2. Nick Perito, interview by Alan Cass for the American Music Research Center (University of Colorado, Boulder), 18 March 2005.

3. Tony Mottola, interview by Michael Rosen for the Television Academy Foundation, 24 October 2000. https://interviews.televisionacademy.com/interviews/tony-mottola

4. Thornton F. Bradshaw, 'Perry Como's 40th Anniversary with RCA Records, 50th in Show Business Saluted at Rainbow Grill Ceremonies', RCA Press Release, June 1983.

5. Robert D. Summer, 'Perry Como's 40th Anniversary with RCA Records, 50th in Show Business Saluted at Rainbow Grill Ceremonies', RCA Press Release, June 1983.

6. Ronald Reagan, 'Perry Como's 40th Anniversary with RCA Records, 50th in Show Business Saluted at Rainbow Grill Ceremonies', RCA Press Release, June 1983.

7. Perry Como, 'Perry Como's 40th Anniversary with RCA Records, 50th in Show Business Saluted at Rainbow Grill Ceremonies', RCA Press Release, June 1983.

8. Perry Como, *Entertainment Tonight*, June 1983.

9. Marvin Hamlisch, *Entertainment Tonight*, June 1983.

10. Sarah Litzsinger '"It's My Life," Carmel Native Living Out Childhood Dream on Stage', by Michael Hartz, *WRTV (ABC Indianapolis) (Scripps Media, Inc.)*, 14 December 2023.

11. *Variety*, 21 December 1983.

12. Perry Como, 'Val Doonican's Very Special Christmas', 24 December 1984.

13. Perry Como, *Regis Philbin's Life Styles*, August 1984.

14. Lucinda Cummings Kilmer, email message to Matthew Long, 25 January 2008.

15. Greg Dawson, *Orlando Sentinel*, 23 December 1987.

16. Perry Como, interview by Arlene Herson, *The Arlene Herson Show*, 1984.

17. Ray Charles, email message to Malcolm Macfarlane, 18 April 2007.

18. Beverly Beckham, 'Perry Como Made It the Best Night of Her Entire Life', *The Boston Herald*, 7 July 1989.

19. John Williams, *Evening at Pops*, 14 August 1988.

20. Nick Perito, *I Just Happened to Be There: Making Music with the Stars*, Xlibris, 2004.

21. Cassie Miller, email message to Matthew Long, 16 September 2007.

22. Yuzo Kayama, 'Friendship Concert', 22 October 1989.

23 Perry Como, 'Friendship Concert', 22 October 1989.

24 Perry Como, interview by Chris Stuart, *Perry Como* (80th Birthday Tribute), 18 May 1992.

Chapter 8

1 Frank Sinatra, *Academy of Television Arts & Sciences Hall of Fame*, 24 January 1990.

2 Perry Como, *Academy of Television Arts & Sciences Hall of Fame*, 24 January 1990.

3 Bob Wynn, file note of interview by Malcolm Macfarlane, 1 August 2007.

4 Jim Santella, *The Buffalo News*, 9 December 1990.

5 Perry Como, concert at Westbury Music Fair, Long Island, New York, 30 November to 2 December 1990.

6 Dr Robert F. Vizza, interview by Diane Ketcham, *New York Times*, 10 June 1990.

7 Perry Como, interview by Diane Ketcham, *New York Times*, 10 June 1990.

8 Sister Jean, interview by Diane Ketcham, *New York Times*, 10 June 1990.

9 Perry Como, interview by Diane Ketcham, *New York Times*, 10 June 1990.

10 Anon., 'A Brief History of the Duke Children's Classic: 16 Years and Growing', Duke University Press Release, May 1990.

11 Perry Como, *Hard Copy*, 14 June 1991.

12 Perry Como, interview by Chris Stuart, *Perry Como* (80th Birthday Tribute), 18 May 1992.

13 Perry Como, 'The Barber Comes to Town', 14 December 1975.

14 Ray Charles, file note of interview by Malcolm Macfarlane, 20 September 2007.

15 Roy Clark, Charity Concert in Florida, c. 10–11 April 1993.

16 Perry Como, 'Perry Como's Irish Christmas', December 1994.

17 Christopher Logan, email message to Matthew Long, 15 February 2025.

18 Perry Como, *Duke Children's Classic*, 20 May 1995.

19 Roselle Como, 'Perry Como's Wife Sings His Praises at 65th Wedding Anniversary', *Pittsburgh Post-Gazette*, c. July 1998.

20 Perry Como statue inscription, Canonsburg, Pennsylvania.

21 Bernie Miller, liner notes for compilation *Make Someone Happy*, 1962.

22 Vox Pop, 'The Barber Comes to Town', 14 December 1975.
23 Benny Green, liner notes for the album *The Best of British*, 1977.
24 Nick Perito, 'Christmas at the Hollywood Palace', December 2004.
25 Perry Como, 'Mr. Nice Guy? Perry Como Wonders "What Do They Expect Me To Do?"' by Gilbert Millstein, *TV Guide*, 14 January 1961.

Bibliography

Books

Gelatt, Roland. *The Fabulous Phonograph 1877 to 1977*, 2nd edn. London: Cassell, 1977.

Harmon, Jim. *The Great Radio Heroes*, rev. edn. Jefferson, North Carolina: McFarland, 2001.

Lissauer, Robert. *Lissauer's Encyclopedia of Popular Music in America 1888 to the Present*. New York: Paragon House, 1991.

Macfarlane, Malcolm and Ken Crossland. *Perry Como – A Biography and Complete Career Record*. Jefferson, North Carolina: McFarland, 2009.

Millard, Andre. *America on Record – A History of Recorded Sound*. Cambridge University Press, 1995.

O'Connor, Des. *Bananas Can't Fly!: The Autobiography*. London: Headline, 2002.

Perito, Nick. *I Just Happened to Be There: Making Music with the Stars*. Bloomington: Xlibris, 2004.

Roberts, David. *British Hit Singles and Albums*, 18th ed. Guinness World Records Limited, 2005.

Scholes, Percy A. *The Oxford Companion to Music*, 10th ed., edited by John Owen Ward. Oxford University Press, 1970

Walker, Leo. *The Big Band Almanac*, rev. ed. New York: Da Capo Press, 1989.

Whitburn, Joel. *Pop Memories 1890–1954 – The History of American Popular Music*. Menomonee Falls, Wisconsin: Record Research Inc., 1986.

Whitburn, Joel. *Pop Hits 1940–1954*. Menomonee Falls, Wisconsin: Record Research Inc., 1994.

Whitburn, Joel. *Top Pop Albums 1955–1996*. Menomonee Falls, Wisconsin: Record Research Inc., 1996.

Whitburn, Joel. *Top Pop Singles 1955–1999*. Menomonee Falls, Wisconsin: Record Research Inc., 2000.

Websites

45cat - 45cat.com
DAHR (Discography of American Historical Recordings) - adp.library.ucsb.edu/index.php
Discogs - discogs.com
Hymnary.org - hymnary.org
IMDb (Internet Movie Database) - imdb.com
IMSLP Petrucci Music Library - imslp.org
Internet Archive - archive.org
The Online Books Page - onlinebooks.library.upenn.edu
A Perry Como Discography and Digital Companion - kokomo.ca
SecondHandSongs - secondhandsongs.com
Sheet Music Singer - sheetmusicsinger.com
YouTube - youtube.com

Index

Ace, Goodman 72
Adams, Don 97
Adamson, Harold. 30–1
albums and compilations
   The Best of British 130–1
   Como's Golden Records 57
   Como Swings 80
   I Believe 61–2
   And I Love You So 118–20
   It's Impossible 116
   Lightly Latin 104
   Look to Your Heart 104–6
   Perry Como (1980) 139–40
   The Perry Como Christmas Album 107–8
   Perry Como in Italy 105
   Perry Como in Person at the International Hotel, Las Vegas 115–16
   Perry Como Live on Tour 140
   Perry Como Sings Merry Christmas Music 81–2
   Perry Como Today 148–9
   The RCA Victor Platter Party 47
   By Request 99
   Saturday Night with Mr. C. 74
   The Scene Changes 102–3
   Season's Greetings from Perry Como 81–2
   So It Goes 148
   So Smooth 63–4
   We Get Letters 80
   When You Come to the End of the Day 77
   Yesterday & Today A Celebration in Song 162
Alessandroni Singers, Alessandro 105
Allyson, June 101
Altschuler, Ernie 115
Ameche, Don 97, 147
Andrews, Jack 70
Andrews, Julie 121
Arena, Jay 159
Arlen, Harold 54
Armstrong, Louis 70
Artane Boys Band 163
Atkins, Chet 102, 118, 124
Austin, Gene 16
awards and commemorations
   Academy of Television Arts & Sciences Hall of Fame 157
   American Music Awards 134
   Billboard 120, 169
   British Phonographic Industry (BPI) 120
   Emmys 74, 128
   gold records 31, 34, 36, 53, 57, 75, 85, 143
   Grammys 83
   Guinness Book of Records 114
   Kennedy Center Honours 147
   Most Romantic Singer of 1944 32
   Nielsen ratings 71, 145
   Peabody Award 71

Index

Perry Como Avenue   37
Perry Como Statue   168–70
Perry Como Week   37
RCA Victor anniversaries   52, 142–3, 162
Ayres, Mitchell   46, 62, 69, 103–4, 161

Bacharach, Burt   82, 99–100
Balducci family, The   145
Ballard, Kaye   97
Bancroft, Anne   92, 95
Banner, Bob   128, 144, 146
Barbour, Dave   34–5
beginnings
    barbering   13–14, 16
    Canonsburg Italian Band   14
    double-bell euphonium   14
    Perry & Lou – The Comedy Boys   16
Begley, Ed   107
Berger, Senta   130
Berle, Milton   157
Berlin, Irving   54, 57, 97
Berliner, Emile   28
Berniker, Mike   139–40, 148
Bigard, Barney   76
Blaine, Vivian   31
Blair, Janet   97
Block, Martin   32, 50
Blondell, Joan   52
Blue, Ben   52
Boone, Debby   134
Boone, Pat   168
Borge, Victor   32, 101
Boswell, Connee   32
Boys' Choir of St. Peter of Alcantara, The   43
Bradshaw, Thornton F.   143
Brewer, Teresa   51
Brown, Nacio Herb   78
Burns, George   97
Burton, Jay   72
business
    contracts, fees and royalties   60, 76–7, 89–90, 100–1, 142
    philosophy   72

popular music charts and record sales   74, 75–6, 83
recording bans and disputes   22, 27, 28, 44, 45
retirement   168
Roncom   56, 60, 89
song pitching, plugging and publishing   53–4, 56, 60
USP (Unique Selling Point)   171
Bygraves, Max   78

Caesar, Sid   69, 130
Cahn, Sammy   54
Canova, Diana   133, 134
Captain and Tennille   139
Carlone, Freddie   11, 13, 17
Carmichael, Hoagy   51
Carney, Art   117
Carroll, Diahann   113–14, 147
Carson, Johnny   92
Carson, Mindy   51
Caruso, Enrico   12, 82
Case, Russ   36
Cavallaro, Carmen   32
Charisse, Cyd   31, 101
charity
    Duke Children's Classic   159, 166–8
    John Gary charity fundraiser   159–60
    philosophy   61
    Sister Jean   159
    St. Francis' Hospital Celebrity Golf Classic   158–9
Charles, Ray   46, 53, 70, 71, 75, 83, 99, 104, 148, 161, 170
Cherico, Gene   142
Clark, Buddy   46
Clark, Petula   132
Clark, Roy   162
Clooney, Rosemary   69
Collins, Joan   70
Columbo, Russ   16, 17
concerts
    Boston Pops   150–2
    Chicago Theatre   20–1, 37
    Christmas tours   158–9

Copacabana   29
    fiftieth anniversary tour   145
    Harrah's, Lake Tahoe   118, 128
    International Hotel (Hilton), Las
        Vegas   115–16, 118
    Japan   127, 152–3, 161–2
    London Palladium   121–3
    Mill Run Theatre, Niles, Illinois   140
    National Memorial Day Concert   161
    Palmer House, Chicago   18
    Paramount Theatre, New York   29
    The Point Theatre, Dublin,
        Ireland   162–6
    South Shore Music Circus, Cohasset,
        Massachusetts   149–50
    20th Century-Fox studios, Hollywood,
        California   142
    UK tour   125–7
    Versailles Club   29
    White House, Washington,
        D.C.   141–2
Conway, Russ   92
Cooley, Lee   50, 65, 72
Costa, Don   116, 131
Cottler, Irving 'Irv,'   142
Covington, Warren   54
Cramer, Floyd   102, 124
Craven, Gemma   132
Crosby, Bing   16–18, 91–2, 107, 150–2

Damone, Vic   29, 105–86
DaPron, Louis   69
David, Hal   82, 99
David, Mack   48
Davis and the Nashville Brass,
    Danny   124
Davis Jr, Sammy   158
Day, Doris   117
Dennis, Clark   20
Derringer, Glenn   77
Dickinson, Angie   146
Disney, Walt   48–50
Domingo, Placido   152
Donahue, Phil   61
Donegan, Lonnie   78

Doonican, Val   91, 116
Dorsey, Jimmy   51
Dorsey, Tommy   45
Douglas, Kirk   48, 70
Drake, Ervin   76
Drake, Tom   31
Duke of Bedford, The 13th   92
Durante, Jimmy   95

Ellington, Duke   76
Everly Brothers, The   78

Falcone, Vincent 'Vinnie'   141
family
    Christmas   118
    David Como   38, 168
    Dee Belline   38, 56
    Lucia Como   11–12
    Pietro Como   11–12, 14, 29–30, 35
    Ronnie Como   22, 43, 52
    Roselle Como   13, 23, 65, 142, 157,
        167, 168
    Terri Como   37–8, 161
Fans
    bobby-soxers   29–30, 51
    England   121, 125–7, 170
    Ireland   164–6
    Scotland   125
    United States   149–50, 158–9
Fargo, Donna   124
Faye, Alice   97
Ferrer, José   92
Fielding, Fenella   92
Fields, Dorothy   78
Fifth Army Band and Air Force Band of
    the West   146
film
    And the Angels Sing   29
    Blast from the Past   97
    Cinderella   48–50
    Doll Face   30–1
    film making   30
    If I'm Lucky   31
    March of Time Upbeat in Music   27
    The Odessa File   130

script writing   72
Somebody up There Likes Me   70
Something for the Boys   30
stereo soundtracks   31
Swing Frolic   21
Words and Music   31
Finkel, Bob   72, 79
Fisher, Eddie   160
Fitzgerald, Ella   134
Fodor, Eugene   133
Fonda, Henry   70
Fontane Sisters, The   44–5, 48, 50, 54, 57–8
Fonteyn, Dame Margot   92
Ford, Gerald   159
Forever Plaid   167
Foster, George   72

Gabriel, Ethel   76
Gallop, Frank   69
Gary, John   159–60
Gaynor, Mitzi   117
Gibbs, Parker   98
Gigli, Beniamino   12
Glass, Mickey   56, 148–51, 168
Gleason, Jackie   70–2, 160
Goodman, Benny   58, 91
Gordon, Mack   54
Grant, Cary   48
Grean, Charlie   108
Green, Mort   72
Greene, Shecky   113
Griffith, John   159

Hall, Ray   107
Hamilton, Vera   168
Hamlisch, Marvin   143
Hammerstein II, Oscar   78
Hampton, Lionel   51
Harmonizers, The   147
Harnick, Sheldon   143
Harris, Phil   91
Hart, Lorenz   31
Hemion, Dwight   94, 147
Hilliard, Bob   99

Hirt, Al   102
Hoffman, Al   48, 50
Hope, Bob   114–15, 128, 134, 159, 160
Horne, Lena   97, 101, 134
Howes, Sally Ann   78
Hudson, Rock   70
Hugo and Luigi   99
Hutton, Betty   29
Hutton, Marion   32

images
    Early 1950s hand-signed publicity photo   55
    Jupiter Lighthouse   146
    London Palladium   123
    MacGregor Putters   144
    1940s portrait   36
    Odeon Theatre autograph signing   127
    Odeon Theatre ticket stub   126
    paperweight souvenir   171
    Perry Como Album (Dell magazine)   49
    Perry Como statue   169
    with Pete Murray and Johnny Mercer   120
    Point Theatre (shaking hands with fans)   164
    Point Theatre (with Liam and Christopher Logan)   166
    between rehearsals   96
    with Rocky Marciano   73
    The Sons of Italy   15
    St. Jude Catholic Church   151
    Ted Weems and his Orchestra   19
Ingle, Red   17, 20, 98

James, Harry   31
Jarrett, Art   17
Johnson, Sterling   128
Jolson, Al   17, 60
Jones, Clark   72
Jones, Tom   117

Kaiser, Fred   13
Kanaga, Larry   52

Kapp, Dave   18, 52, 53
Kapp, Jack   53
Katz, Sam   159
Kayama, Yuzo   152
Kenny, Pat   163
Kerr, Anita   102
Kilmer, Lucinda Cummings   146–7
King, Adele 'Twink'   163, 165
King, Billie Jean   128
King Cole Trio, The   32
Klenner, John   34
Koch, Ed   145
Kukla and Ollie   113

La Rosa, Julius   69
Laine, Frankie   69, 77
Lamour, Dorothy   29, 48
Langford, Frances   97
Lee, Brenda   77
Lee, Gypsy Rose   30
Lee, Michele   144–5
Lee, Peggy   34–5, 51
Lenassi, Lennie 'Buzz'   13
Leno, Jay   140–1
Leyrac, Monique   113
Linden, Hal   134
Lipman, Joe   70
Littlewood, Yvonne   74, 93–4, 132–3
Litzsinger, Sarah   144–5
Livingston, Jerry   48
Lockwood, Grey   72
Loftus, Tommy   130
Lollobrigida, Gina   78
London, Julie   70
Lovano, Nick   13
Lucas, Nick   16
Lynde, Paul   95–6
Lynn, Loretta   124–5

MacMurray, Fred   29
Mann, Jerry (and Betty Linde)   33
Manning, Dick   50
Mansell, Tony   121, 122
Margolis, Jeff   144
Martin, Dean   101–2

Martin, Lew   35
McHugh, Jimmy   30–1, 78
McLerie, Allyn Ann   31
Mercer, Johnny   54, 78
Merman, Ethel   95
Metropolitan Opera House
    headliners   45
Migenes-Johnson, Julia   146
Miller, Branda S.   128
Miller, Cassie   151–2
Miller, Glenn   34, 58
Miller, Walter, C.   124
Mills, Irving   76
Mills Brothers, The   27
Miranda, Carmen   31
Monroe, Vaughn   45
Moore, Garry   21
Mottola, Tony   26–7, 142
Murray, Anne   128, 135

Nash, Clarence   49–50
Nicklaus, Jack   100

O'Hara, Maureen   78
Oberstein, Eli   53
Olaf, Pierre   100
Olsen, Byron   140
Osmond, Marie   145

Page, Patti   52
Paley, William   47
Palmer, Arnold   100, 159
Palmer, Sandra   128
Parish, Mitchell   76
Parnell, Jack   121
Pearl, Minnie   124
Perito, Nick   77, 81, 104–4, 106, 115, 127,
    131, 141, 148–50, 161, 167, 170
personal life
    Christmas   22–3, 118
    faith and philosophy   61, 77, 162
    family and home   12, 105–6, 171–2
    lifestyle   142, 161
    reflections   160, 162, 171–2
    sport   61, 72, 100, 106, 118, 168

Pertini, Sandro   141
Peterson, Oscar   113
Petrillo, James C.   27, 45
Pick and Pat   33
Pizzarelli, Bucky   142
Player, Gary   100
Pockriss, Lee   82–3
Porter, Cole   28, 30
Pride, Charley   124
Puleo, Johnny   48

Queen Elizabeth II   142
Queen Mother (of Queen Elizabeth II)   122

radio
  Armed Forces Radio Service (AFRS)   32
  Beat the Band   21–2
  British Broadcasting Corporation (BBC)   35
  The Chesterfield Supper Club   31–5, 43, 45, 48–50
  Columbia Presents Perry Como   26, 44
  Fibber McGee and Molly   18, 20
  Smoke Dreams (theme)   34
  WCFL   21
  WMAQ   20
Randolph, Boots   102, 124
Ray Charles Singers, The   57, 69, 107
Raye, Martha   97
Reagan, Nancy   152–3
Reagan, Ronald   143, 147, 152–3
recordings and audio formats
  acoustic and electrical recording (wax discs)   16, 28
  alternative takes   59
  Battle of the Speeds   46, 64
  electronic stereo   62–3
  extended play (EP) records   47
  45 rpm single records   46–8, 64
  long-playing (LP) records   43–4, 46–8, 64
  master recordings   28, 132

methodology   59–9, 102, 104–6, 131
mono and stereo compatibility   93
overdub and multi-track recording (magnetic tape)   131–2
76 rpm records   43–4, 46
unreleased recordings   59, 132
Reed, Alan   32–3
Reichner, Bix   50
René, Henri   45–6
Reynolds, Burt   145
Rich, Charlie   124
Richardson, Sir Ralph   92
Rockwell, Tommy   25, 27
Rodgers, Richard   31, 54, 78
Rogers, Ginger   70
Rooney, Mickey   31, 102
Roosevelt, Franklin D.   11, 35
Rose, Billy   78
Rowland, Billy   27

San Antonio Symphony Orchestra and Master Singers   146
Sarnoff, Robert   47
Savo, Jimmy   32
Sayer, Leo   132
Scott, Howard 'Scotty'   47
Scott, Raymond   26
Secombe, Harry   92
Seiler, Lewis   30
Shaffer, Lloyd   34
Shaw, Artie   51
Sherman, Bobby   114
Sholes, Steve   102
Shore, Dinah   75, 159
Sigman, Carl   69
Silvers, Phil   31
Simpson, Bob   107, 115, 132
Sinatra, Frank   27, 77, 107, 141–2, 157, 159
Sinatra, Nancy   114
Singers of Praise, The   129
singing style and technique
  approach   63, 106
  bel canto   16
  crooning   16

development   17–18, 21, 22
influences   17
Italian ethnic humour   141
legacy   170
personality and public persona   60, 71, 79, 107, 133, 147, 170–1
preparation   160–1
versatility and longevity   58, 83, 116
Sistine Chapel Choir   129
Smith, Gary   94
Snow, Hank   52
St. Patrick's Cathedral Choir   145
St. Paul's Cathedral Choir   132
Stafford, Jo   34
Stark, Dick   50, 56
Steele, Ted   34
Stevens Jr, George   147
Stewart, Sandy   97
Stoneham, Harry   133
Strait, George   146
Styne, Jule   78
Summer, Robert D.   143
Sweeney, Warren   26
Swit, Loretta   139

Tanner, Elmo   17, 20–1, 98
Television
    British Broadcasting Corporation (BBC)   92–4
    camerawork, set design and technique   48–50, 95, 97, 128–30
    Chesterfield cigarettes   56
    colour and stereo broadcasts   72–4, 95
    cue cards and ad-libs   50, 79, 92
    Dream Along with Me (I'm on My Way to a Star)   69–70
    Fifty Nifty United States   98
    influence and impact   74, 90–1, 129
    King of Saturday Night   70
    The Kraft Music Hall Players   95–7
    rehearsals   64–5, 71, 77, 79
    schedule   147
    script writing   72
    simulcast   43
    Sing to Me, Mr. C   94
    songwriter medleys   78–9
    The Story of the First Christmas   52
    television sales and impact   50–1
    touring   100–2
    We Get Letters (aka Dear Perry)   70
    You Are Never Far Away   95
television shows and specials
    The All-Star Revue   52
    Austria   130
    The Bahamas   139
    Colonial Williamsburg   133–4
    Como Country Perry and His Nashville Friends   124
    England   132
    French Canada   139–40
    Hawaii   145
    The Hollywood Palace   113–14
    The Holy Land   128–30
    Ireland   162–6
    Lake Tahoe   128
    The Many Moods of Perry Como   114
    Mexico   138, 139
    New Mexico   135
    New York   144–5
    Paris   146
    Perry Como – In Person   117
    The Perry Como Show (CBS)   50–2, 56, 57, 64–5
    The Perry Como Show (NBC)   69–71–74, 77–9
    Perry Como's Kraft Music Hall   89–102, 113
    Rome   129
    Sands Point Golf Club   100
    Texas   146–7
    Winter Show (1971)   117–19
Tiu, Ginny   95
Tormé, Mel   31, 51
Truman, Harry S.   45

Valdés, Miguelito   32
Vallée, Rudy   16, 107
Van Heusen, Jimmy   78

Vance, Paul   82–3
Vanoff, Felisa   94, 114
Vanoff, Nick   94, 113, 147
variety acts
   minstrelsy   33
   pantomime   132
   vaudeville   16
   ventriloquism   33–4
Villella, Edward   113
Vizza, Robert F.   159

Wald, Jerry   29
Wallerstein, Bill   47
Warren, Fran   45
Washburn, Country   17, 98
WAVES (Women Accepted for Volunteer Emergency Service) singing platoon   46

Wayne, John   133–4
Weems, Ted   17–22, 98
Wesson Brothers, The   33
West, Mae   48
Weston, Paul   34
Whiting, Margaret   33
Williams, Andy   90–1
Williams, Hank   51–2
Williams, John   150
Williams, William B.   61
Wilson, Flip   114, 117, 170
Winterhalter, Hugo   52–4, 62
Wiswell, Andy   104, 107
Wiswell, Hank   104
Woods, Ilene   49–50
Wynn, Bob   146, 158

Zappia, Marco   128